DATE DUE			
NB 12-65			
GAYLORD			PRINTED IN U.S.A.

THE DOMESTIC SERVANT CLASS
IN EIGHTEENTH-CENTURY ENGLAND

THE
DOMESTIC SERVANT CLASS
IN
EIGHTEENTH-CENTURY
ENGLAND

J. Jean Hecht

ROUTLEDGE & KEGAN PAUL
London

*First published in 1956
by Routledge & Kegan Paul Ltd.,
Broadway House, Carter Lane, E.C.4
Printed in Great Britain
by Butler & Tanner Ltd.,
Frome and London*

To
MY MOTHER

CONTENTS

		Page
	ACKNOWLEDGEMENTS	ix
	INTRODUCTION	xi

Chapter

I	THE DEMAND AND SUPPLY OF SERVANTS	1
II	THE SERVANT HIERARCHY	35
III	THE RELATIONSHIP OF MASTER AND SERVANT	71
IV	THE CONDITIONS OF SERVICE: HOUSING, DIET, CLOTHING	102
V	THE CONDITIONS OF SERVICE: RECREATION	125
VI	THE REWARDS OF SERVICE: PECUNIARY PROFITS	141
VII	THE REWARDS OF SERVICE: SOCIAL ADVANCEMENT	177
VIII	THE SERVANT CLASS AS A CULTURAL NEXUS	200
	BIBLIOGRAPHY	229
	INDEX	231

ACKNOWLEDGEMENTS

LIKE the authors of most scholarly works, I have incurred heavy obligations in many quarters. Among those to whom my thanks are especially due are Professor Bernard Barber of Columbia University, who guided me past some of the most treacherous reefs and shoals of sociological misinterpretation, Professor Thomas C. Cochran of the University of Pennsylvania; who helped me to achieve a fuller comprehension of certain crucial methodological problems; Professor David E. Owen of Harvard University, who suggested several lines of investigation that proved extremely fruitful; and Dr. Elliott Perkins of Harvard University, who clarified a number of points that perplexed me about eighteenth-century English society. My principal debt is to Professor Ruth Emery of Rutgers University and Professor Harry M. Johnson of Simmons College, both of whom promoted the progress of my labours at every stage, Professor Emery by giving me the benefit of her rare critical judgement and her detailed knowledge of English social history, Professor Johnson by giving me expert counsel on the application of sociological concepts to historical material.

London,   J. J. H.
   July 5, 1955

INTRODUCTION

THE importance of the domestic servant class in eighteenth-century England has long been recognized. From Lecky onwards, both literary and scholarly surveys of the social life of the period have generally devoted a certain amount of attention to the group; and several monographs have dealt with it incidentally, as relevant to their special subjects. With the exception of a single brief article by Dorothy Marshall, however, no serious effort has been made to treat it in detail.

It is this lack that the present study attempts to supply. In the pages that follow an effort has been made to reconstruct the principal lineaments of the servant class and to show the significance of the group in relation to the society of which it formed a part. Its composition, size, and structure, the means by which it was recruited, the hopes or ambitions of its members, the nature of their social status, and the conditions under which they lived and laboured have all been fully treated. In no sense, however, does the study pretend to be definitive. Much of the inexhaustible material on the subject necessarily remains unexamined; since they deserve separate investigation, certain tempting by-ways, such as the success of Wesley and Whitefield among servants and the reputed criminality of a large part of the class, have been left unexplored.

A good deal of the material employed in the study has been extracted from the usual quarries of the social historian: diaries, memoirs, letters, magazines, newspapers, the accounts of travellers, and literary works. Much has also been taken from pamphlets and treatises on social and economic problems of the day. And, of course, a wealth of data has been drawn from contemporary works on service, servants, and household management.

Since relatively little of what servants committed to paper has survived, the bulk of the material derives from the employer class. Some of it naturally reflects the prejudices of that group. To a considerable extent, however, it presents data that are uncoloured by

INTRODUCTION

class bias. Moreover, even where such bias does exist, careful weighing and assessment have made it possible to assign a proper value to the material. Thus, although it is largely through the eyes of the employer class that servants are viewed in the study, it is by no means a one-sided presentment that emerges from the assembled facts.

In treating the material, the descriptive or impressionistic method, traditional tool of the social historian, has been used throughout the study. Here and there a more scientific approach might perhaps have been employed: bits of evidence might have been counted and conclusions drawn on the basis of quantitative appraisal. But it is extremely doubtful whether so limited an application of the statistical method would have added to the study; and in the main, the material is unsuited to such treatment.

The material has imposed on the study a more or less static character. Evidence of change is far from abundant. In consequence, while it has been possible to note some of the modifications that service and the servant class underwent during the period, many of the main lines of growth and development could not be traced.

Chapter One

THE DEMAND AND SUPPLY OF SERVANTS

WERE it possible to chart accurately the relative size of occupational groups in eighteenth-century England, the servant class would undoubtedly rank with the largest. A variety of economic developments and resulting social changes created a steadily increasing demand for domestics throughout the period; multiple sources furnished a constantly increasing, though generally inadequate, supply.

I

The chief stimulus to demand was the accelerated growth of the middle classes that accompanied the commercial and industrial expansion of the century. Land no longer remained unrivalled as the principal source of wealth; trade in its various aspects presented numerous possibilities for the acquisition of new fortunes and the improvement of old. For the merchant who imported foreign luxuries and exported domestic staples, for the shipper engaged in the carrying trade and the shopkeeper concerned with the retail market there existed almost unlimited opportunity. Speculation and promotion also enriched a host of obscure men. And manufacturing—particularly during the second half of the period—brought wealth to entrepreneurs such as Joshua Fielden, Jedediah Strutt, Sir Richard Arkwright, and the first Sir Robert Peel. This increase in the number and size of individual fortunes meant new households in some cases, more elaborate households in others. Wealthy merchants like the elder Beckford, desiring to equal the magnificence of the upper classes, made certain that their tables were as luxurious, their clothes as fashionable, and their houses as fine as those of their social superiors. Fully alive to the value of a large complement of domestics as a symbol of wealth, they also took care that their establishments were no less extensive than those maintained by the nobility and gentry. Thus in *Humphry Clinker* Matt Bramble remarked:

> About five and twenty years ago, very few even of the most opulent citizens of London kept any equipage, or even any servants in livery. ... At present, every trader in any degree of credit, every broker and attorney, maintains a couple of footmen, a coachman, and a postillion.[1]

Lesser men followed suit to the best of their ability, so that a letter to the *Craftsman* could make the exaggerated complaint: 'There is scarce a mechanick in town who does not keep a servant in livery. ...'[2] The *Female Tatler*, striking a similar note, could declare that in former times tradesmen did not maintain their coaches, 'nor did ev'ry petty Merchant keep a Butler out of livery....'[3] And one of the participants of a pseudo-Socratic dialogue, when asked whether it was only people of fashion who kept livery servants, could be made to reply: 'I have known many a Doctor and Apothecary... starve themselves, that they may maintain their footmen.'[4]

For the nobility and gentry the importance of maintaining a numerous train of servants was greatly intensified by this challenge from the middle classes. Since a lord or squire was not only forced to meet the competitive ostentation on his own level but that of the mercantile community as well, the medieval dictum that an establishment ought to be no larger than demanded by its master's social status gave way completely to the rule that it should be as extensive as his fortune would permit. Servants were, of course, only one of the evidences of wealth that gained increased significance as wealth became a more potent criterion of social status. But for the nobleman and the gentleman a large establishment was indispensable. It might be argued that the size of the house or the complexity of the household paraphernalia necessitated a large domestic staff; but this is merely to say that the servant not only put his master's

---

[1] Tobias Smollett, 'The Expedition of Humphry Clinker', *The Works of Tobias Smollett, M.D.*, ed. John Moore, 1797, VII. 108.
[2] Reprinted in *London Magazine*, 1756, XXV. 225.
[3] *Female Tatler*, 1709, No. 24, Aug. 29–31, 2a.
[4] *London Chronicle*, 1762, XI, 204a.

wealth into evidence directly but also indirectly, by supporting a style of living that was expensive and ostentatious. The importance of servants as symbols of status is revealed by Mrs. Harrison Cappe, the daughter of a well-to-do clergyman. Describing how she was questioned by her fellow students at a fashionable boarding school, she writes:

> . . . I was interrogated by many of the young ladies as to the station of my father, or rather respecting the figure he made in the world. 'Does your papa keep a coach?'—'No'—'How many servants have you?'—'Four'—'Dear; only think Miss's papa does not keep a coach, and they have only four servants.'[1]

It was particularly important to have a large retinue in London, where, owing to the impersonality of urban society, the visible indications of social position assumed a greater consequence than in the country. But even in the country, members of the nobility and gentry were highly conscious of how their households compared with those of their neighbours. Smollett effectively portrays this in his account of the vain and extravagant Mrs. Baynard, who on discovering 'that Sir John Chickwell had a house-steward and one footman in livery more than the complement of Mr. Baynard's household', plagued her husband until two more servants were added.[2]

Compared with the medieval household, however, the upper-class establishment of the eighteenth century was extremely small. During the Middle Ages the retainers of a great lord might run into the hundreds.[3] When the Earl of Warwick went up to Parliament in the middle of the fifteenth century, he was accompanied by 600 liveried servants; a much less important personage, the deputy-steward of Kendal in Westmorland, had a retinue of 290 about the same time.[4] But in the transitional period that witnessed

---

[1] *Memoirs of the Life of the Late Mrs. Catherine Cappe*, 1824, p. 40. Cf. Thomas Gisborne, *An Enquiry into the Duties of the Female Sex*, 1794, pp. 87–8.

[2] Smollett, 'Humphry Clinker', *Works*, VII. 368.

[3] Mary H. Perkins, *The Servant Problem and the Servant in English Literature*, Boston [1928,] p. 14; A[nnie] Abram, *English Life and Manners in the Later Middle Ages*, 1913, p. 14; William E. Mead, *The English Mediaeval Feast*, Boston, 1931, p. 145 and *passim*.

[4] Frances E. Baldwin, 'Sumptuary Legislation and Personal Regulation in England', *Johns Hopkins Studies in Historical and Political Science*, Series XLIV, Baltimore, 1926, p. 73.

the disintegration of medieval society and the reshaping of social life, the number of dependents in most upper-class houses was gradually reduced. Such factors as the increasingly high cost of maintenance, the replacement of the autarchic castle and manor house, with their host of quasi-domestics, by the country seat, at least partially provisioned from the near-by market town, and the effective suppression of the serving-men, who had taken the place of the old feudal retainers, were accountable for the change. Harrison's *Descriptions*, which appeared in the last quarter of the sixteenth century, refers to the 'great swarmes of idle seruing men' and moralizes:

> It were verie good therefore that the superfluous heapes of them were in part diminished. And sith necessitie inforceth to haue some, yet let wisdome moderate their numbers, so shall their masters be rid of vnnecessarie charge.... No nation cherisheth such store of them as we doo here in England, in hope of which maintenance many giue themselues to idlenesse, that otherwise would be brought to labour, and liue in order like suiects.[1]

The 166 servants kept by the Earl of Northumberland in 1521[2] and the hundred maintained by the Bishop of Ely before his death in 1533[3] exemplify the swollen households that so exercised Harrison.[4] By the beginning of the following century such establishments had become relatively few. Fynes Moryson's *Itinerary*, written between 1609 and 1617, speaks of 'the great trains and large howse keepinges of lords and gentlemen' as things of the past.[5] And succeeding decades saw no reversal of this trend towards smaller retinues. Hence in 1713 Bishop Burnet, contrasting the upper-class households of that year with those of former times,

---

[1] *Descriptions of Britaine and England*, ed. Frederick J. Furnivall, Bk. II. 134–5 (New Shakespeare Society Series VI), 1887.

[2] Thomas Percy, *Regulations and Establishment of . . . the Fifth Earl of Northumberland*, 1770, pp. 253–8.

[3] Thomas Hearne, *Collections* (Oxford Historical Society), Oxford, 1885–1921, IV. 240.

[4] For other examples of the size of Tudor households see H. F. M. Prescott, 'The House and Household in the Sixteenth Century', *Transactions of the Architectural and Archaeological Society of Durham and Northumberland*, X. 155; Paul Van Brunt Jones, *The Household of a Tudor Nobleman*, Cedar Rapids, 1918, p. 10.

[5] Fynes Moryson, *Itinerary*, ed. Charles Hughes, 1903, p. 476.

declared: '... it is a happiness to the nation that the great number of idle and useless retainers that were about noblemen anciently, is much reduced....'[1]

But if the establishments of the eighteenth century were only fractional vestiges of the staffs that had served in medieval houses, by modern standards they appear impressively large. La Rochefoucauld, who visited England in 1784, observes: '... there are certain English noblemen who have thirty or forty men-servants. ...'[2] And no doubt female servants in such households were at least equally numerous. The retinue maintained by the sixth Duke of Somerset was said to have contained more than a hundred servants in the 1690's;[3] during the early years of the eighteenth century it probably ran to about fifty or fifty-five. Between 1700 and 1724 he employed more than twenty-six menservants alone.[4] Very little smaller was the fourth Duke of Bedford's London family. In 1753 it included forty servants of both sexes and in 1771 forty-two.[5] Lord Stormont's household in 1784 was probably of similar size. He employed nineteen male servants and perhaps as many more women.[6] Only slightly less impressive was the thirty-odd servants retained by the first Duke of Newcastle at Claremont in 1734;[7] the thirty servants with which the ninth Duke of Norfolk came down to Arundel in 1775;[8] the thirty or more who constituted Lord Gage's family when Thomas Hutchinson, the American, visited him in 1774;[9] and the thirty Hutchinson found in the employ of Lord Hardwicke in 1778.[10] Of course, the regal state supported by these employers was not duplicated by every member of the nobility. The first Earl of Bristol, for example, paid poll tax

[1] [Gilbert Burnet,] *History of His Own Times*, Oxford, 1833, VI. 219.
[2] Jean Marchand, *A Frenchman in England 1784*, Cambridge, 1933, p. 25.
[3] Julia G. Longe, *Martha Lady Giffard Her Life and Correspondence*, 1911, p. 192.
[4] *Gentleman's Magazine*, 1791, LXI. 199.
[5] Gladys S. Thomson, *The Russells in Bloomsbury*, 1940, p. 238.
[6] Elizabeth and Florence Anson, *Mary Hamilton, at Court and at Home*, 1925, p. 236.
[7] Stebelton H. Nulle, *Thomas Pelham-Holles, Duke of Newcastle*, Philadelphia, 1931, App. D, pp. 184–5.
[8] *The Diary of John Baker*, ed. Philip C. Yorke, 1931, p. 308.
[9] *The Diary and Letters of ... Thomas Hutchinson*, ed. Peter O. Hutchinson, Boston, 1884–6, I. 224. Cf. *ibid.*, I. 523.
[10] *Ibid.*, II, 218.

in 1702 for only twenty servants;[1] and at the time of her death in 1722 the great Duchess of Marlborough employed only thirteen.[2] But it is unlikely that many noble households fell much below these in size.

The households of the wealthier gentry were hardly less elaborate than those of the nobility. That of the Duke of Grafton's brother, Lt.-Gen. Fitzroy, for instance, was composed of forty servants in 1779.[3] Writing in 1786, Mrs. Powys describes a household that was probably not much smaller:

> Their establishment is very large; so numerous I style it uncomfortable—house-steward, man-cook, two gentlemen out of livery, under-butler, Mrs. Pratt's two footmen, Mr. Pratt's two, upper and under coachmen, two grooms, helpers, &c., &c. These are menservants; female ones, I dare say, in proportion.[4]

But according to Giles Jacob, the average large country family would include twenty servants; and in his estimate of the cost of keeping that number he provides for eight or ten liveries, thus indicating that half or almost half of them would be men.[5] Peter Legh's household must have been about this size in 1760. His menservants included a butler, an under-butler, a cook, a coachman, a groom, a groom's helper, a postillion, two footmen and a park-keeper—ten in all.[6]

Most country gentlemen were not so well attended. John Custance of Ringland in Norfolk had a staff of ten in 1776.[7] Horace Walpole probably kept about the same number at Strawberry Hill in 1781, his menservants including a valet, a coachman, two footmen, and a gardener,[8] his female servants presumably being no fewer than the men. But a staff of about seven domestics seems to have been much more usual amongst this class of employers.

---

[1] *The Diary of John Hervey, First Earl of Bristol*, Wells, 1894, p. 129.
[2] [Olivia] Colville, *Duchess Sarah*, 1904, p. 371.
[3] *Beneden Letters, 1753–1821*, ed. Charles F. Hardy, 1901, p. 169.
[4] *Passages from the Diaries of Mrs. Philip Lybbe Powys, 1756–1808*, ed. Emily J. Climenson, 1899, pp. 222–3. Cf. Maud M. Wyndham, *Chronicles of the Eighteenth Century*, 1924, II. 170.
[5] G[iles] Jacob, *The Country Gentleman's Vademecum*, 1717, pp. 46–7.
[6] [Evelyn] Newton, *Lyme Letters*, 1925, p. 317.
[7] *The Diary of a Country Parson: the Reverend James Woodforde, 1758–1802*, ed. John Beresford, 1924–31, I. 235.
[8] *The Letters of Horace Walpole*, ed. [Helen] Toynbee, Oxford, 1903–5, XII. 10.

Francis Sitwell appears to have found three men and four women adequate during the 1730's;[1] Henry Purefoy, a Buckinghamshire squire, usually kept three maids, three men, and a boy between 1735 and 1753;[2] Sanderson Miller had an identical staff in 1748;[3] and the Rev. George Betts, a substantial landholder in Suffolk, employed two male and five female servants in 1784.[4]

The London establishments of the moderately well-to-do gentry were of similar proportions. The servants in Mrs. Boscawen's town house, for instance, numbered seven in 1748.[5] And Horace Walpole's friend, Mary Berry, estimated in 1796 that in order to live comfortably in London, without 'pinching economy and pitiful savings', she required three menservants and four women.[6]

Amongst the lesser gentry still smaller establishments were the rule. The minimal needs of a country squire with limited funds were set by the Rev. Trusler at five servants: a man 'to act in the capacity of coachman and to manage the farm', a second man to serve as a combination footman-gardener, a boy and two maids.[7] Between 1776 and 1802 the Rev. James Woodforde, whose income was about £300 a year, maintained a household on precisely this scale. He employed a 'farming-man', who, though not properly classed as a domestic, occasionally aided within the house, a footman, a 'skip-jack' or yard boy, an upper maid, who did the cooking, and an under maid, who, in addition to her regular duties, took care of the dairy.[8] Woodforde's friends, the Rev. Du Quesne and the Rev. Jeanes, were similarly served.[9] And towards the close of the century 'a discreet management' enabled the Rev. William Gilpin, who had an income of £700 a year, to keep two male and two female domestics.[10] To contemporary eyes these establishments appeared extremely modest; in retrospect they seem far from diminutive.

[1] George R. Sitwell, *The Hurts of Haldworth*, 1930, p. 257.
[2] *Purefoy Letters 1735–1753*, ed. G[eorge] Eland, 1931, I. 132, 142, 150.
[3] Lilian Dickins and Mary Stanton, *An Eighteenth Century Correspondence*, 1910, p. 58.
[4] Katharine F. Doughty, *The Betts of Wortham in Suffolk*, 1912, p. 242.
[5] Cecil A. Oglander, *Admiral's Wife*, 1940, p. 77.
[6] *The Berry Papers 1763–1852*, ed. Lewis Melville, 1914, p. 179.
[7] [John Trusler,] *The Way to be Rich and Respectable*, [1777,] pp. 18–19.
[8] *Diary of a Country Parson, passim*.
[9] *Ibid.*, introd., p. xi.
[10] Richard Warner, *Literary Recollections*, 1830, I. 362.

In the middle classes the gamut of variation in the size of families was somewhat broader than that which existed amongst the gentry. Typical of the larger households were the eighteen or twenty servants employed at Streatham by Henry Thrale, England's most successful brewer during the third quarter of the century.[1] Most well-to-do commercial and professional men, however, kept only a fraction of this number. In the 1770's John Baker, a lawyer affiliated with the West Indian interest, retained a valet, a coachman, a postillion, a gardener, a boy, a housekeeper, a housemaid, a laundry maid, a dairy maid, and a general maid—a total of eleven.[2] The households maintained by the different branches of the Milnes family, prosperous entrepreneurs of the Yorkshire woollen trade, also indicate the number of servants kept by employers of this class. In 1780 James and Robert Milnes each kept three menservants; Peter Milnes had four, and John six;[3] assuming the women in each case to have been at least equally numerous, these households ranged in size from six to twelve domestics. The number of servants employed by men of more limited income is suggested by the designs of the architect Isaac Ware. His small London houses intended for 'the middle rank of people' included living quarters for three or four domestics.[4] And below this stratum there existed a large group of employers who kept but a single maidservant or, at most, a maid and a footboy. In such families it was often an apprentice who played the role of footboy, dividing his time between the shop and attendance on his mistress.

Rural counterparts of these lower middle-class families existed in the houses of the farmers, both tenants and yeomen.[5] But only a small portion of the average farmer's household consisted of menial servants. Except for an occasional footman, the men were hired as servants in husbandry. Some of the women, on the other

[1] *The Intimate Letters of Hester Piozzi and Penelope Pennington 1788–1821*, ed. Oswald G. Knapp, 1914, p. 119.

[2] *Diary of John Baker*, p. 53.

[3] J[ohn] W. Walker, *Wakefield Its History and People*, Wakefield, 1934, p. 398.

[4] Isaac Ware, *A Complete Body of Architecture*, 1756, p. 347. See also James P. Malcolm, *Anecdotes of the Manners and Customs of London During the Eighteenth Century*, 1810, II. 417.

[5] [Arthur Young,] *A Six Months' Tour Through the North of England*, 1770, *passim*; [Arthur Young,] *The Farmer's Tour Through the East of England*, 1771, *passim*.

hand, were domestics. But frequently those who performed the duties of an indoor servant did outdoor work as well. Not that the distinction between indoor and outdoor servants was always clear in upper-class families. Dairy maids, for example, usually were engaged as domestics and were on the same general footing as other domestics; yet their work was essentially that of farm servants. Moreover, other types of domestics might be called on to do agricultural work. When Elizabeth Purefoy sought a coachman in 1738, she required one who understood 'Husbandry businesse & cattle'.[1] And the possibility was not absent in establishments of the first order. A visitor who inspected Holkham on a July evening in 1792 found 'a fine group on the lawn of valets, footmen, grooms, cooks, women and labourers to the amount of 60 persons, all busy getting hay up into cocks'.[2] But such servants remained primarily domestics whereas the farmer's maid often devoted most of her time to outdoor work, her duties as a domestic being a secondary concern. Obviously maids of this sort can no more be considered domestics than the parish apprentices so frequently taken by artisans both to aid them in their work and to do the drudgery of the home. How many true domestics the average farmer kept cannot be discovered.

II

If farmers as a class contributed little to the demand for domestics, their offspring, together with those of agricultural servants and labourers, comprised the chief source of supply.[3] The children of farmers were considered the most suitable for service, as is made clear by a writer who in 1766 saw the decay of small farms as the root cause of the scarcity of good domestics:

> ... small farmers were the people that used to stock the country with the best of servants: these were the nurseries for breeding up industrious and virtuous young men and women; whereas the generality of servants, now-a-days, are such as have had but little opportunity of learning how to do business so as to be fit to make good servants; for the labourer cannot be expected to be able to give

---

[1] *Purefoy Letters*, I. 134.
[2] *Annals of Agriculture*, 1793, XIX. 116, quoted in A[nna] M. W. Stirling, *Coke of Norfolk and His Friends*, 1908, I, 283.
[3] J[ames] E. T. Rogers, *Six Centuries of Work and Wages*, New York, 1884, p. 463.

his children that learning which is proper to fit them for good places; whilst those who rent small farms have generally wherewithal to give their children learning sufficient to qualify them to read virtuous books, and to know how to behave in a proper and decent manner. Besides, the girls have opportunities of learning at home how to brew, bake, cook, knit, sow, and get up linnen, &c., whereas poor people's children have not such advantages.[1]

To obtain good domestics large landholders often drew directly on their own tenantry, a practice generally regarded as commendable and at the same time highly beneficial to the employer. Thus a writer in the *Westminster Journal* in 1745 recommended it with warm approval:

I have often thought of the great interest a nobleman, or gentleman of large estate, might always secure by only the proper choice of his *domestics*. Such an one cannot be without a great number of tenants, who might think their children honoured in the *service* of his lordship, and whose tenures would be a sort of *security* for the honesty and good behaviour of the servant.[2]

Lesser landowners frequently took their menials from the agrarian population in the vicinity of their estates. The possibilities of this variety of recruitment are suggested by a letter that Henry Purefoy wrote on behalf of a tenant's boy:

Here is a ffarmer's son of this parish who is out of place & has lived with a clergyman three years; hee waits at table very well, & can do almost any sort of Businesse. His master parted with him because hee outgrew his wages & will give him a Character. Wee are provided, otherwise would have him ourselves. If you hear of ever such a place for him, should take it as a favour if you'll let mee know thereof. . . .[3]

But of the candidates for servitude who came of farming people, the majority did not hire themselves in the country, but in London, where during the course of the century a broadening devotion to 'the Season', the requirements of the growing middle classes, and

---

[1] *An Address to the P———t in Behalf of the Starving Multitude*, 1766, p. 39.
[2] Reprinted in *Gentleman's Magazine*, 1745, xv. 544–5. Cf. *The Batchelor's Monitor*, 1743, p. 64.
[3] *Purefoy Letters*, I. 154.

an extremely high death rate created an abundance of places. A characteristic instance of this abandonment of the country by a young man seeking employment in the Capital is recorded by the Rev. William Cole. Having advised the son of a neighbouring farmer to remain at home to help his father, Cole was later obliged to enter in his diary: 'Tom Watts dined in the Kitchen with Wm Grace: he told me he had been at Mr Selby's . . . but that he was too big for a Postilion, & that he was determined to go to London for a Place. . . .'[1]

Such young people were welcomed as servants in the Metropolis because of the ill-repute of the local species. The lower classes of London were thought to be vicious and dishonest, hence entirely unfit for service. 'London is so much the sink of vice,' warns the Rev. Trusler, 'that the lower class of people are very much corrupted.'[2] London servants were considered the worst of the lot. They were said to be wanton in habit and unscrupulous in practice. Moreover, urban living was supposed to have given them a sophistication characterized by a highly insubordinate spirit and an exceptionally self-interested attitude. It was therefore customary to compare them unfavourably with domestics in the country. Mrs. Elizabeth Carter, the bluestocking, was almost unique in taking a charitable view. 'I do not', she wrote, 'think London servants are by any means more wicked than others. On the contrary it seems rather a matter of surprise that of such a number so few should be notoriously bad.'[3] The general opinion was well expressed by a newspaper correspondent who signed himself 'Pro Bono Publico': 'In the remote parts of the kingdom, which have little connection with the capital, servants are tractable and industrious; at least they are infinitely more so than those to be met with in London and its environs.'[4] Indeed, so great was the prejudice against the domestics of the Metropolis that those who had lost their places would not infrequently leave the city and return again,

---

[1] *The Blecheley Diary of the Rev. William Cole 1765–67*, ed. Francis G. Stokes, 1931, p. 52.
[2] [John Trusler,] *The London Adviser and Guide*, 1786, p. 47. Cf. *Oxford Magazine*, 1771, VI. 82.
[3] *Letters from Mrs. Elizabeth Carter to Mrs. Montagu, 1755–1800*, ed. Montagu Pennington, 1817, III. 298.
[4] *London Packet*, 1772, No. 454, Sept. 18–21, 4a. Cf. *London Chronicle*, 1758, III. 116c.

posing as fresh arrivals. A letter addressed to the editor of a London newspaper exposes this stratagem:

> ... the servant-maids of London are well apprized of the eagerness of people to snap at any thing that comes out of the country; and therefore when their misconduct has made it difficult for them to get a service, they go out of town and return perhaps with the next waggoner; and being made free of the waggon (which is the phrase amongst those sort of gentry for the last favour) the honest fellow gives them a character. . . .[1]

But despite the preference accorded country servants, employers often were forced to take those from London, since they alone were fit for positions requiring experience and special skills. It was essentially the simpler type of place for which country servants were in demand. Nevertheless, much truth is reflected in Huntingford's contention that 'a poor girl who has the misfortune to be born in London, cannot get a place because she knows the town. . . .'[2]

The preference accorded country-bred servants brought recruits into London in droves. Of the young people who went up to the Capital every year, a large proportion were destined for service. Charging abortionists with responsibility for seriously lowering the birth rate, 'Philo-Britanniae' argued in 1762 that 'London would soon become depopulated, if it was not for the waggon loads of poor servants coming every day from all parts of this kingdom. . . .'[3] Jonas Hanway, likewise concerned with problems of population, in 1777 set the number of migrants at five thousand annually, 'chiefly for service'.[4] And a letter published in the *Gentleman's Magazine* in 1793 commented on 'what vast numbers [were] continually drawing off from the country . . . to the metropolis, to the service of noblemen and gentlemen. . . .'[5]

---

[1] *London Chronicle*, 1758, III. 116c. Cf. [Daniel Defoe,] *Street Robberies Consider'd*, 1728, p. 68; J[ames] Huntingford, *The Laws of Masters and Servants Considered*, 1790, p. 107.

[2] Huntingford, *Laws of Masters and Servants*, p. 107. Cf. *London Chronicle*, 1757, II. 572a.

[3] *London Chronicle*, 1762, XII. 58a. Cf. *Court Miscellany*, 1766, II. 10.

[4] Jonas Hanway, *Virtue in Humble Life*, 1777, I. introd., p. vi. Cf. Mabel C. Buer, *Health, Wealth and Population in the Early Days of the Industrial Revolution*, 1926, p. 75.

[5] *Gentleman's Magazine*, 1793, LXIII. 35.

But the probability of easily finding employment cannot be held solely accountable for this movement. London seemed attractive because it offered better wages and larger perquisites than could be obtained in the country. Thus in 1762 a writer who denounced the rate of remuneration that prevailed in the Capital maintained that it had the 'pernicious consequence of draining the country of necessary hands, many of whom flock to London in expectation of high wages. . . .'[1] And another writer declared in 1771: 'The grand supply of servants . . . comes from the country; and I believe more *women* from the north of England, than from any other quarter. These are allured to London with the prospect of high wages. . . .'[2]

Almost equally magnetic was the charm of urban life. The fascination London exercised over a broad segment of the upper classes gradually came to be felt by an increasing number amongst the lower classes. Many were lured from the country by the beckoning glitter, excitement, and novelty of the Metropolis. Archenholz, who was in England about 1780, describes the powerful spell it cast over the minds of the young:

> The idea of the pleasures to be enjoyed in the capital inspires the girls in the country with the most longing desire to participate in them. Imagination inflames their little heads, and presents every object under an exaggerated appearance. The young people of both sexes, who have been educated at a distance from town, imagine the metropolis to resemble that paradise promised to the mahometans by their prophet.[3]

The same phenomenon was depicted in a magazine article in 1793. The writer inquires: 'What lass, in the rural village, that hears the name of London, but wishes to be there? What young Damsel that knows of the Lord Mayor's show, that don't wish to be a witness of its splendour?'[4] Responsibility for the spread of this enchantment among the lower classes lay in no small measure with servants returning to visit their parents or accompanying their masters into the country at the end of 'the Season'. The tales of a footman

---

[1] *London Chronicle*, 1762, XI. 165a.
[2] *Oxford Magazine*, 1771, VI. 82. Cf. *Gentleman's Magazine*, 1791, LXI. 803.
[3] J[ohann] W. Von Archenholz, *A Picture of England*, Dublin, 1791, p. 191.
[4] *Carlton House Magazine*, 1793, II. 505. Cf. [Arthur Young,] *The Farmer's Letters to the People of England*, 1768, 2nd ed., p. 340.

might set a whole village in ferment, as Vicesimus Knox observed: 'The lads and lasses of the village listen to his lesson with mouths open, and hearts panting to imitate their kind instructor. Many immediately relinquish the plough and dairy, and hasten up to London in pursuit of fine clothes, money and pleasure.'[1] Smollett's Matt Bramble also noted the unsettling influence of town servants on the rustic mind:

> 'The plough-boys, cow-herds, and lower-hinds, are debauched by the appearance and discourse of those coxcombs in livery, when they make their summer excursions. They desert their dirt and drudgery, and swarm up to London, in hopes of getting into service, where they can live luxuriously and wear fine clothes. . . .'[2]

Even the parents of the young folks appear to have fallen under the spell. A satirist who in 1725 ridiculed the fantasies that country people wove about the Metropolis, represented the typical farmer as 'charmed by the Sight of every Jackanapes in Livery' and as resolving that 'My Jack shall be a footman in London'.[3] The same reaction was ascribed to the farmer's wife by a newspaper correspondent in 1780. In what purports to be a characteristic monologue he makes Dame Susan say to Dame Deborah:

> Ah Bless me, . . . what a charming place London must be! Who would have thought that *Nanny Ginger* would have cut such a tearing figure—a poor aukward, clumsy creature as ever was seen? 'Twas but the June before I lay in with my *Johnny* she got a place in London; and last summer she came down to her friends, all bedizened over from top to toe with silks and sattins and laces, and fine cloaths, as grand I warrant you, as any princess in the land.—Lord!—I wish my *Polly* had such a place!

And the writer then adds: '. . . and on some happy early day, the dear girl is sent off.'[4]

While thus in various ways London drew potential servants from the farms, many were driven to make their exit from the country by other forces. Perhaps foremost of these was the operation of the law of settlement, under the influence of which parish officers

---

[1] Vicesimus Knox, *The Works of Vicesimus Knox*, 1824, I. 346; *London Chronicle*, 1782, LII. 287b.
[2] Smollett, 'Humphry Clinker', *Works*, VII. 108.
[3] *Rural Folly*, 1725, p. 6.
[4] *London Packet*, 1780, No. 1501, Jan. 31–Feb. 2, 2ab.

forcibly expelled or encouraged the migration of all who seemed likely to become chargeable. The manner in which this swelled the number of arrivals in London is illustrated by a news item that appeared in a metropolitan paper in 1772:

> Yesterday, a decent looking girl about thirteen, whom some *humane* Churchwardens at Bristol had given the Coachman a trifling fee to drop in London, came into the Bell in Bell Savage Yard, and enquired for a place; on being interrogated, she said, that her father ... and her mother were both dead, and that fearing she would become chargeable to the parish, this cruel scheme had been taken as a preventative.[1]

Only a minority of the undesirables reached London under such auspices; many more found their own way up to the Capital. Prominent amongst them were pregnant women whose unborn children it was feared would become a burden on the local rates. Hence Defoe thought nothing more natural than the common jest put upon country girls who sought service in London: '*viz.* to ask them *if they had been Church'd before they came from home.*'[2]

Although probably less important than the brutality of parish officials, the enclosure movement, especially after 1760, also promoted an exodus from the countryside. One of the principal effects of the enclosures was the partial disruption of rural society. Small freeholders sometimes sold out the compact allotments they had received in exchange for their scattered strips and pasture rights. Tenants able to rent farms under the new system were often unable to adjust themselves to the altered conditions, eventually being forced to relinquish their land and become ordinary labourers. Other tenants who, because of the consolidation of holdings that usually accompanied enclosure, could not obtain farms, found themselves immediately reduced to the labouring class. Cottagers lost their common rights and in some instances the houses they rented. Squatters were summarily evicted from the waste on which they had encroached. Whether or not such changes resulted in radical depopulation depended on the use to which the enclosed land was put. Where tillage was converted into pasture, as in the Midland counties, the need for labour decreased, and many therefore left the countryside. Where tillage was maintained or extended

[1] *London Chronicle*, 1772, XXXI. 472b.
[2] Daniel Defoe, *The Great Law of Subordination Consider'd*, 1724, p. 86.

THE DEMAND AND SUPPLY OF SERVANTS

and new agricultural methods were introduced, an increased amount of labour was required, so that all of the uprooted population could be reabsorbed. But even when this was the case, the unsettling effects of the sale of land, the loss of common rights, reduction in circumstances, and eviction ultimately caused some to drift away from their native villages. Hanway is therefore substantially correct, when, in discussing the influence of the enclosure movement on the 'Political œconomy' of the nation, he concludes that 'it drives people into great towns'.[1] And he might have added with equal accuracy that after they arrived there, a good many entered service.

In addition to the agrarian population the artisan class of the rural regions also contributed to the supply of domestics. It was not uncommon, asserted a magazine article in 1779, 'for a ploughman to bring up his son to be a postillion, or to wear a livery'; and it maintained that the same thing was done 'by the country bricklayer, mason, carpenter, weaver, &c. . . .'[2] Their daughters, it might have said, were likewise often sent into service. Catherine Hutton, whose father was a woolcomber in Derbyshire, is a case in point.[3]

In London, too, and in the smaller towns, the children of craftsmen and manufacturers were taken as domestics. Thus, arguing in 1763 that certain industries were undermanned, an essayist lamented the diversion of young hands from productive work: 'Many of the very prime of the people are taken from labour, to be attendants on the Opulent.'[4]

Tradesmen, likewise, sent their children into service. '. . . sometimes', writes Defoe, 'Tradesmen, &c., reduced are glad when their Children cease to hang upon them, by getting into Service. . . .'[5] But it was not necessarily financial reverses that prompted members of the shopkeeper class to dispose of their sons and daughters in this fashion. Boys were urged to become domestics when their fathers could not afford to set them up in business or even appren-

[1] Jonas Hanway, *Virtue in Humble Life*, 1774, I, introd., p. xxix.
[2] *London Magazine*, 1779, XLVIII. 16.
[3] Llewellyn Jewitt, *The Life of William Hutton and the History of the Hutton Family*, [1872,] p. 26.
[4] *London Chronicle*, 1763, XIII. 171b.
[5] [Daniel Defoe,] *Augusta Triumphans*, 1728, p. 24. Cf. [Mary Johnson,] *Madam Johnson's Present*, 1769, 5th ed., p. 52.

tice them in a lucrative trade. A letter to a newspaper in 1777 makes this clear:

> Suppose . . . a man gets one hundred pounds a year by trade . . . and that he has four or five sons, is it in his power to make mechanics or tradesmen of them all?—I will answer no;—the sums that must be given as apprentice fees with them would ruin him, was he to do it with more than one or two of them; the consequence is that he has no other resource than to make them servants, to get their living.[1]

Young girls of this class were even more commonly designed at an early age for service. In 1712 Lady Wentworth wrote of one 'who was put out only to improve her, a ritch groser's daughter in the sety'.[2] A host of private schools, particularly in and around London, existed expressly to prepare such girls for the better places.[3] Thus Saunders Welch, the magistrate, observed:

> The maxim of the parents of these children is to give them what they call a good education; and if Miss happens to be pretty her vanity is indulged by dress, &c. in hopes that she may mend her fortune by captivating some rich gudgeon, or be qualified to wait upon a lady, or at least to be a chambermaid. . . .[4]

It was not only the young people of this class, however, who entered service; tradesmen themselves sometimes forsook their shops in order to become menials in upper-class homes. One of Lord Dacre's servants in 1763, for example, had been a butcher 'with his father in Norfolk'.[5] Peter Legh took a barber into his employ in 1765.[6] And Thomas Marchant noted in his journal that he had signed 'a sort of petition in the nature of a certificate for Thos: Hart, the butcher, in order of his being taken into some nobleman's service'.[7]

---

[1] *Morning Post*, 1777, No. 1456, June 20, 4b.
[2] *The Wentworth Papers 1705–1739*, ed. James J. Cartwright, 1883, p. 274.
[3] *Annual Register*, 1759, II. 424–5; *London Chronicle*, 1759, v. 116bc.
[4] Saunders Welch, *A Proposal to Render Effectual a Plan, to Remove the Nuisance of Common Prostitutes from the Streets*, 1758, quoted in the *Grand Magazine of Magazines*, 1758, I, 43.
[5] *Gentleman's Magazine*, 1763, XXXIII. 94.
[6] *Lyme Letters*, p. 318.
[7] 'The Marchant Diary', *Sussex Archaeological Collections*, xxv. 185–6.

The lower strata of the mercantile community were by no means the most elevated levels from which servants were drawn. Domestics, says a newspaper writer who in 1723 attacked the charity schools,

> are generally the Children of the lesser Shopkeepers, though sometimes of decayed Merchants and Gentlemen, who have given them an Education above the Rank of People, which has qualified them to earn a comfortable Subsistence this way, without much Labour; to which they have never been used.[1]

Conspicuous amongst these domestics of good family were the unmarried daughters of impecunious clerics. Their situation, declared 'Humanus', 'is truly deplorable, ... if they have beauty or admiration, or both, they are obliged to be sent out into the world as upper servants. ...'[2] And the destiny of the resourceless widow was often the same as that of the portionless girl. The lot of these poor women is clearly depicted in the fiction of the period.[3] Clara Reeve, the authoress, is an actual example. According to a lady who knew her case, 'She was a clergyman's daughter, who had a large family and a very small living. She, the eldest, was forced to be a common servant.'[4] John Cowslade records another instance in describing the Earl of Hertford's household about 1735:

> The establishment of the family in point of servants was large, and those of the second table, particularly the women, had had a good education, and had the behaviour of real gentlewomen. Mrs. Rothery, Lady Hertford's first woman ... was a widow of genteel extraction; and her niece, Mrs. Nevinson, the second woman, was the daughter of a clergyman in the North. ...[5]

Some of these servants from clerical homes could boast of blood ties with peers and gentlemen. As in earlier centuries, members of the nobility and gentry sometimes employed their poor relations. More often, however, such persons took service with strangers. A male domestic whom Lady Wentworth described in 1710 as 'a

---

[1] *British Journal*, 1723, June 15, 2a.
[2] *County Magazine*, Salisbury, 1786, I. 94.
[3] See, for example, *The History of Lavinia Rawlins*, 1756, I. 35; *Town and Country Magazine*, 1772, III. 232.
[4] H. M. C. Du Cane, p. 238.
[5] Helen S. Hughes, *The Gentle Hertford*, New York, 1940, p. 96.

THE DEMAND AND SUPPLY OF SERVANTS

decaid gentleman's son' is a representative case.[1] Lady Fermanagh's cousin, who until 1736 lived as waiting-woman to a Mrs. Stone, is another.[2]

The servant class, then, was composed of recruits from social levels as diverse as the gentry and the rural proletariat; many sections of the population were represented in its ranks. It included, besides, servants from Scotland and Ireland, some of whom had been brought into the country by their masters, as Swift brought over Patrick, while others had come on their own initiative. Finally, it included continentals, Negroes from Africa and America, and Indians from Asia.[3] Those from abroad were far fewer, however, than the servants recruited from the various classes at home.

III

The principal motives that sent members of these different classes into service were the desire for security and the desire to rise in the economic and social scale. Service was both a refuge and a means whereby improved social status could be attained.

As a refuge it chiefly benefited women, especially those who possessed any semblance of what was termed a 'polite education'—music, dancing, needlework, and perhaps a smattering of arithmetic. When forced to provide for themselves, women of this sort had little choice of occupation. '. . . women', writes Sir John Fielding, 'have but few trades and fewer manufactures to employ them. . . .'[4] To open a boarding-school, to become a milliner or dressmaker, to go to service constituted almost the whole range of possibility for a woman of 'good family'. The means by which Laurence Sterne thought that his sister might maintain herself are revealing in this connexion. He had suggested, he says in a letter,

> that if She would set herself to learn the Business of a Mantua-maker, as soon as she could get Insight enough into it, to make a Gown & set up for herself, *That* we would give her 30. pounds to

---

[1] *Wentworth Papers*, p. 116. Cf. *Purefoy Papers*, I. 141.
[2] *Verney Letters of the Eighteenth Century*, ed. Margaret M. Verney, 1930, II. 171.
[3] See J. Jean Hecht, 'Continental and Colonial Servants in Eighteenth Century England', *Smith College Studies in History*, XL.
[4] *London Chronicle*, 1758, III. 327c. Cf. *Parliamentary History*, 1785–6, XXV. 569.

begin the World & Support her till Business fell in.—Or if she Would go into a Milliners Shop in London, My Wife engaged not only to get her into a Shop where she should have Ten pounds a Year Wages, But to equip her with Cloaths &c: properly for the Place: or lastly if she liked it better, As my wife had then an Opportunity of recommending her to the family of the first of our Nobility —She undertook to get her a creditable place in it where she would receive no less than 8 or 10 pds a Year Wages with other Advantages.[1]

As occupations, millinery and dressmaking had serious drawbacks. They required apprentice fees or working capital; they left a woman completely exposed to the vicissitudes of commercial life. In addition, they were fields in which the encroachment of male competition made it increasingly difficult for women to establish themselves.[2] Similar disadvantages attached to the setting up of a seminary. Service, on the other hand, demanded little or no financial outlay and had the virtue of insuring a sheltered existence. Largely because of these attractions it was the most frequently chosen of the possible careers. Thus Sir John Fielding remarks: '... the general resource of young women is to go to service....'[3]

Besides women of good family, young people of more humble origin also found a haven in service. It was the occupation offering the greatest degree of security and protection and so considered the most suitable for poor children. This attitude is implicit in a letter addressed to the editor of a London periodical in 1769. Concerned with the preservation of poor girls, 'Cornelius' supposes that they could be

> provided for in some cheap-rented, convenient house in any part of town, cloathed and maintained in the plainest manner; and ... habituated to cleanliness and works of industry till they were of an age to be received into families (that were known) as common servants.[4]

[1] *Letters of Laurence Sterne*, ed. Lewis P. Curtis, Oxford, 1935, pp. 37–8.
[2] Hanway, *Virtue in Humble Life*, 1774, I. 410; Huntingford, *Laws of Masters and Servants*, p. 106; *Gentleman's Magazine*, 1795, LXV. 980; *Further Humble Advice from Job Nott*, Birmingham, 1800, p. 8; *Memoirs of Mrs. Ann Radcliffe in Familiar Letters*, Edinburgh, 1810, pp. 405, 419.
[3] *London Chronicle*, 1758, III. 327c. Cf. *Manufactures Improper Subjects of Taxation*, 1785, p. 48.
[4] *London Magazine*, 1769, XXXVIII. 146. See also Sir John Fielding, *An Account of the Origin and Effects of a Plan of Police*, 1758, p. 52.

THE DEMAND AND SUPPLY OF SERVANTS

Institutions devoted to the care of the orphaned, the degraded, and the destitute operated on this plan. The Foundling Hospital,[1] the Magdalen Hospital,[2] the Asylum for Orphan Girls,[3] the Orphans' Working School,[4] and the Philanthropic Society[5] prepared most of their girls for service, apprenticing them at an early age.

The charity schools followed a similar course in disposing of their charges. In the hot debate that raged over the value and propriety of educating the children of the 'labouring poor', one of the arguments most frequently pressed by apologists for the schools was that they produced a supply of good servants. Quantitatively, at least, the contention was in accordance with the facts; for in the first thirty-three years of the century the charity schools of London and Westminster alone bound out 3,873 girls and 3,366 boys as domestics.[6]

The parochial system of poor relief also sent young people into service in order to secure their maintenance. The parish was obliged to support foundlings, children of the 'settled poor', and bastards whose parents, in order to be relieved of their care, surrendered them together with a lump sum. The initial stage of its obligation was fulfilled either by putting the children out to nurse or by rearing them in the local poorhouse or workhouse. Later, as provided in the Act of 1601, those who survived were apprenticed at the expense of the parish. Masters in a wide variety of trades took such children as apprentices. But domestic service was the occupation to which girls were most frequently bound.[7]

Those apprenticed to service by philanthropic institutions and

[1] A[nthony Highmore,] *Pietas Londinensis: the History, Design and Present State of the Various Public Charities in and near London*, 1810, pp. 728–9; R[eginald] H. Nichols and F. H. Wray, *The History of the Foundling Hospital*, 1935, pp. 5, 150.

[2] [Jonas] Hanway, *Reflections, Essays and Meditations on Life and Religion*, 1761, I. 64.

[3] Highmore, *Pietas Londinensis*, p. 603. See also the advertisement published in the *London Chronicle*, 1759, v. 576c.

[4] Highmore, *Pietas Londinensis*, p. 837.

[5] *Ibid.*, p. 868.

[6] M[ary] G. Jones, *The Charity School Movement*, 1938, p. 51.

[7] The apprenticing of parish children is treated extensively in M. D[orothy] George, *London Life in the XVIII Century*, New York, 1925, pp. 215–67; Dorothy Marshall, *The English Poor in the Eighteenth Century*, 1926, pp. 181–206.

parish officers did not always become true domestics. Sometimes instead of being given household tasks they were compelled to labour at their masters' trades; sometimes they were forced to combine such work with the legitimate duties of service. Perversions of this sort resulted from a policy that allowed young people to be bound to irresponsible masters, often engaged in the lowest trades and often not far removed from poverty.

Masters and mistresses, however, were not all of this kind. In many instances the young people apprenticed to service were placed in middle-class families. The first girl admitted to the Female Orphan Asylum, for example, having received a thorough course of training in housework, became Sir John Fielding's servant.[1] Many charity school-children were similarly placed, being bound to respectable tradesmen and professional men.[2] And such servants were not unknown in upper-class households. Sanderson Miller, country gentleman and dilettante, for instance, had a bluecoat boy among his domestics.[3] In the homes of masters of this type the apprenticed menial received the same treatment accorded other servants; the only essential differences in his position were that he was paid no wages and that he was unable to leave his place until the expiration of his indenture.

Numerous as were those who thus in one way or another entered service in order to gain shelter and maintenance, many more were led to embrace it as an occupation by its promise of economic and social advancement. Such people were, of course, not unmindful that service was a comfortable mode of existence. There were probably very few amongst them who did not feel the attraction of a life in which most necessities were supplied and many luxuries made accessible, in which work was relatively light and diversion seldom lacking, in which employers often displayed a genuine solicitude and frequently offered a more than nominal protection. The attraction of these aspects of service was pointed out by a writer alarmed at the number of agricultural workers who went up to London:

> Noblemen and gentlemen of fortune keep a vast many unnecessary servants, . . . which is another great drain of labourers, for no man

[1] R[onald] Leslie-Melville, *The Life and Work of Sir John Fielding*, [1935,] p. 125.
[2] Jones, *Charity School Movement*, p. 50.
[3] Dickins and Stanton, *Eighteenth Century Correspondence*, p. 58.

THE DEMAND AND SUPPLY OF SERVANTS

that can live the idle and luxurious life of a livery servant in town, will live on plain food and work hard for the farmer in the country.[1]

But as an incentive to enter service, the prospect of a comfortable life operated far less powerfully than the hope of profit and increased prestige. Hanway is instructive on this point. 'As to servants,' he writes, 'they often entertain each other, with accounts of *profitable places*; as how much wages some have more than others. They do not consider so much the comfort and peace, the s fety and good treatment they enjoy, as how much they may get. . . .'[2] The same basic motivation is also suggested by a pamphleteer who writes that, in general, the aim of country people is 'to get a servitude in London, or to use their own words *to better themselves*. . . .'[3] Of course, for many country people the transition to the Metropolis in itself meant a certain increment in prestige. Much more fundamental in their attitude, however, was the conviction that a place in London provided the best chance of improving their condition. To the daughters of tradesmen as well as to the sons of cottagers, then, service had an appeal because it meant the possibility of substantial pecuniary rewards and the possibility of social elevation.

IV

Since these chances were most fully realized by servants who held the higher posts in upper-class families, such positions were the most coveted. As a consequence, although the over-all demand for servants generally exceeded the supply, aspirants for employment as upper servants greatly outnumbered the available places. At least one contemporary observer held that this was not so. The author of *An Appeal to the Public against the Growing Evil of Universal Register Offices* insisted in 1757 that 'The number of Masters and Mistresses who are in Want of good Servants in every Capacity, is infinitely superior to the number of good Servants out of Place'.[4]

---

[1] *Considerations on the Dearness of Corn and Provisions*, p. 7. Cf. Oliver Grey, [James Townley] *An Apology for Servants*, 1760, p. 19.
[2] Jonas Hanway, *Domestic Happiness Promoted in a Series of Discourses from a Father to His Daughter*, 1786, p. 89. Cf. Hanway, *Virtue in Humble Life*, 1774, I. 344.
[3] *Considerations on the Dearness of Corn and Provisions*, p. 7.
[4] Quoted in *London Chronicle*, 1757, II, 574b.

But the best authorities were of a contrary view. Writing in 1758, Sir John Fielding declares 'that there is always in London an amazing number of women servants out of place', and he proceeds to identify them as 'those of a higher nature, such as chambermaids, &c. whose numbers far exceed the places they stand candidates for. . . .'[1] And in 1790 Huntingford repeated Fielding's remarks almost verbatim, a fairly certain indication that conditions had not changed.[2] Jonas Hanway had an experience that reflects the truth of these observations. When he advertised for a cook, he received more than a hundred applications.[3]

The reverse side of the situation was naturally a scarcity of women willing to serve as domestics in less opulent families. The well-informed Saunders Welch speaks in 1758 of 'the great difficulty of getting servants for all work. . . .'[4] Sir John Fielding likewise notes in the same year that despite the many unemployed female servants, 'the useful housewifery servant, commonly called maids of all work, are not sufficiently numerous to supply the wants of the families in town'.[5]

A similar reluctance characterized the attitude of women towards occupying the lesser posts in upper- and middle-class households. Thus, defending the establishment of foundling homes on the grounds that they would become 'Nurseries' from which upper-class women could 'pick out Servants for the meanest Offices of their Houses', a writer, possibly Thomas Bray, remarks in 1727 'That there has been of late a great Out-cry for want of such Servants. . . .'[6]

As in the case of maidservants, the demand for men far outran the supply. But men as well as women directed their endeavours towards securing the better places, with the inevitable result that a great number were frustrated in their ambitions. Their attitude is laid bare by John Macdonald, the footman, when he details his course of action during an interval of unemployment: 'I took things

---

[1] *London Chronicle*, 1758, III. 327c.

[2] Huntingford, *Laws of Masters and Servants*, p. 107.

[3] John Pugh, *Remarkable Occurrences in the Life of Jonas Hanway*, 1788, 2nd ed., p. 233.

[4] Saunders Welch, *A Proposal*, quoted in *Grand Magazine of Magazines*, 1758, I. 43.

[5] *London Chronicle*, 1758, III. 327c.

[6] *A Memorial Concerning the Erecting in the City of London . . . an Orphanotrophy or Hospital for the Reception of . . . Foundlings*, 1727, p. 29.

very easy, . . . I went after none but a place with a single man, as I wanted for nothing.'¹ The condition which the prevalence of this attitude produced is revealed by Hanway when he describes the unemployment among livery servants in 1760: '. . . it is computed that here [London] are above *Two Thousand*, in a kind of rotation, always *out of place*, and in search of *good Services*; so much is our office of a *domestic* Servant preferable to most other occupations.'² Menservants do not appear to have grown less selective as the century progressed; for Patrick Colquhoun, whose position as magistrate enabled him to collect a wealth of accurate information on the London of the period, calculated in 1796 that there were 'seldom less than *Ten Thousand Servants*, of both sexes, at all times out of place in the Metropolis'.³

Many men, rather than accept inferior positions, seem to have turned to other fields. A newspaper essay written in 1723 insists that 'multitudes of them daily, for want of Employment, betake themselves to the Highway, Housebreaking, other Robbing and Sharping, or to the Stews. . . .'⁴ And Joseph Massie, discussing the young men who left the country for London, gave a similar account in 1758: '. . . if they cannot get such Employment as they expected, . . . many of them will not go Home again to be laughed at . . . but inlist for Soldiers, go to the Plantations &c. if they are well inclined; otherwise they probably commence Thieves or Pickpockets. . . .'⁵

In the country unemployment among servants can never have assumed such proportions, since the unemployed tended to go up to London. But whatever unemployment did exist arose from the same causes that produced it in London.

Thus, with the exception of those disqualified by loss of character or other personal disability, servants out of place were

[1] *Memoirs of an Eighteenth-Century Footman*, ed. John Beresford, [1927,] p. 235.
[2] Jonas Hanway, *The Sentiments and Advice of Thomas Trueman*, 1760, p. 50.
[3] P[atrick] Colquhoun, *A Treatise on the Police of the Metropolis*, 1797, 5th ed., p. 423*n*. Cf. [Louis Simmond,] *Journal of a Tour and Residence in Great Britain, during the Years 1810 and 1811*, New York, 1815, II. 142.
[4] *British Journal*, 1723, June 15, 2a.
[5] J[oseph] Massie, *A Plan for the Establishment of Charity Houses*, 1758, p. 16.

victims of their own selectivity. Much of the demand for domestics simply went unheeded.

V

The demand for servants was fed by a complex machinery of recruitment. Master and servant were brought together by a number of different devices.

One of the commonest ways of procuring domestics, both in London and the country, was through friends or through other servants. Employers often canvassed such sources when faced with the necessity of filling vacancies in their households. Thus on one occasion Mrs. Piozzi asked Mrs. Pennington to find her a capable person to head her establishment: 'You must enquire me a Housekeeper such as you *know* will suit us; a good country housewife, who can salt Bacon, cure Hams, see also to the baking, etc., and be an active manager of and for a dozen troublesome servants. . . .'[1] And Horace Walpole, when in need of a combined steward and butler, asked his business agent to undertake a similar mission: 'If you could find a very good servant for me it would be of great use. . . . His chief business will be to look after my family, in which he must be strict; and he must understand buying and selling. . . .'[2]

Tradesmen also served as recruiting agents. A guidebook suggests that the newcomer to the Metropolis 'get a servant recommended by a friend, or some tradesman, with whom he deals, such as the baker, butcher, poulterer, green-grocer, tallow-chandler, publican, or the like. . . .'[3] And in the country tradesmen were called upon to perform the same service. 'I desire you still to enquire after a maid for mee,' writes Elizabeth Purefoy to a village shoemaker at a time when her household lacked an essential

---

[1] *Intimate Letters of Hester Piozzi*, pp. 132–3. For other examples see Francis Bamford, *Dear Miss Heber. An Eighteenth Century Correspondence*, 1936, p. 133; *The Autobiography and Correspondence of Mary Granville, Mrs. Delany*, ed. Lady Llanover, Second Series, 1862, I. 328; *Elizabeth Montagu the Queen of the Bluestockings Her Correspondence from 1720 to 1761*, ed. Emily J. Climenson, 1906, I. 225; *Private Letters of Edward Gibbon*, ed. Rowland E. Prothero, 1896, I. 248, 250.

[2] *Letters of Horace Walpole*, v. 245.

[3] Trusler, *London Adviser*, p. 48.

member; and on a similar occasion she instructed another tradesman to get her a footman.[1]

When the efforts of tradesmen and other intermediaries proved unsuccessful, employers in the country could fall back on the local mop or statute fair, a public hiring held once or twice a year in many villages as well as in most county towns. Although the origin of the institution is sometimes traced to the Elizabethan Statute of Apprentices (1563),[2] its earliest appearance probably occurred in the years succeeding the passage of the Statute of Labourers (1351),[3] which enjoined the unemployed to proceed to the nearest market town, implements in hand, and offer themselves for hire. It retained its vitality until the end of the nineteenth century,[4] and vestiges of it survived into the third decade of the twentieth.[5] In the eighteenth century its existence was not universal: no statutes were held in Devonshire and in some of the other southern counties.[6] Nor was the time for holding them everywhere the same. In Cumberland, for instance, they took place at Whitsuntide and Martinmas;[7] in Yorkshire Martinmas was the date;[8] and in some other sections they were held at Michaelmas.[9]

The original form of the statute fair remained unaltered in the eighteenth century. At the customary time masters and servants converged on the appointed place: street, churchyard, or market square. Each servant usually wore or carried an emblem to indicate

[1] *Purefoy Letters*, I. 143, 136–7.
[2] R[aymond] W. Muncey, *Our Old English Fairs*, [1935,] p. 160; Daniel Defoe, *Tour thro' the Whole Island of Great Britain*, ed. G. D. H. Cole, 1927, II. 430.
[3] W[ilhelm] Hasbach, *The English Agricultural Labourer*, 1908, p. 23; Russell M. Garnier, *Annals of the British Peasantry*, 1895, p. 58; *Notes and Queries*, First Series, 1851, II. 157.
[4] T[homas] E. Kebbel, *The Agricultural Labourer*, 1893, pp. 173–82.
[5] E[phraim] Lipson, *The Economic History of England*, 1929–31, III. 301*n*.
[6] [William] Marshall, *The Rural Economy of the West of England*, 1796, I. 108–9, II. 227; *The Rural Economy of the Southern Counties*, 1798, I. 55, II. 233.
[7] John Housman, *A Topographical Description of Cumberland, Westmorland, Lancashire, and a Part of the West Riding of Yorkshire*, Carlisle, 1800, p. 71.
[8] K. L. McCutcheon, 'Yorkshire Fairs and Markets to the End of the Eighteenth Century', *Thoresby Society Publications*, 1940, XXXIX. 158; Walker, *Wakefield*, p. 405.
[9] *Purefoy Letters*, I. 126.

the type of work he was accustomed to do. Defoe comments on this:

> ... the poor Servants distinguish themselves by holding something in their Hands, to imitate what Labour they are particularly qualify'd to undertake; as the Carters a Whip, the Labourers a Shovel, the Wood Men a Bill, the Manufacturers a Wool Comb, and the like.[1]

Guided by these symbols an employer inspected and interviewed a number of candidates. When he had finally made his selection a verbal contract was concluded and earnest money given. Sometimes a court of Petty Sessions was held concurrently with the fair, so that contracts could be sworn and registered without delay;[2] sometimes they were registered when the court met a month or two later.

The statute fair also had a lighter side. A writer reporting on this aspect of the institution says that

> when the hiring is over and the fiddlers tuning their fiddles in public houses, the girls begin to file off, and gently pace the streets, with a view of gaining admirers; while the young men, with equally innocent designs, follow after, and having eyed the *lasses*, pick up each a sweetheart, whom they conduct to a dancing room, and treat with punch and cake. . . .[3]

Because of these activities moralists and economists regarded statute fairs with an intolerant eye, the former claiming that they were conducive to roistering and profligacy, the latter holding that they rendered servants indisposed to work for a long period afterwards. The servants themselves, however, looked forward all the year to the local statute as one of the high points of their social life.

Servants in husbandry were predominant amongst those who offered themselves at statute fairs. But there were also many domestics, as is evident from a picture of the Waltham Abbey hiring which Samuel Curwen, an observant American, drew in 1782. The men, he wrote, 'appear with the tools or insignia of their respective employments; the females of the domestic kind are distinguished by their aprons, viz. cooks in colored, nursery-

---

[1] Defoe, *Tour*, II. 430.
[2] [William] Marshall, *The Rural Economy of Norfolk*, 1787, I. 40.
[3] Housman, *Topographical Description*, p. 71.

maids in white linen, and chamber and waiting-maids in lawn or cambric.'[1] Thus, while farmers resorted to the statutes to look for ploughmen, the gentry went to staff their houses. Elizabeth Purefoy, for example, occasionally sought servants at a near-by statute.[2]

No statutes were held in the Metropolitan area. But the existence of other devices through which servants could be obtained partially compensated for their absence.

The inns at which country wagons concluded their trips up to the Capital served as centres where domestics could be engaged.[3] Employers often met the wagons in order to make their selection from amongst the latest arrivals. It was also a common practice for innkeepers to put employers in touch with young people from the country who desired places.

Register offices or intelligence offices, as they were called before the establishment of the Fieldings' agency in 1749, were another means whereby Londoners could find servants. Originating in early seventeenth-century schemes for bringing together buyer and seller, worker and employer, the idea of a register office had been translated into practice long before the dawn of the eighteenth century.[4] By the time of the Restoration London possessed a number of such agencies, and in the decades that followed the register office became a permanent fixture of the metropolitan scene.

In operation the register office of the eighteenth century greatly resembled its modern equivalent. Fees were exacted both from the applicants for places and the applicants for domestics. A notice of a register office explained in 1717 that 'all Masters wanting Servants of any Denomination (do enter for three pence) as likewise Servants for Places. . . .'[5] Some offices charged annual rates, which entitled subscribers to use their facilities as often as necessary within the course of the year. In 1780 the London General Office, for instance, offered to supply employers 'with any

---

[1] *Journal and Letters of the Late Samuel Curwen*, ed. George A. Ward, New York, 1842, p. 389.

[2] *Purefoy Letters*, I. 126, 144–5, 156.

[3] *London Chronicle*, 1758, III. 116c.

[4] M. Dorothy George, 'The Early History of Registry Offices', *Economic Journal* (Supplement), Jan., 1929, IV. 570–9.

[5] *Weekly Journal*, 1717, No. 2, Mar. 4, 126.

servant they may want' for two shillings the first year and one shilling every year thereafter; servants who applied for upper stations were asked one shilling and sixpence, those who applied for inferior posts one shilling.[1] Register offices sometimes notified an employer of the availability of a servant by messenger or post; sometimes he had to call in person to receive such information. The early agencies issued advertisement sheets which, along with commercial news and miscellaneous notices of articles for sale, included listings of servants out of place. With the multiplication of newspapers and their gradual development as vehicles for advertisement, however, this practice was abandoned.

A more direct process of selection was made possible by the statute hall, a variant of the register or intelligence office which had established itself in London by the middle of the eighteenth century. Like the register office, the statute hall was privately owned and privately operated. Yet, as its name suggests, it imitated the statute fairs of the country by gathering together a number of servants whom an employer could inspect before making his choice. A news item that appeared in 1774 describes it as a place 'where servants, like cattle, are viewed. . . .'[2] Some statute halls also sent domestics to be interviewed at the employer's home. The Rev. Trusler informed those unacquainted with London that 'by sending a shilling to the keepers of such offices, and a description of the servant wanted, they will send one, day after day, till you are suited. . . .'[3] It is highly possible that in the second half of the century some register offices likewise employed the practice.

Neither register offices nor statute halls enjoyed the confidence of the public. Both, in fact, laboured under a popular disrepute which, in the case of register offices, dated from the last years of the seventeenth century.

The unsavoury reputation of register offices derived in part from the victimization of domestics that many of them practised. Their principal ruse was to take fees when the only vacancies known to them were imaginary ones. Richard King includes this stratagem in his catalogue of London chicanery: 'It is customary for keepers of Register Offices, to put advertisements into papers, relative to

---

[1] *General Advertiser*, 1780, No. 879, Jan. 27, 3d.
[2] *London Chronicle*, 1774, XXXVI. 46b.
[3] Trusler, *London Adviser*, p. 47.

THE DEMAND AND SUPPLY OF SERVANTS

places, which in fact they have not to dispose of. . . .'[1] In Joseph Reed's play about a register office Gulwell, the keeper, pursues precisely this course.[2] And news items confirm the impression that it was a fraud often attempted. In 1764 it was reported in the press that the keeper of a register office had been summoned before a magistrate for having accepted five shillings from a girl to get her a place and then having refused to return the money, when it became apparent that he had no place for her.[3] A similar account was published in 1765. A keeper was said to have been called before a magistrate for having taken seventeen shillings from five servants 'under pretence of helping them to places, which, on enquiry they found had been gone several days before their application'[4]. Still another case was reported in 1766. In this instance the court ordered the register office to pay all of the expenses of the servant during the period he had waited for a non-existent place.[5] A more flagrant malpractice of which some register offices were undoubtedly guilty was procurement for prostitution. Thus one writer calls them 'the markets of pimps and procuresses',[6] and another refers to them as 'warehouses of iniquity'.[7] Reed's play also attacks them on this score. Frankly, one of the characters tells of an old man in the neighbourhood who had built up a fortune by including among the conveniences of his register office 'the good old Trade of *Pimping*'.[8] It was with ample reason, then, that in one of his moral tracts Hanway cautions the young girl to investigate her employer with special care if her position had been obtained through a register office.[9] In some instances register offices must have been the unwitting instruments of evil designs. This is strongly suggested by a case reported in 1767. A young man was approached through a register office and told to go to a certain address; but the suspicions of the keeper had been aroused, so the address was investigated and found to be a lockup for recruits gathered by the press gang.[10] But the

[1] [Richard King], *The New Cheats of London Exposed*, n.d., pp. 24–5. Cf. *The New Cheats of London Exposed*, 1792, p. 44.
[2] Joseph Reed, *The Register Office*, 1771, pp. 8–9.
[3] *London Chronicle*, 1764, XVI. 514a.   [4] *Ibid.*, 1765, XVIII. 95b.
[5] *Ibid.*, 1766, XX. 178c.
[6] King, *New Cheats*, n.d., p. 25; *New Cheats*, 1792, pp. 44–5.
[7] *Oxford Magazine*, 1771, VI. 82.   [8] Reed, *Register Office*, p. 7.
[9] Hanway, *Domestic Happiness*, p. 229.
[10] *Annual Register*, 1767, X. 60.

use of register offices for such artifices redounded as much to their discredit as the transgressions some of them actually committed.

The disrepute register offices earned by their mistreatment of servants was equalled by that which they gained from their disservice to employers. They were constantly reprobated for giving or aiding in the acquisition of false characters. The attitude of the employer class is exemplified by Huntingford's insistence in 1790 that 'they ought to be under some better regulation; and not to be left at liberty to impose a profligate woman, or a villain, upon a family, where one or the other may prove the destruction of it.'[1] Moreover, they were frowned on for encouraging in domestics an independent spirit. A letter published by a newspaper in 1772 maintains that the intractability of servants is due to

> the ease with which they find it possible to provide themselves with one place, when turned out of another. There are so many register and intelligence offices, so many statute halls . . . where they may hear of employment for sixpence, a shilling or half a crown, that they laugh at any threats of dismission for misbehaviour.[2]

No such odium attached to the use of the newspaper advertisement as a means of securing servants. Except perhaps for personal recommendation, it was the most respectable of the possible methods. It is significant that Jonas Hanway, who knew the virtues and defects of all the devices of recruitment, habitually advertised for his domestics.[3] The practice of advertising grew as newspapers expanded in size. Occasional notices appeared in the small sheets of the early century; they became a regular feature of the larger morning papers later on.

Advertising in these journals was a particularly effective technique because they reached more candidates than could be approached in any other way. Thus when recommending the *Daily Advertiser* in 1786 as the best medium through which an employer could make his wants known, the Rev. Trusler points out that it 'is taken in by almost all the publicans in London' and then states with assurance: 'Such an advertisement will bring you scores of servants.'[4]

[1] Huntingford, *Laws of Masters and Servants*, p. 106.
[2] *London Packet*, 1772, No. 454, Sept. 18–21, 4a.
[3] Pugh, *Life of Jonas Hanway*, p. 233.
[4] Trusler, *London Adviser*, p. 48.

THE DEMAND AND SUPPLY OF SERVANTS

The advantages of a wide circulation also led domestics to publish their availability in the press. The amount of advertising space they purchased seems to have been at least as great as that taken by employers.

VI

Unfortunately no accurate figures exist for the supply of servants enlisted through these various devices. The returns are available for the tax of a guinea a head that Lord North levied on male domestics in 1777. But the imposition was so widely evaded and its collection so inefficiently executed that the yield cannot be taken as an index of the number of menservants. No more informative are the returns for the taxes on male and female domestics which the younger Pitt imposed in 1785. Their progressive nature; their exemptions and special features, such as the provision for double payment by bachelors; their inclusion of such groups as waiters in inns and taverns; their circumvention by employers all conspire to render the intake useless as a basis for calculating the number of servants.

This lack of explicit data makes precise measurement impossible. But some notion of the size of the servant class may be gained from contemporary opinion.

To contemporaries the servant class seemed a numerous group. Mary Johnson, author of a work for domestics, declared: '. . . the Number . . . of Servants (both Male and Female) throughout his Majesty's Dominions is very large. . . .'[1] A newspaper correspondent in 1760 noted 'the prodigious number of your Youth of both sexes entertained as servants. . . .'[2] And Sir John Fielding remarked: '. . . the Body of domestic Servants is very large. . . .'[3]

The speculations made during the period are in complete harmony with these comments. Several of the speculations deal solely with the London area. Assuming in 1767 that the population of London within the bills was 650,000, a cautious figure, Hanway reckoned that one in every thirteen was a domestic—a

---

[1] Johnson, *Madam Johnson's Present*, pp. 1–2.
[2] *London Chronicle*, 1760, VIII. 196a.
[3] Sir John Fielding, *Extracts from* . . . *the Penal Laws*, 1769, 3rd ed., p. 141. Cf. Huntingford, *Laws of Masters and Servants*, p. 97.

THE DEMAND AND SUPPLY OF SERVANTS

total of 50,000.[1] The ratio he employed in 1767 was conservative compared with that which he adopted later on. In 1775 he calculated that of the 650,000 persons in London within the bills one in every eight was a servant, which meant an aggregate of 80,000.[2] Even this is dwarfed by the estimate made in 1796 by Patrick Colquhoun, the magistrate. Basing his calculations on the assumption that there were about 240,000 families in the metropolitan area, he concluded that 100,000 of them kept an average of two servants or a total of 200,000.[3] Since the census of 1801 credits Greater London with a population of 900,000, this would mean that one in every four and a half persons was a domestic. Estimates similar to these were made for the country as a whole. When Lord North proposed his servant tax in 1777, he computed the number of male servants at 100,000.[4] Colquhoun arrived at a slightly higher figure in 1806. He put the number of menservants at 110,000. At the same time he supposed the number of maidservants to total 800,000.[5] When Colquhoun made these estimates the first census had already revealed the population of England and Wales to be a little over 10,400,000; so he evidently thought that about one in every eleven was a servant.

In contrast to the meticulous counting of political arithmeticians like Gregory King all these calculations are mere guesswork. Yet it seems likely that the general impression they give of the size of the servant class closely resembles its true proportion.

[1] Jonas Hanway, *Letters on the Importance of Preserving the Rising Generation of the Labouring Part of Our Fellow Subjects*, 1767, II. 158. See also *Virtue in Humble Life*, 1774, I. introd., p. xxiin.
[2] Jonas Hanway, *The Defects of Police the Cause of Immorality*, 1775, p. 267.
[3] Colquhoun, *Police of the Metropolis*, p. 151.
[4] *Parliamentary History*, 1777–8, XIX. 245. Cf. *Morning Post*, 1777, No. 1429, May 20, 2b; No. 1439, May 31, 2b.
[5] Patrick Colquhoun, *A Treatise on Indigence ... with Proposals for Ameliorating the Condition of the Poor*, 1806, p. 253.

Chapter Two

THE SERVANT HIERARCHY

AMONG the many domestics who comprised the servant class there existed distinct gradations. Household function was the essential basis of this differentiation: the nature of the work that a servant performed determined his nominal rank, and although only one of the factors that defined his occupational status, nominal rank was by far the most powerful.

I

The principal line of cleavage was that which divided upper and lower domestics. The former included those servants whose work was executive and supervisory, and those who possessed special skills developed through long and sometimes expensive training. The latter category was composed of servants whose activities were controlled and directed, and whose work was of a relatively unskilled, manual variety.

Differences in living quarters, in dress, in diet, in leisure time and in a host of minor particulars signalized this division; and some of the differences were pronounced. Upper menservants, for example, wore ordinary clothes while their subordinates wore livery. Again, in large establishments, upper servants dined together at the second table while the lower servants sat at the third.[1] It was, of course, in the large households, where specialization of function was carried furthest, that such distinctions were most marked; but they were to be found in some degree wherever the staff included both upper and lower domestics.

Domestics were acutely conscious of the disparity in rank that these differences reflected. A new cook engaged by John Spencer,

---

[1] *A Treatise on the Use and Abuse of the Second, Commonly Called, the Steward's Table*, n.d., *passim*.

for example, announced that 'she expected to dine in ye housekeeper's Room, as it was Always ye Custom where there was a second Table for ye cook to dine at it. . . .'[1] Similarly, his housekeeper expressed 'a very great objection' to sleeping 'with ye other Maids'.[2] The general attitude of such domestics is well described by an anonymous pamphleteer who, flaying them for their arrogance and pretensions, complains that they 'endeavour to imprint the strongest Idea they possibly can of their own Consequence and Authority on the Minds of every menial Servant. . . .'[3] It is also effectively laid bare by the protests of Frank, an upper servant in John O' Keeffe's play *Tony Lumpkin in Town* (1782):

> Do you make no difference between a servant in livery, and a gentleman's gentleman? In the country, I suppose it's 'hail fellow well met'; but here, Sir, we are delicate, nice in our distinctions; for a valet moves in a sphere, and lives in a stile as superior to a footman, as a Pall-mall groom porter to the marker of a tennis-court.[4]

The functional differentiation that underlay the major division also created a number of minor ones. Although the outward marks that set these subdivisions off from each other were not numerous, servants were well aware of the differences in prestige. This is apparent from the admonition an author of a handbook for servants addressed to the genus footman: 'Never treat those with contempt whose station in the house may happen to be inferior to yours, considering they are placed there by the will of Providence. . . .'[5] Moreover, it is perfectly mirrored in the seating arrangement that generally prevailed in the steward's or housekeeper's room, on the one hand, and in the servants' hall, on the other. In the smaller households, where the entire staff dined together, those servants who held the highest posts occupied seats at the head of the table, the others sitting according to rank in descending order. In the large establishments, where upper and lower servants dined separately, the same strict observance of precedence governed the disposition of places at both tables, so that at mealtime the two sections of the household were arrayed in all the gradations of their hierarchy.

[1] A[nna] M. W. Stirling, *Annals of a Yorkshire House*, 1911, I. 125.
[2] *Ibid.*, I. 127.
[3] *Treatise on the Use and Abuse of the Second . . . Table*, p. 6.
[4] *The Dramatic Works of John O'Keeffe*, 1798, I. 228.
[5] Anthony Heasel, *The Servants Book of Knowledge*, 1773, p. 72.

THE SERVANT HIERARCHY

But the individual domestic's occupational status was not wholly determined by his nominal rank. Personal background also counted. The readers of a vade-mecum for servants were told: '... your birth and education will shine through whatever station you serve in.'[1] Thus a butler who was the son of a comfortable tradesman possessed greater prestige than one whose father had been an agricultural labourer. A still more important factor was the social position of the employer; for a certain amount of his prestige was imparted to the servant, who not only identified himself with him but was also closely identified with him by others. 'You will be known by your master's rank and fortune,' runs a contemporary description of the servant's position in the occupational hierarchy.[2] Thus the butler of a nobleman was held in higher regard than the butler of a country gentleman, and the butler of a country gentleman enjoyed greater esteem than the butler of a merchant.

The social standing of the employer did not exert an equal influence on the occupational status of all his domestics. Those whose functions brought them near to his person and who consequently were treated with a relatively high degree of familiarity, were more profoundly affected than those whose household tasks fixed them at a distance. Hence the prestige that a scullery maid acquired by being employed in a ducal household was negligible compared with that which accrued to a valet or steward, whose duties entailed frequent and prolonged contact with his master. Referring to the post of scullery maid, a writer remarked that 'as for the honour, it matters little whether it be with a duke or earl. . . .'[3]

Nevertheless, whatever his nominal rank, the average domestic was keenly aware that his occupational status derived in part from the social standing of his employer. This awareness is amusingly parodied in Townley's piquant *High Life Below Stairs* (1759). Emphasizing external differences but at the same time evincing a lively appreciation of the distinction in status they represent, the Duke's servant says:

> What Wretches are ordinary Servants that go on in the same vulgar Track ev'ry Day! Eating, working, and sleeping!—But we, who have the Honour to serve the Nobility, are of another Species. We are above the common Forms, have Servants to wait upon us, and are as lazy and luxurious as our Masters.[4]

---

[1] *Servants Pocket-Book*, 1761, p. 7. [2] *Ibid.*, p. 8. [3] *Ibid.*, p. 10.
[4] [James Townley,] *High Life Below Stairs*, 1775, 9th ed., p. 11.

The domestics of the gentry regarded those of the mercantile classes with a similar condescension; while those employed by great merchants felt themselves distinctly superior to those who lived in the homes of petty tradesmen, calling them 'pitiful creatures'.[1]

But the transfiguration effected by the aura of the master was always of a very limited nature. While the social status of a duke, for instance, normally invested his butler with a prestige considerably in excess of that possessed by the butler of a country squire, it did not elevate his footman above the squire's valet. 'Though your master wear a coronet,' the ambitious livery servant was informed by a writer concerned with the aspirations of domestics, 'you will be less valued than the servant who dresses an honest country gentleman.'[2] In short, although the social status of the employer dictated variations in prestige among servants of the same nominal rank, it was incapable of endowing a particular post with prestige equivalent to that ordinarily derived from a post much higher or lower in the hierarchy.

More than any other factor, then, nominal rank defined a servant's occupational status. His position in the hierarchy was decisive in fixing his position in the servant class.

Many details in the structure of the hierarchy elude definition. Its main outlines are disclosed by such information as exists about wages: the scale of wages suggests the main differences in status.[3]

II

At the top of the servant hierarchy was the land steward, an official whose duties were both manifold and diverse. He managed his master's estate, leasing the farms, collecting the rents, surveying the boundaries, settling disputes between tenants and keeping a detailed record of receipts and expenses.[4] He was also expected to superintend the cultivation of the land his master retained in his own hands and to supervise the tenants in their practice of husbandry, giving advice and acquainting them with the latest improvements in agricultural method.[5] Thus, among other things,

---

[1] *Servants Pocket-Book*, p. 10.   [2] *Ibid.*, p. 8.   [3] See chap. VI.
[4] Edward Laurence, *The Duty of a Steward to His Lord*, 1727, pp. 21, 82–3, 85, 133.
[5] *Ibid.*, pp. 22, 23; Thomas Stone, *An Essay on Agriculture*, Lynn, 1785, pp. vii–ix; John Lawrence, *The Modern Land Steward*, 1801, p. 45.

according to Edward Laurence, who had himself been steward to the Duke of Buckingham, he was supposed to '*ride over the whole Estate once a month*, in order to view both the Lands and Stock of the Tenants carefully and distinctly. . . .'[1] Timber land was no less his concern than arable. He inspected the trees and had them cut and marketed at the proper time.[2] Where a court leet or court baron was held on the estate, that, too, came within his province. In the former he served as judge; in the latter the free suitors were the judges 'and the steward merely their president'.[3] Finally, in some instances he played a leading role in parish affairs, acting as his master's representative and at the same time looking out for his master's interests.

Candidates for the post obviously had to possess a real versatility. It was not only necessary 'that a Steward should be a good Accomptant, but also that he should have a tolerable degree of Skill in *Mathematics*, Surveying, Mechanicks, and Architecture. . . .'[4] He likewise had to have 'some skill and knowledge in the law (*especially parish-law*). . . .'[5] Another important qualification was to be familiar with agriculture in all its branches. This was considered particularly essential, as both Edward Laurence and John Mordant make clear in their extensive handbooks on the occupation of steward.

Those who met the requirements were a heterogeneous lot. They numbered amongst them lawyers, yeomen, and country gentlemen of small fortune as well as men who had been lower domestics, farmers, and clerks in mercantile houses.

In some instances lawyers and men of property maintained outside interests while serving as stewards. Edward Laurence strongly disapproved of the employment of country attorneys for that reason, arguing that 'A Steward's Business is not such as may be done as it were *by the by*; 'Tis his *whole* Employment, and a full one too. . . . The Attorney, if he has any Character, has Business enough of his own, of the Law, and therefore should not undertake the Office of a Steward. . . .'[6] Much the same thing might

---

[1] Laurence, *Duty of a Steward*, p. 24.   [2] *Ibid.*, pp. 66–73.
[3] F[ossey] J. C. Hearnshaw, 'Leet Jurisdiction in England', *Southampton Record Society Publications*, v. 91.
[4] Laurence, *Duty of a Steward*, p. 50.
[5] Mordant, *Complete Steward*, I. p v.
[6] Laurence, *Duty of a Steward*, p. 5.

have been said of those gentlemen who combined a stewardship with the care of their own property. Most stewards, however, devoted all their time to the management of their masters' affairs.

Some large estates required even more attention than could be supplied by a steward who gave full time to his duties. Especially was this likely to be true of those made up of scattered holdings. For such estates several stewards were employed and the work divided between them. Sometimes an agent-in-chief was also retained.[1] The principal function of the agent-in-chief was the supervision of the other stewards. After inspecting their accounts, says Mordant, 'he either draws up an abstract, or passes them separately: and he likewise occasionally looks over and inspects every estate and agent of his *Lord's*. . . .' At the same time he might also be 'absolutely steward to that estate belonging to his *Lord's* chief seat'.[2]

On many small estates and on large estates where the farm lands lay near the house, there was, of course, no need for a land steward. Where this was the case, the land steward's duties were often performed by the house steward—the *maître d'hôtel*, as he was often called; the 'steward and *Domo-fac-totum*, or *Major Domo*', as Mordant styles him.[3]

The primary concern of the house steward was the management of his employer's residence. He controlled its staff; he regulated its economy. It was his duty

> to take and state all Accompts, receive and pay all Monies, buy in the Provision for the Family, hire all Livery-men, buy all Liveries, pay all Wages, direct and keep in order all Livery-men (except the Coachman and Groom) to be at his Master's Elbow during Dinner, and receive all Orders from him relating to Government; to oversee and direct the Bailiff, Gardener, &c. in their Business; and also the Clerk of the Kitchen, Cook, Butler, &c. to whom he delivers the Provision, Wine, Beer, &c. who give him an Account of the spending it, Weekly or otherwise.[4]

In addition to these cares, as has been pointed out, he also sometimes assumed those of land steward.

---

[1] Mordant, *Complete Steward*, II. 33; Edward Hughes, 'The Eighteenth Century Estate Agent', *Essays in British and Irish History in Honour of James Eadie Todd*, [1949], p. 188.
[2] Mordant, *Complete Steward*, II. 33.   [3] *Ibid.*
[4] Jacob, *Country Gentleman's Vademecum*, p. 45.

THE SERVANT HIERARCHY

When the two posts were thus combined, the office demanded all the ability required in a land steward. Ordinarily, however, the house steward was a man of slighter stature. He had to possess dependability, a certain degree of executive talent, and a thorough familiarity with social rites and forms; but no special skills were a necessary part of his equipment.

The house steward was a domestic in a much fuller sense than the land steward. Regular visits to the house, where he always had an office and often a bedroom, and frequent meals at the second table, made the land steward share actively in the life of the family. Thomas Marchant, for example, who in the early century was steward to the Duke of Somerset, mentions in his diary having dined with the housekeeper and having been at prayers along with the rest of the household staff.[1] But he usually maintained a home of his own where he spent a good deal of his time. The house steward, on the other hand, almost always lived in, his role in the establishment requiring his presence at all times.

The authority he wielded in the execution of that role varied. He was responsible to the land steward, where such an official was employed; where there was no land steward, he ruled supreme over the household, being answerable to no one save his master.

In the early years of the century the pre-eminence of the land and house stewards within the servant class and the authority they wielded within the individual establishment were shared by other domestics. One of these was the gentleman-in-waiting, a masculine counterpart of the lady's maid or waiting-woman. Drawn whenever possible from the lesser gentry, he acted as both confidential adviser and personal attendant. Of equivalent household rank was the master of the horse. Although, like the gentleman-in-waiting, he was often a man of good family, his work had a far more utilitarian character. The stables were in his charge; and all the livery servants connected with them, from the coachman down to the helpers and boys, were under his sole superintendence. It was his duty, writes Giles Jacob, 'To buy Coaches, Saddles, and Furniture, and all Horses; to buy in Corn, Hay and Provender for Horses, direct the Coachman, Postilion, and Groom, and, during Travelling, the other Livery-men; order all Horses, &c.'[2] Like the

[1] 'The Marchant Diary', *Sussex Archaeological Collections*, xxv. 196.
[2] Jacob, *Country Gentleman's Vademecum*, p. 45.

gentleman-in-waiting, he was exempt from all superior control, except that imposed by his master.

By the end of the first quarter of the century, the posts of gentleman-in-waiting and master of the horse had nearly disappeared from English households. Most of the functions performed by the gentleman-in-waiting devolved upon the *valet de chambre* and the house steward; while the master of the horse was replaced by the clerk of the stables.

The clerk of the stables, together with his fellow clerk who presided over the kitchen, stood just below the house steward in the scale of rank. Both were subject to his authority, submitting their accounts for his inspection and approval, and receiving directions from him as to the management of their departments.

As a rule, the clerk of the stables was probably not so well-born as his predecessor, the master of the horse, had been. His duties were substantially the same. 'His use', affirms an anonymous pamphleteer who was thoroughly acquainted with the structure and operation of upper-class households,

> is to act as Purveyor, and see that the servants under him do the business he commands; he ought to be a judge of hay, corn, straw, physic, roads, carriages, horses, and the intire decorum of stables, with regard to race-horses, hunters, coach-horses, and hacks.[1]

He also acted as a sort of travel counsellor. From a fund of knowledge, presumably gathered at first hand, he supplied his master with detailed information on the condition of roads and inns.[2]

Somewhat lighter demands were made upon the clerk of the kitchen. He ordered the provisions for the table, negotiating with the butcher, the baker, and the greengrocer, and disbursing the funds allocated by the house steward for the payment of those tradesmen.[3] It was likewise his task to dispense the foodstuffs he had purchased. Orders were presented to him periodically by the cooks; and these he passed on, keeping a careful record of whatever provisions he released. His role as guardian of supplies is well illustrated by a set of directions drawn up by the second Earl of Nottingham. It is stipulated therein that the clerk of the kitchen 'must deliver out to ye cooks wtever is to be by ym used, and not

---

[1] *Treatise on the Use and Abuse of the Second . . . Table*, p. 54.
[2] *Ibid.*, p. 55.
[3] Pearl Finch, *History of Burley-on-the-Hill*, 1901, I. 233.

THE SERVANT HIERARCHY

give ye key to any person wtsoever on any pretense wtsoever'.[1] But something more than management of the larder was expected of the clerk of the kitchen. It was part of his duty 'to make [the] Bills of Fare'.[2] He also saw to it that the meals were properly prepared and punctually served. 'Fail not', he is admonished in the Earl of Nottingham's directions, 'to have ye dinner ready by 12 of ye clock and lett the bell then be rung and dinner sert up, likewise supper at 7.' In addition he shared in the actual serving. 'You must wait at ye lower end of ye Parlour table,' read the Earl's instructions, 'yt you may be in My Lady's eye and be directed, when to go for the second course, or desert wch must be brought into ye parlour in like manner.'[3]

Immediately beneath the clerk of the kitchen and the clerk of the stables ranked the man-cook, the confectioner, the baker and the bailiff.

The duties of the man-cook varied, depending on whether or not a clerk of the kitchen was employed. When there was no clerk, his control over the culinary department was complete. The kitchen staff worked under his direction; the whole process of making up menus, buying victuals, preparing and serving meals was his responsibility, and his alone. But where a clerk was retained, authority in the culinary sphere was divided; and the cook, although not in all things directly subordinate to the clerk, was distinctly the lesser personage.

Whether he presided over the kitchen alone or in conjunction with a clerk, the first qualification in a cook was familiarity with the arcana of French cuisine; for the upper classes and their imitators grew increasingly devoted to Parisian diet as the century advanced. When there was no clerk, the cook's abilities had to extend far beyond this. What was considered essential in such circumstances is well-summarized by a writer intimately acquainted with the details of domestic economy. A cook, he states,

> should be a man of thorough knowledge in his profession, capable of forming a bill of fare, and dressing it when approved of. He should be well versed in what is a sufficiency for the support of the family which he is to provide for, be they more or less in number.

---

[1] Finch, *History of Burley* I. 232.
[2] B[ernard] Clermont, *The Professed Cook*, 1769, 2nd ed., p. v.
[3] Finch, *History of Burley*, I. 233, 232.

He should also be a judge of the goodness of each sort of provisions for which he goes to market. . . .[1]

Not infrequently Frenchmen were employed, since it was assumed that they knew best how to prepare their native dishes and since they possessed a high honorific value.[2] But it was not exceptional to find an Englishman in the post of chief cook.

Some of the larger establishments included other culinary experts besides the chief cook. It was not unusual for a servant to be employed solely to make pastry and other sweets, nor was it uncommon for a specialist in baking to be retained to make bread. Both the confectioner and the baker were very likely to have received their training outside the field of domestic service, the former in a sweet shop such as Betty's, the latter in a bakery. Both were as likely as not to be French.

A very different kind of preparation was required in a man who filled the post of bailiff. The holder of that office, serving either as the subordinate of a land steward or as an independent agent, was entrusted with the management of his master's home farm. It was his task 'to buy and sell all Cattle and Horses for the Plow, direct and order Plowmen, buy Corn for Seed, inspect Plowing, Sowing and all Manner of Husbandry Affairs'.[3] Frequently his work also entailed assisting the land steward in administering that part of the estate leased out to tenants. Such being the nature of his province, he had to have an extensive knowledge of agriculture. 'A bailiff', wrote 'A Farmer and a Breeder', 'ought to have had some years experience of, at least, the common methods of husbandry and gardening, of the management of all kinds of live stock, and of buying and selling; he should be able to keep common accounts. . . .'[4]

Although the bulk of his time was devoted to the administration of the estate, a pursuit that tended to keep him out of doors, the bailiff had work to do within the house as well. The Earl of Nottingham expected the bailiff at Burley to 'Attend and wait at

[1] *Treatise on the Use and Abuse of the Second . . . Table*, pp. 65–6.
[2] See Hecht, 'Continental and Colonial Servants', *Smith College Studies in History*, XL. 5, 7.
[3] Jacob, *Country Gentleman's Vademecum*, p. 45. Cf. Finch, *History of Burley*, I. 233.
[4] [John Lawrence,] *The New Farmer's Calender*, 1800, p. 122.

table and also in ye Hall' whenever guests were being entertained.[1] A friend of Sanderson Miller's made approximately the same demands. Soliciting Miller's aid in searching for a bailiff, he explained that the man must be willing to assist in the dining-room whenever he was called upon to do so: '. . . I want . . . a baliff . . . who will when I have company or whenever I require it wait at table as a gentleman out of livery, as 'tis at Lord North's. . . .'[2]

The valet, who ranked just below the bailiff, also had both indoor and outdoor duties.

Essentially a personal servant, the *valet de chambre's* chief responsibility was his master's appearance; for the figure his master cut in the world depended much on the expertness of his ministrations. Hence Anthony Heasel's manual for servants reminds him that the surest way to distinguish himself is to make his master appear as modish as possible: '. . . the more care you take in dressing your master in a fashionable manner, the more respect you show for him, and you will be much taken notice of for your fidelity.'[3] The process of dressing his master involved literally helping him on with his clothes. Discussing the importance of having a competent valet, John Moore, the physician-novelist, comments on the complete dependence of many masters on this sort of assistance:

> Many of our acquaintances seem absolutely incapable of motion, till they have been wound up by their valets. They have no more use of their hands for any office about their own persons, than if they were paralytic. At night they must wait for their servants, before they can undress themselves, and go to bed: In the morning, if the valet happens to be out of the way, the master must remain helpless and sprawling in bed, like a turtle on its back upon the kitchen table of an alderman.[4]

The valet was necessary too for the preparation of his master's coiffure. He was expected to have 'a perfect knowledge of hairdressing',[5] and often this was acquired by studying with a professional *friseur*. John Macdonald, who at various times had served as

---

[1] Finch, *History of Burley*, I. 233.
[2] Dickins and Stanton, *An Eighteenth Century Correspondence*, p. 116.
[3] Heasel, *Servants Book of Knowledge*, p. 75.
[4] John Moore, *A View of Society and Manners in France, Switzerland and Germany*, 1786, 6th ed., I. 15.
[5] Heasel, *Servants Book of Knowledge*, p. 74.

a footman-valet, recounts how at one point in his career he 'went and lived with Mr. La Motte, the hairdresser, for four months' in order to bring his 'hand into hairdressing again'.[1]

No such special training was required for the services the valet performed outside the closet. Foremost among these was attendance on his master as a sort of servile companion. Master and man went everywhere together: shopping, visiting, travelling. While thus accompanying the master, the valet was called upon to undertake minor tasks; but his chief value was honorific. Regardless of his birth and background, his deportment invariably suggested the gentleman. A valet, says Heasel, 'must be master of every sort of politeness, to which he must take care to accustom himself without stiffness or affectation'.[2] He had, moreover, to be thoroughly conversant with French modes and customs, and to speak some French, even though the extent of his mastery was a small number of polite phrases learned by rote. Candidates from Paris were naturally favoured for the position, but many English servants were sufficiently Frenchified to prove acceptable. Describing his nephew's new valet, Matt Bramble limns the type: 'The fellow, whose name is Dutton, seems to be a *petit-maître*. He has got a smattering of French, bows, grins, and shrugs, and takes snuff *à la mode de France*. . . .'[3] To be attended by a servant of this kind stamped a master as a man of wealth and fashion.

If the valet's role as companion and escort demanded a polished exterior, often other duties, also unconnected with the routine of the dressing-room, required more substantial qualities. In establishments where the valet was the male domestic of the highest rank, he commonly assumed most, if not all, of the business that would have been undertaken by a house steward had such an official been employed. He directed the household staff, purchased provisions, kept accounts. The satisfactory fulfilment of these duties naturally depended on his possessing, in some measure, the abilities requisite in a house steward.

Next to the valet in the scale of rank came the butler and the gardener.

A servant with diverse functions, the butler gave his attention to the pantry and the wine cellar. As custodian of the wines and

---

[1] *Memoirs of an Eighteenth Century-Footman*, p. 93.
[2] Heasel, *Servants Book of Knowledge*, p. 74.
[3] Smollett, 'Humphry Clinker', *Works*, VII. 193.

liquors, he was accountable for their preservation. This meant that he had to guard against depredations and spoilage alike. 'Take great care of your wine and other liquors,' Heasel warns him, 'not only to keep them in good order, but likewise to prevent their being embezzled, or given away to any person besides those who have a right to them according to your instructions.'[1] He served as well as kept the wine, hence Heasel reminds him to observe the niceties when officiating at mealtime: 'Be ready when the company are at table to attend them with the greatest exactness; taking care that the glasses are kept extremely clean, and the wine poured into them in a genteel and easy manner. . . .'[2] Where there was neither house steward nor clerk of the kitchen, it was especially important that he perform smoothly; for in such establishments the butler served as a model for the footmen when they were waiting at table: it was from him that they took their cue. But the butler was much more concerned with the appointments of the table and the sideboard than with the pouring of drinks and the serving of meals. The glass and plate were his responsibility. Heasel instructs him to 'Take great care in cleaning [the] plate, not to scratch it, nor suffer any thing to remain in the crevices of such as is chased'.[3] His concern with the plate was not confined to merely cleaning and polishing it; he was its keeper, answerable for its safety. This responsibility moved Heasel to caution him as to how circumspect he must be: 'As all the plate will be committed to your care, never suffer strangers to come into the place where it is kept; nor let the place be ever left open.'[4]

Since the post of butler involved guardianship of the wine and plate, it called for 'a man of known integrity'; since deft and punctilious service was expected from its occupant, it called for a man with 'a becoming carriage'.[5] The butler, moreover, was supposed to have a knowledge of vintages and to understand the more technical aspects of the care of liquors. An acquaintance with French was also sometimes insisted upon, especially by upper-class employers.

---

[1] Heasel, *Servants Book of Knowledge*, p. 70. Cf. *The Letters of Philip Dormer Stanhope 4th Earl of Chesterfield*, ed. Bonamy Dobree, 1932, v. 2356.
[2] Heasel, *Servants Book of Knowledge*, pp. 70–1.
[3] *Ibid.*, p. 71. Cf. *Letters of . . . Chesterfield*, v. 2356.
[4] Heasel, *Servants Book of Knowledge*, p. 70.   [5] *Ibid.*

Other household offices were often merged with the post of butler, the most usual combination being that in which the butler acted as valet in addition to performing his regular duties. Another very common arrangement, popular among families in which the butler headed the roster of male domestics, gave him the powers and functions of house steward besides those he ordinarily possessed. These dual posts, of course, demanded an unusual range of accomplishments. The butler called upon to act as a body servant had to know the rudiments of hairdressing; the butler who doubled as a steward had to be able to manage the complex affairs of a household.

More highly trained than the butler, the gardener was a skilled technician whose work was of major importance to his employer. Much of its consequence derived from the *furor hortensis* that swept through the century making the grounds of the country seat a new medium of competitive display. Far more than in the previous age, landscape gardening became the index of wealth and taste; and the owners of estates strove to surpass each other in embellishing and improving them.

In consequence, the gardener was expected to be accomplished in many branches of horticulture. To begin with, he had to know how to plant and maintain a kitchen garden and flower beds, as Heasel makes abundantly clear: 'The person who acts as gardener to noblemen or gentlemen must take care to make himself well acquainted with the cultivation of fruits, flowers, vegetables, and in general every thing growing in gardens either for pleasure or use.' Moreover, he had to have such skills as the ability to handle hotbeds and the faculty of managing greenhouses and orangeries.[1] Thus a characteristic advertisement announced in 1798 that 'a Single, Young, Active Man', who desired employment as a gardener, had had 'the greatest experience in every Branch of his Profession, particularly in the Pinery and Forceing Houses'.[2]

More often than not, the gardener also had to understand something of the elements of landscape-gardening; for with the development of the mania for natural gardens, the landowner bent upon making 'improvements' tended to lean heavily upon him. Either acting on his master's suggestions or drawing on his own ingenuity, he laid out walks, devised prospects, arranged urns, obelisks and

---

[1] Heasel, *Servants Book of Knowledge*, pp. 76–7.
[2] *Sun*, 1798, No. 1941, Dec. 12, 4d.

THE SERVANT HIERARCHY

benches, rigged up waterworks and executed a multitude of similar projects.[1] Thus a gardener who advertised for a place in 1773 stated that he understood 'laying out Ground Work, in the modern Taste, perfectly well. . . .'[2] The reliance that was often placed on such a man is revealed by a letter Shenstone sent Lady Luxborough in 1749. Responding to a request for instructions on how to make a turf seat, the poet writes: 'If you have Roots enough, & will give Tom leave when he comes with me to build himself such a *trophy* or two at Barrels, he will do it with great *inward* Satisfaction. He is my only Architect for this kind of Work. . . .'[3]

Yet another essential in the equipment of the average gardener was a courteous manner, for he was often obliged to guide visitors about the grounds. Heasel evidently thought this an important part of the work, since he supplies pertinent advice on how to behave when acting as cicerone: 'Take every opportunity of entertaining those who come to visit your master, with a particular description of every thing in the garden, and have always some places ready for them to rest themselves on, while passing from one part to another.'[4]

Although the gardener was not housed with the main body of the domestic staff, he must have been readily available as a guide. Ordinarily he occupied a cottage on the estate; sometimes he had an office in the main house as well.

Curiously enough, in many instances the gardener was a Scot, a fact of which contemporaries were well aware. Matt Bramble, Smollett's Welsh squire, was told 'that almost all the gardeners of South-Britain were natives of Scotland'.[5] Similarly, Dr. Alexander Carlyle 'had often heard, that most of the head-gardeners of English noblemen were Scotch'; and when he visited England in 1758, he discovered for himself the truth of the report.[6] Walpole, too, had probably observed that the gardeners on English estates were nearly all emigrants from the northern Kingdom; for, commenting to the Countess of Ossory in 1777 on the ridiculous

---

[1] Heasel, *Servants Book of Knowledge*, p. 77.
[2] *Bristol Gazette*, 1773, No. 290, Mar. 4, 3b.
[3] *Letters of William Shenstone*, ed. Duncan Mallam, Minneapolis, [1939,] p. 162.
[4] Heasel, *Servants Book of Knowledge*, p. 76.
[5] Smollett, 'Humphry Clinker', *Works*, VII. 298.
[6] *Autobiography of the Rev. Dr. Alexander Carlyle*, ed. John H. Burton, Edinburgh, 1860, 2nd ed., p. 362.

THE SERVANT HIERARCHY

lengths to which luxurious living was currently carried, he writes: 'Our ancestors had more sense. . . . They were not so absurd as to import peaches, and nectarines, and pine-apples from the south, and highlanders from the Orcades to look after them.'[1] Since at home the Scots followed rather than led the English in all branches of horticulture, this circumstance appears the more remarkable. Its causes, whatever their nature, remain obscure.

Lowest among male upper servants stood the groom of the chambers, a functionary whose major task was the maintenance of the furniture but who also attended to a number of other matters. The full scope of his work is revealed by the instructions the Earl of Nottingham composed for the benefit of the man who held the office at Burley:

> You must be careful of the furniture, brushing and cleaning every morning that wch is in constant use, and the rest also once in the week or oftener if need be.
>
> You must make fires in the hall, parlour, etc., where required keeping clean the hearths and often coming in to repair them, and at night to snuff ye candles.
>
> You are to attend in the Hall when there is Company, and also at other times, but in this last you shall be relieved by ye footmen in turns.
>
> You must take care of all keys in your costody, not to break them, but especially yt they be not lost.
>
> You must bar all the windows, *lock all the outward doors every night when the family is in bed, and rise so early as to open them in time for such as have occasion to come into the house,* and to take care to put out all fires and candles at night.
>
> When any strangers lodge here you must diligently attend ym. taking care that there be fires, candles, etc., in good order, and that nothing be wanting.
>
> You are to *ring the bell for prayers* and lay the cushens and take them away when done, and to keep them and all the furniture of the chappell (when ready) clean.[2]

Employment in the post of groom of the chambers presupposed training in upholstery work. This is implied by a writer who, regarding the groom of the chambers as an official valueless except for show, declared: '. . . he is of no other use than to take upon him the business of an upholsterer. Unless he has been brought up

---
[1] *Letters of Horace Walpole,* x. 68.
[2] Finch, *History of Burley,* I. 230–1.

to that trade I think he can know but little of the matter. . . .'[1]
Perhaps typical of those who qualified was 'A Young Man aged about twenty-five years' who recommended himself in the press in 1777, stating that he 'would be glad to serve any nobleman or gentleman as groom of the chambres having served his apprenticeship in a very capital house in the Upholstery and Paper-hanging branches, and is very well acquainted with the practical part thereof. . . .'[2]

Of the inferior manservants—those who wore livery—the coachman ranked highest. His activity was restricted to mere driving where a master of the horse or clerk of the stables was employed; but where he had no superior directly above him, the governance of the stables lay entirely in his hands. He directed the grooms, postilions, and stable-hands, when such subordinates were employed; he bought the fodder; he looked after the coaches and chariots, making certain they were kept in good condition. When unassisted, he took care of the horses and made minor repairs on the coaches; when he had helpers, he delegated at least some of the work to them.

A relatively simple kind of preparation, such as could be found in many men of rural background, fitted him for the post. Dexterity with the reins was the first requirement. In their advertisements candidates for the post frequently mentioned their ability in this respect. A young man, for example, who advertised in 1794 that he had 'no objection to engage in a small Family as Coachman', asserted that he could 'ride and drive well'.[3] Usually, however, an employer looked for something more in his coachman than competence on the box; he expected some knowledge of farriery, some understanding of the care of coaches.[4] Yet all of this could easily be picked up by any country boy.

Several domestics occupied the hierarchical level just below the coachman. These included the footman, the groom, the under-butler, the under-coachman, the park-keeper, and the gamekeeper.

Charged with multifarious duties, the footman was the mainstay of the household. His work fell essentially into two parts: that which was executed within the house and that which was performed

---

[1] *Treatise on the Use and Abuse of the Second . . . Table*, p. 57.
[2] *Morning Post*, 1777, No. 1390, Apr. 4, 4c.
[3] *Morning Chronicle*, 1794, No. 7715, July 2, 4a.
[4] *Treatise on the Use and Abuse of the Second . . . Table*, p. 55.

outside it. Within the house he laid the cloth, waited at table, served tea, cleaned the knives and, where there was no butler, the glass; he was also supposed to help out in any department where his services were needed.[1] Outdoors he acted as both messenger and escort. In the role of messenger he made formal calls known as 'how d'ye's', paying his employer's respects to friends and acquaintances by enquiring after their health.[2] He also delivered many of his master's notes and letters, thus providing a means of communication that custom preferred to the postal system as more polite and that, in some instances, had the additional advantage of being more rapid. Indeed, in some circles a footman was considered the only proper medium by which a note might be transmitted from one friend to another.[3] This is clearly indicated by a story Sir Joshua's sister, Frances Reynolds, told Fanny Burney:

> ... I had nobody to send to her that was proper to appear before Mrs. Montagu; for, to own the truth, you must know I have no servant but a maid, and I could not think of sending such a person to Mrs. Montagu. So I thought it best to send a chairman, and to tell him only to ring at the bell, and to wait for no answer; because then the porter might tell Mrs. Montagu my servant brought the note, for the porter could not tell but he might be my servant.[4]

The footman was no less essential in the role of escort. He rode on the back of the coach, walked before the sedan chair,[5] to clear the way, and followed close behind when his master or mistress went on foot.

This attendance served several practical purposes. For one thing, it was highly convenient for a master or mistress to have someone always at hand to open the door of the coach or chair, to run an errand or to carry a parcel. Then, too, the darkness of

---

[1] His duties are itemized in [Robert Dodsley,] 'The Footman', *A Muse in Livery*, 1732, pp. 18–19.

[2] For references to the practice see *Spectator*, 1753, II. 236; Jonathan Swift, *The Journal to Stella*, ed. George A. Aitken, 1901, p. 338; [Thomas] Baker, *Tunbridge Walks*, 1764, p. 57; *Bruford Papers*, ed. William H. Hutton, 1905, p. 59; *Letters of Horace Walpole*, XV. 102.

[3] Alice C. C. Gaussen, *A Later Pepys*, 1904, II. 273; *Public Advertiser*, 1767, No. 10296, Oct. 30, 1c.

[4] *Diary and Letters of Mme. D'Arblay*, ed. [Charlotte Barrett,] 1842, II. 220.

[5] *Public Advertiser*, 1767, No. 10296, Oct. 30, 1c.

London streets, even after the system of lighting had been greatly improved in the second half of the century, and the total absence of lighting in most of the lesser towns made it necessary for everyone to provide his own illumination. Of course, linkboys could usually be hired; but their lack of dependability made it safer and far more comfortable to bring footmen along to carry the flambeaux.[1] Yet another service rendered by the omnipresent footman was to protect his master's person and property—a service he inherited from his predecessors, the feudal retainer and the serving-man of Tudor times.[2] Urban streets and country roads alike were infested with highwaymen; hold-ups, such as Walpole experienced at the hands of the gentlemanly Maclean, were not uncommon, as newspaper accounts attest. Hence to venture abroad at night without a servant was to invite robbery and possibly death.

But the chief value of the footman lay in none of these services directly. It was the efficiency with which he advertised the extent of his master's wealth. All domestics served that end, since their presence in an establishment demonstrated their master's ability to pay and maintain them in return for little or no productive work. But all were not equally effective in this respect. Those whose uncommon skills and specialized training commanded a high remuneration reflected more credit upon their employers than those who were paid at lower rates; those whose duties brought them obtrusively into view more effectively suggested their master's wealth than those whose work kept them constantly out of sight. Livery servants, from the coachman down to the footboy, were among the most effective of the lot. Their routines endowed them with the highest visibility. Moreover, the livery itself emphasized their remoteness from productive labour. Their effectiveness achieved its maximum in the footman, for his routine exposed him to view more consistently than did that of any of the

---

[1] For references to this function of the footman see Stirling, *Coke of Norfolk*, I. 32–3; [Charlotte] Papendiek, *Court Life in the Time of Queen Charlotte*, 1887, II. 164.

[2] For illustrations of footmen acting as guards see Mrs. Montagu, 'Queen of the Blues', *Her Letters and Friendships from 1762 to 1800*, ed. Reginald Blunt, 1923, I. 117–18; *A Series of Letters of the First Earl of Malmesbury*, ed. Lord Malmesbury, 1870, I. 236; *Letters of Horace Walpole*, XII. 343, 366; A[rthur] S. Turberville, *A History of Welbeck Abbey and Its Owners*, [1939,] II. 156–7.

others. He was, in consequence, one of the most vital parts of his master's equipment of display.

Large establishments usually included a considerable corps of such servitors; smaller ones contained as many as the master could afford. For, as employers generally recognized, a number of them together formed an imposing and arresting retinue. The impression they created on the beholder is amusingly described by an American who came to England shortly after the close of the century. Commenting on an equipage he had seen, he says that on it there

> were four stout fellows, such as Hannibal would have chosen for his companions through the Alps. Three of these gentleman had their station behind, and so dignifiedly did they carry themselves, with so much lace were they puffed off, and so elegantly trimmed were their cocked hats, one might easily in the hurry of novelty have mistaken them for men of high rank, who were disposed to amuse the populace. . . .
>
> An Englishman accustomed to see such things daily, may probably have but one reflection on such an exhibition—'*The owner of that chariot must be very rich*'. . . .[1]

Since the more footmen a master kept the better figure he cut, attempts to outstrip rival establishments in point of size and magnificence often took the form of increasing the number of such servants. 'One great point of emulation,' writes Silliman, whose observations, though made in 1805 and 1806, are generally valid for the whole of the preceding century, 'is to excel all rivals in the number of footmen. Some of the coaches had two, three, and even four footmen, standing up, and holding on behind the carriage, not to mention occasionally a supernumerary one on the coachman's box.'[2] How invidious the retention of a large complement of footmen must have been is suggested by a letter that passed between Lady Wentworth and Lord Raby in 1710. Sketching the style of living maintained by a Mrs. Lewis, Lady Wentworth wrote: 'She keeps a coach and six horssis and fower footmen, did keep six but she being very discreet desired twoe might be put ofe, for soe many would but make them envyed. . . .'[3]

The requirements for the post of footman were relatively simple. To qualify a youth had to have a good carriage and a good

[1] William Austin, *Letters from London*, Boston, 1804, p. 10.
[2] Benjamin Silliman, *A Journal of Travels in England, Holland and Scotland . . . in the Years 1805 and 1806*, New Haven, 1820, 3rd ed., 1. 219.
[3] *Wentworth Papers*, p. 113.

physique. The lustier he appeared the greater his suitability; for, as Veblen has pointed out, the more robust the servant the more emphatically he proclaimed the 'waste' of time and energy of his unproductive routine, the more effective his performance of vicarious leisure. Besides a powerful body, it was essential that he have a familiarity with the system of forms that governed such activities as waiting at table and serving tea. And though not absolutely necessary, it was preferable that he should know how to read and write.

Other abilities were needed in the running footman, a special variety of the species. Like the ordinary footman, he was a highly conspicuous part of his master's entourage. When his master travelled the road in state, accompanied by a retinue of mounted servants, he ran just ahead of the coach, adding a spectacular touch to the cavalcade.[1] But he also served more practical purposes. 'His use', remarks the playwright John O' Keeffe in recollecting the heyday of the running footman, 'was to carry a message, letter or despatch; or, on a journey, to run before and prepare the inn, or baiting-place, for his family or master. . . .'[2] Yet another service he performed was to win prizes and wagers for his master by means of his speed. Races between running footmen were a frequent occurrence, especially during the early decades of the century.[3] In 1718, for instance, the Duke of Wharton 'made a Match with Captain Lane of Staffordshire, for his running Footman to run with a servant of the said Captain Lane's from Woodstock Cross in Oxfordshire to Tyburn, near Paddington, for 1000 Guineas. . . .'[4] Sometimes the swiftness of the running footman was put to the test in another way. A course would be fixed upon and then bets taken that he would complete it within a specified time. In 1769, for example, 'the Running-Footman of the Rt. Hon. the Earl of March, undertook, for a considerable Wager, to run from Rochester Bridge to Westminster Bridge. . . .'[5] Obviously, the essential quality of a running footman was physical prowess.

[1] For an account of a running footman thus engaged see *London Chronicle*, 1770, XXVIII. 472b.
[2] *Recollections of the Life of John O'Keeffe*, 1826, I. 121.
[3] Louis C. Jones, *The Clubs of the Georgian Rakes*, New York, 1942, p. 5.
[4] *Weekly Journal*, 1718, No. 84, July 19, 500. Cf. *Whitehall Evening Post*, 1721, No. 403, Apr. 11–13, 3a; No. 460, Aug. 19–22, 2a.
[5] *St. James's Chronicle*, 1769, No. 1309, July 18–20, 3c.

'... his qualifications', writes John O' Keeffe, 'were fidelity, strength and agility.'[1] It was with agility that employers were most concerned. Lord March, later the notorious Duke of Queensberry, for instance, always carefully checked the speed of a running footman with a stop watch before engaging him.[2]

When dashing before the coach or acting as courier, the running footman cut an even more impressive figure than the ordinary footman in his flamboyant livery suit. The unusual clothes that he wore were largely responsible. John O'Keeffe gives a graphic description of them in his memoirs. Speaking of running footmen, he says: '... one of them I particularly remember, his dress a white jacket, blue silk sash round his waist, light blue velvet cap, with a silver tassel on the crown, round his neck a frill with a ribbon, and in his hand a staff about seven feet high with a silver top.'[3] An entry, dated 1741, in William Hutton's *Book of Recollections* also supplies a glimpse of the running footman's attire: 'Saw a running footman, belonging to a gentleman's equipage, pass over Leen bridge at Nottingham, and thought him dressed in beautiful style. His cap, black velvet; his jacket white dimity fringed with black.'[4] The trappings of the running footman included some unusual features. According to a note written about 1780 by the Rev. George Ashby, he did not wear breeches but was clothed instead in a short silk petticoat, which was kept down by a deep gold fringe.[5] The fringe does not appear to have been too effective, for in 1725 a somewhat ribald observer remarked 'how our Village Maids delight to see the Running Footman fly bare-ars'd o'er the dusty Road'.[6] Another unusual feature mentioned by Ashby was that the large silver ball surmounting the pole carried by the running footman contained white wine for his refreshment.[7] Undoubtedly the singularity of their equipment contributed to the impression that running footmen created.

[1] *Life of John O'Keeffe*, I. 121. C[harles] H. C. and Muriel I. Baker, *The Life and Circumstances of James Brydges First Duke of Chandos*, Oxford, 1949, p. 175.
[2] John R. Robinson, *Old Q*, 1895, p. 251; *Notes and Queries*, Second Series, 1856, I. 9.
[3] *Life of John O'Keeffe*, I. 120-1.
[4] *Catherine Hutton and Her Friends*, ed. Catherine H. Beale, [Birmingham, 1895,] pp. 118-19.
[5] *Notes and Queries*, Second Series, 1856, I. 9.
[6] *Rural Folly*, p. 7. [7] *Notes and Queries*, Second Series, 1856, I. 9.

The practice of keeping these strikingly clothed servants did not long survive the end of the century.[1] The fourth Duke of Queensberry, who died in 1810, was reputed to have been the last to employ one. The gradual improvement of the roads and the introduction of more swiftly moving vehicles may have been the causes of their disappearance; for as travel became more rapid, they may have found it impossible to keep ahead of the equipage. At any rate, about 1780 the Rev. Ashby wrote: 'Since the roads have been made good, the carriages and cattle lightened, we have had little of them. . . .'[2]

On the same level of the hierarchy with the footman and the running footman was the groom. 'The business of a groom', writes Heasel, 'is to take care of the horses, to see that they be properly fed, watered, cleaned down, and when hurt, or labouring under any disorder, to administer proper remedies to them.'[3]

This called for a real knowledge of equine lore. But such knowledge was very common, most men raised in the country having picked it up incidentally, as part of their general preparation for rural life. Especially was this true in the northern counties, the great horse breeding region. Thus, speaking of Yorkshire, Defoe remarks that 'the young Fellows are naturally Grooms, bred up in the Stable, and used to lie among the Horses. . . .'[4]

The under-butler and second or under-coachman, servants whose position in the scale of rank was identical with that of the footman and groom, had duties closely akin to those of the butler and head coachman respectively. Each in his own department assisted the man who bore the full title of the office and who, presumably, had a greater familiarity with its routine, greater experience, or both.

The porter, whose position in the hierarchy was also on this level, acted as guardian of the gate. In the country he occupied a lodge at the entrance of the estate, and there he inspected and questioned all who sought admittance. At some of the London mansions, those surrounded by a large court or garden plot, he was similarly situated. But in the smaller London dwellings, when a porter was kept, he was lodged within the house and while on duty was stationed in the foyer, at the front door. The details of

---

[1] *Notes and Queries*, Second Series, 1856, I. 80, 178, 383.
[2] *Ibid.*, I. 9.   [3] Heasel, *Servants Book of Knowledge*, p. 73.
[4] Defoe, *Tour*, II. 629.

his routine may be gleaned from the Earl of Nottingham's instructions for the man who kept the gate at Burley:

> You are to keep ye Ct. Yards constantly lockt.
>
> You must not permitt any person to come up to the house but to stay in ye Lodge till ye clark of ye kitchen be called wch. may be done by ringing a bell.
>
> You are to be carefull not to suffer unknown persons to come in or others without businesse. In this there is need of great discretion, yt you may not needlessly give offence nor on ye other hand expose my house and yards to Pilferers.
>
> You must not fail to lock up ye gates so soon as ye bell rings and afterwards not open ym to any person unlesse to such as are sent abroad by order, give an acct every morning who are so admitted after ye time of shutting ye gates as also of all whom you shall know are lockd out or gett in by indirect ways.
>
> After ye bell has rung to dinner shutt ye gates and come into ye house, and after prayers return to ye lodge.[1]

Reliability and the appearance of physical strength were necessary for the successful discharge of the duties of the post. The Swiss were generally believed to possess both of these qualities in an exceptional degree, hence they were often preferred as porters.[2]

The same qualities must have been welcome in two other servants who ranked beside the porter. These were the park-keeper and the gamekeeper.

The park-keeper devoted himself chiefly to the care of the deer on his master's estate. 'He must', runs Giles Jacob's summary of his duties,

> daily take a Turn round his Park, and keep a constant Account of the Number of his Deer; and oftentimes watch them at Night, for their Preservation against unlawful Hunters, especially in Moonshiny Nights and the Rutting Season. He must take care to calculate an exact Number of Bucks and Does proper to be kill'd in each Season, . . . so as not to make any Destruction, or lessening of his Park, and at the same Time not to over-stock the same, preserving a proper number of young Fawns to be bred up in the steads of those he kills; and having always a Regard to Casualties, which some will happen in the Winter, unavoidably.[3]

---

[1] Finch, *History of Burley*, I. 230.

[2] See Hecht, 'Continental and Colonial Servants', *Smith College Studies in History*, XL. 28-9.

[3] [Giles Jacob,] *The Compleat Sportsman*, 1718, p. 67. Cf. Joseph Wilkinson, *Worthies, Families and Celebrities of Barnsley and the District*, [1883,] p. 400.

THE SERVANT HIERARCHY

He was also supposed to keep 'the Pales or Walls entire', so that the deer could not stray out of the park.[1]

He was usually quartered in a lodge in the grounds of the estate. His meals, however, were taken in the main house with the other servants, at least when his master was in residence.[2]

In order to carry out his trust satisfactorily he had to be 'a careful vigilant Man'.[3] Moreover, he had to know the needs and habits of the game over which he stood warder.

Far heavier responsibilities rested on the shoulders of the gamekeeper; for, whereas the park and its deer were the sole concern of the park-keeper, the gamekeeper's province coincided with the limits of the estate, and he was expected to prevent the destruction of most forms of wild life to be found upon it. 'On all acounts', writes Edward Laurence, 'the Game ought to be preserv'd by the diligence and care of the . . . Gamekeeper, for the sake of [his] Lord's Diversion and Table.'[4]

The gamekeeper was invested with special police powers. A parliamentary act passed in 1671 granted to every landowner who was Lord of a manor, and to him alone, the right to appoint a gamekeeper; at the same time it authorized that official to confiscate dogs, firearms, and other implements of the chase from persons suspected of being unqualified to hunt and to bring before the local justice such actual poachers as he might apprehend.

The man appointed might be the park-keeper, the land steward, a tenant farmer, or even a gentleman with a small estate of his own. Most often, however, he was a servant who devoted himself exclusively to patrolling the fields and copses. Like the park-keeper, he usually lived in a cottage on the grounds.

The gamekeeper had to know the game laws and, by the middle of the century, how to breed game, for the ravages of enthusiastic hunting were necessarily repaired by systematic replenishment.

Below the main body of livery servants, which included domestics as different in function as the footman and the gamekeeper, were youths who bore such titles as postilion, yard boy, provision boy, footboy, and page. The postilion was probably much superior to the others in the scale of rank, and as a rule was

---

[1] Laurence, *Duty of a Steward*, p. 62.
[2] Mordant, *Complete Steward*, II. 384.
[3] Jacob, *Compleat Sportsman*, p. 67.
[4] Laurence, *Duty of a Steward*, p. 57.

somewhat older. He rode one of the left-hand horses that drew the coach, helping to guide the team from that position. When not on the road he made himself generally useful about the stables. The yard boy, provision boy, or footboy—the titles were more or less interchangeable—was the lowest ranking male servant. His youth—he could be as young as eight or nine years—and inexperience no doubt account for his position at the bottom of the scale. In some families he served as a sort of factotum, helping out in all departments; in others he was footman of smaller growth, running errands, carrying messages, bringing in the tea-tray.

The page was a special variety of footboy. Of the same age as the youths who bore that title, he was identical in function to such of them as were footmen in miniature.[1] But there did exist an essential difference. The page came from a higher social stratum than the average footboy. In a letter to the Duke of Dorset Lord Chesterfield speaks of one of his pages as 'a gentleman of extreme good Derbyshire family.'[2] Hearne, the antiquarian, writing in 1708, observed that Admiral Byng, who sprang from the gentry, had in his youth been page to Lady Middleton.[3] Like his medieval predecessor, the page of the eighteenth century was placed in a family with the understanding that after a number of years of service he would receive preferment, either within the family itself, or, through his master's efforts, outside it.[4] This, too, distinguished him from the ordinary footboy, who had no such expectations. The essential difference between the two was strikingly symbolized by the difference in their dress: the page wore a much more costly livery than that of the ordinary footboy.

III

Primacy among maidservants belonged to the lady's maid, waiting-woman or, as she was called in the early century, tirewoman, a

---

[1] For the routine of the page see *Letters Books of John Hervey, First Earl of Bristol*, Wells, 1894, I. 285; *H. M. C. Portland*, II. 231; Thomas Whitehead, *Original Anecdotes of the Duke of Kingston and Miss Chudleigh*, 1792, p. 194.
[2] *Letters of . . . Chesterfield*, IV. 1633.   [3] Hearne, *Collections*, II. 107.
[4] For examples see Swift, *Journal to Stella*, p. 283; *Letters of . . . Chesterfield*, III. 684; IV. 1633, 1634; Baker, *James Brydges First Duke of Chandos*, pp. 174–5.

servant equal in rank to the gentleman-in-waiting and comparable in function with the *valet de chambre*. Personal attendance normally consituted her entire work. It involved dressing and undressing her mistress, arranging her head, mending and altering her clothes. In addition she accompanied her mistress abroad and offered her companionship at home. A French traveller who visited England in 1765 noted: 'Les servantes de la petite bourgeoisie, les femmes-de-chambre de la haute & petite noblesse, sont cortège à leur dames dans les rues & dans les promenades publiques. . . .'[1]

To fill the post satisfactorily a considerable number of accomplishments were required; and Heasel cautions prospective applicants that since such a maid 'is obliged to be near her lady, it is necessary that none pretend to be properly qualified for it, unless their education has been something above the ordinary rank of other women. . . .'[2] A suitable education consisted of a thorough acquaintance with the niceties of social form, an ability to read well aloud, a knowledge of the French tongue, a familiarity with French modes and customs, and a real proficiency in the arts of the hairdresser, milliner, and modiste. Much of this was regularly acquired at home or at boarding school; much was often gained through self-instruction. But special skills such as hairdressing were frequently studied at first-hand under the tutelage of professional practitioners. It was common for young girls to be placed with milliners and mantua-makers, either as apprentices or as paid assistants, in order to equip them for service as lady's maids; and many who entered a shop through necessity rather than by design later found the training of great advantage in securing places in the better families. That a girl thus prepared could easily step from the shop to the dressing-room is suggested by a notice in a London paper in 1771:

> A Young Woman, who has served an Apprenticeship of three Years to a Coatmaker in the City, and understands the business of making up cloaks, hats, childbed linen, &c. would be glad to be employed to serve in a Shop; or as she has had a genteel Education at a Boarding-School, and speaks French, would wait on a Lady

---

[1] [Pierre Grosley,] *Londres*, Lausanne, 1770, I. 131.
[2] Heasel, *Servants Book of Knowledge*, p. 69.

and make herself useful in any genteel Capacity she may be employed in.[1]

Such applicants knew how to dress hair,[2] and not a few had received special training in the art. Instruction of this kind was provided by experts who catered expressly for the needs of servants. In 1777 one of these specialists publicized herself in an announcement that read: 'To Young Women that wait upon Ladies. The Advertiser hereby informs them that they may be taught to dress Ladies Hair upon reasonable terms. In a short time she will make them fit for places where Hair-dressing is required.'[3]

What was the provenance of those who qualified as lady's maids? The emphasis placed upon the language and ways of France caused many employers to give preference to women from that country.[4] But most lady's maids were native born, almost all social strata contributing to the supply. In fact, it was the post of lady's maid, along with that of housekeeper, that made service a possible refuge for any woman who could pretend to a 'polite education'. Such women might even be fortunate enough to be taken into a family where the post shaded into that of companion.

The position of companion was, as a rule, a highly anomalous one. In a relatively few instances it was genuinely non-servile; upper-class ladies sometimes invited well-bred but necessitous women to live with them so that they might continually be provided with agreeable company. This was evidently the sort of position Sir Joshua Reynolds had in mind when, having been consulted by Boswell about getting the Rev. Temple's niece 'into the situation of a companion', he opined 'that a companion must be a person whom one chuses from one's own knowledge'.[5] Although such women received their expenses and often were given a regular stipend or generous gifts besides, they were treated as social equals, or nearly so. They had no duties to perform; they shared the social life of the ladies to whom they were attached.

---

[1] *Daily Advertiser*, 1771, No. 12534, Feb. 26, 2c.
[2] See, for example, *Lloyd's Evening Post*, 1780, XLVI. 180c; *Morning Chronicle*, 1794, No. 7695, June 7, 4a.
[3] *Morning Post*, 1777, No. 1366, Mar. 7, 3a.
[4] See Hecht, 'Continental and Colonial Servants', *Smith College Studies in History*, XL. 5.
[5] *Letters of James Boswell*, ed. Chauncey B. Tinker, Oxford, 1924, II. 342.

THE SERVANT HIERARCHY

But situations of this kind were exceptional. Usually the title of companion meant little more than its bearer was a lady's maid of a superior sort. Her work was lighter than that of the ordinary lady's maid and far less well defined; she was used with more respect and accorded a greater degree of formal courtesy, as is indicated by the 'Mrs.' generally placed before her surname when she was addressed.[1] In all other respects her position was indistinguishable from that of lady's maid. A fictitious autobiographical sketch in the *Lady's Magazine* fully discloses the resemblance. The narrator describes herself as 'the daughter of a clergyman; who died about three years since, and who, as clergymen of small cures must inevitably do, left [her] mother and family unprovided for'. She tells how at the request of a relative she 'was taken into the house of a lady of quality as her *companion*. . . .' In another passage, however, she identifies her situation by saying: 'I am . . . a *lady's maid*, the humble attendant of a lady of quality. Some, who consider me in a higher rank, call me her *companion*. . . .' And the account she gives of the demands made upon her leaves no doubt about the servile character of her position:

> My business shortly was this; to be always ready at a moment's warning to join my lady in every party of pleasure or business she chuses to mix with. I attended her in the morning to all sales, auctions, exhibitions, &c. and particularly was present at the important affair of *shopping*. . . . I attended my lady on all visits, unless the party was particularly select, and was present in all companies at home, where I acted as a kind of upper servant.[2]

Inferior only to the lady's maid among female servants, the housekeeper was the house steward's opposite number; and, like him, she was occupied for the most part with supervisory work. Where the establishment included a house steward, she served under him, acting as his assistant. In such a household her authority extended only to the female staff, beneath the lady's maid: she had 'the maid servants to look after, and to direct in their proper business'.[3] Where there was no house steward she exercised much broader powers, and the scope of her labours was

---

[1] *Lady's Magazine*, 1789, xx. 235; *World*, I. 232; Defoe, *Law of Subordination*, p. 15.
[2] *Lady's Magazine*, 1789, xx. 235.
[3] Heasel, *Servants Book of Knowledge*, p. 55.

far more extensive. Not only did she supervise the whole establishment, with the exception of whatever stable servants were employed, but she also bought the provisions, dispensed them as they were needed, and kept the household accounts.[1] Like the house steward, she was often entrusted with the important task of hiring the inferior servants.[2] And besides all this, she frequently had special duties in the culinary department. In some homes pickling and preserving made up part of her routine, and often she was expected to turn out the sweetmeats, cordials and desserts.[3] The variety of matters committed to her care is well illustrated by a newspaper advertisement of 1771 that called for

> a very capable Person to undertake the Management of a large Family of Fashion; she must thoroughly understand in what Manner to supply a Table in Town and Country; she must be neat and orderly, a good Oeconomist, and have Authority to oblige the other Servants to be so; she must understand Pickling, Preserving, Potting, Salting Meat, and keeping all sorts of Provisions, to order and keep a proper Supply of them, buying in, paying for and keeping a regular Account thereof, and every Thing under her. . . .[4]

In selecting a housekeeper it was considered 'most prudent' to choose 'a woman of age and experience, well acquainted with the world, and who [had] either kept house herself, or been long in the service of others.'[5] Maturity was insisted upon because it was felt that only a woman who had reached her middle years could have sufficient gravity and decorum to hold the respect of the servants and to enforce discipline amongst them; experience was regarded as highly desirable because it almost certainly meant a thorough initiation in the art of household management. Without such knowledge success was impossible: to be a satisfactory housekeeper a woman had to 'know how to order and keep a good economy throughout the whole family'; she had to be able to keep accounts, she had to 'be well acquainted with the business of a cook and

---

[1] *Every Woman Her Own House-Keeper*, 1796, 4th ed., II. 62–3; Heasel, *Servants Book of Knowledge*, p. 57.
[2] *Every Woman Her Own House-Keeper*, II. 62; Heasel, *Servants Book of Knowledge*, p. 57.
[3] Clermont, *Professed Cook*, p. vi.
[4] *Daily Advertiser*, 1771, No. 12534, Feb. 26, 2c. Cf. *General Advertiser*, 1780, No. 895, Feb. 16, 4d.
[5] Heasel, *Servants Book of Knowledge*, p. 57.

confectioner', she had to know how to plan entertainments and compose menus.[1]

The post of housekeeper was often coupled with other offices.[2] The most usual combinations were housekeeper and lady's maid and housekeeper and cook.

Lowest of female upper servants, the cook ranked directly beneath the housekeeper. Her sphere of activity corresponded exactly to that of the man-cook.

Since this was so, her preparation for the post had to be precisely the same as his. Heasel gives a succinct statement of the essential requisites: 'The young woman who undertakes to be cook in a family ought to have very good knowlege [sic] of provisions in general, and also of the most proper methods used in dressing them. . . .'[3] Included in 'the most proper methods' were the culinary techniques and practices of Paris: an ability to prepare food in the French manner was as necessary to a woman-cook as to a man.

But however accomplished female cooks may have been, they were considered inferior in talent and knowledge to men. Contemporary advertisements furnish clear proof that this was the case, for they make it plain that preference was often given to women who had had experience assisting a man-cook. An employer in search of a cook in 1798, for example, specified that she had to have 'lived under a man cook'.[4] Equally revealing is the way in which cooks were careful to announce that they had had such experience. Thus one who sought employment in 1777 recommended herself as having 'lived under a man cook'; another, advertising in the same year for a place, stated that she had been 'brought up under a man cook'.[5] The conviction that as cooks women were inferior to men is also mirrored in the practice of bringing in a man on special occasions to take over the kitchen from the regular woman-cook.[6]

Lower than the cook but somewhat higher than the other inferior female servants was the chambermaid. The title 'chambermaid'

---

[1] *Every Woman Her Own House-Keeper*, II. 62.
[2] *Ibid.*, II. 61.
[3] Heasel, *Servants Book of Knowledge*, p. 68.
[4] *Morning Chronicle*, 1798, No. 8938, Jan. 16, 1b.
[5] *Morning Post*, 1777. No. 1354, Feb. 21, 3b; No. 1359, Feb. 27, 4b.
[6] William Verral, *A Complete System of Cookery*, 1759, pp. iii–v.

was sometimes confusingly applied to the lady's maid. Fielding, for instance, in *Joseph Andrews* introduces Mrs. Slipslop in a chapter heading as the 'chambermaid' but thereafter refers to her as a 'waiting gentlewoman'. There is no doubt, however, that the two posts were quite distinct. In an essay of the early century a letter purporting to be from a chambermaid who subscribed herself 'Patience Giddy' runs: 'I am the next Thing to a Lady's Woman, and am under both my Lady and her Woman.'[1] Similarly, Swift distinguishes between the two posts in a letter written to the Duchess of Queensberry: 'False spelling is only excusable in a chambermaid, for I would not pardon it in any of your waiting-women.'[2] But if the posts were distinct, their duties might slightly overlap, the chambermaid, for instance, sometimes being called upon to take care of her mistress' clothing. Her proper routine lay 'mostly in the bed-rooms', where she dusted, swept the floor, made the beds in the morning, warmed them at night, and took care of the fires. 'An hour or two before bed-time,' reads a manual of household instruction, 'she ought to attend to the dressing-rooms and bed-chambers, taking care the windows are all properly shut and made fast, lighting fires if necessary, and putting all utensils in their respective places.'[3]

Such work needed no extraordinary abilities. Indeed, the post did not even demand a prepossessing appearance; nor, for that matter, did any other position in the lower ranks of the hierarchy on its female side. For the duties normally delegated to the woman of inferior rank, particularly where the staff was a large one, were not of a conspicuous nature; and it was an established maxim that, as far as possible, such servants were to be kept behind the scenes. 'In a well-governed Family', declares a handbook for bachelors, 'there should be no Excess in any Particular, and if there must be a Want, let it be that which is least visible, such as Maid-servants, for they ought to be least seen in the House. . . .'[4] An observation made by the French traveller La Rochefoucauld suggests that the maxim was closely followed: 'In general the English have many more servants than we have, but more than half of them are never

---

[1] *Spectator*, II. 212.
[2] *The Correspondence of Jonathan Swift*, ed. F. Elrington Ball, 1910–14, IV. 204.
[3] *Every Woman Her Own House-Keeper*, I. 194.
[4] *Batchelor's Monitor*, p. 63.

seen—kitchen-maids, stable-men, maidservants in large numbers. . . .'[1] In a word, maidservants were not an essential part of the equipment of display, although their presence in a household must have had a certain amount of prestige value. Indirectly, of course, they did much to support the style in which their employers lived. Heasel discloses an acute awareness of their contribution when he exhorts the housemaid 'to keep every part of the house and furniture clean, not suffering any dust to be seen, that those who visit the family may take notice of the industry of the servants, and consequently honour their master'.[2]

The maidservants who ranked under the chambermaid, then, had no ornamental function; their roles in the household were essentially utilitarian in character. They included the housemaid, the maid of all work, the laundry maid, and the dairy maid. Some differences in rank may have existed amongst them; but if they were not all on the same level, their relative positions in the hierarchy remain unclear.

The business of the housemaid was

> to keep the whole house in a state of cleanliness, by carefully washing the rooms, stair cases, &c. cleaning the fire-grates, irons, and hearths, dusting carpets, and rubbing the furniture, as well as the locks, knockers, glasses, chimney ornaments, picture frames, &c.[3]

Where a groom of the chambers was employed, the housemaid probably was obliged to assume only part of this burden; but how the work was divided under such circumstances is obscure. Again, where no scullery maid was employed, she may have had to wash the dishes; but this too is uncertain. Like the chambermaid and most other inferior maidservants, the housemaid needed no special training. It was enough if she were an industrious girl.

The same thing cannot be said of the maid of all work; for, as the title suggests, she ran the entire house. This naturally meant that she had to have some of the characteristics and abilities usually sought in both cook and housekeeper. She had to be a responsible person, and she had to be completely at home in the kitchen. Thus a newspaper advertisement that called for 'a Woman Servant,

---

[1] Marchand, *A Frenchman in England*, p. 25.
[2] Heasel, *Servants Book of Knowledge*, p. 57.
[3] *Every Woman Her Own House-Keeper*, II. 73.

thoroughly capable of all Work', stated that 'no person that is not well acquainted with Cookery . . . need offer herself. . . .'[1]

The work of the laundry maid was, of course, more specialized. 'A laundry-maid', writes Heasel, 'is the person to whom the care of the linen is committed. . . .' She washed and ironed on specially appointed days. It was 'most common for her to be brought up to it'. Heasel remarks, however, that 'any young woman of tolerable abilities may soon learn it, as all women are more or less acquainted with washing'.[2]

All that the dairy maid needed to know could be acquired quite as readily. She was employed to milk and to make butter and cheese;[3] generally, the poultry yard also lay within her province.[4] When, as was often the case, the surplus dairy produce was sold to the public, she had to market it. When seeking a dairy maid in 1737, Elizabeth Purefoy wrote: '. . . she must go to market to make the best of my Dairy.'[5] The Rev. Woodforde also expected his maid to sell the products of his dairy for him.[6] The duties of the dairy maid were not light, but in none of her work was there anything with which the average country girl did not have some familiarity.

Even less was required of the scullery maid, who stood at the bottom of the scale of rank on the female side of the hierarchy. Heasel makes her position clear when he speaks of her as 'the woman who does the most servile work in a family. . . .'[7] So does Hannah Glass when she places her last in the roster of maid-servants.[8] Successor to the scullion, who, although virtually extinct, was occasionally to be found in upper-class households during the first half of the century,[9] the scullery maid kept the kitchen, pantry, and wash-house clean, polished the pots and other cooking utensils, washed and put away the dishes. 'Let them', writes Heasel of

---

[1] *Daily Advertiser*, 1771, No. 12538, Mar. 2, 2c.
[2] Heasel, *Servants Book of Knowledge*, p. 62. Cf. Hannah Glass, *The Servants Directory*, 1760, p. vi.
[3] Heasel, *Servants Book of Knowledge*, pp. 65–7.
[4] *Every Woman Her Own House-Keeper*, I. 359.
[5] *Purefoy Letters*, I. 133.
[6] *The Diary of a Country Parson, passim.*
[7] Heasel, *Servants Book of Knowledge*, p. 69.
[8] Glass, *Servants Directory*, pp. III–VI.
[9] Lord March, *A Duke and His Friends*, 1911, I. 330; Baker, *James Brydges First Duke of Chandos*, p. 175.

scullery maids, 'take great care that all the dishes and other things committed to their care be kept in proper order, so that when the cook or any of the servants wants them, they may always be clean and ready for immediate use'.[1]

IV

Extending from the land steward to the footboy and from the lady's maid to the girl in the scullery, this occupational hierarchy was of considerable height. Several kinds of evidence reveal the measure of its elevation. Firstly, there existed an extreme contrast between the wages received by those in the top and bottom ranks. The land steward at the apex of the hierarchy might draw as much as several hundred pounds; the house steward, who ranked second, might have a hundred; the clerk of the kitchen, who came third in order of rank, generally received £30 to £50.[2] At the opposite pole were such servants as the laundry and dairy maids, whose wages, beginning with £2 to £5 during the first years of the period, reached a maximum of £8 to £10 10s. towards its close; and there was also the footboy, who probably at no time received much more than £5 5s. *per annum* and who sometimes had no wages at all.[3] Secondly, within the individual establishment the principal upper servants exercised an extensive control over household affairs, while the lowest of the inferior servants had no voice whatsoever in such matters. Ultimate authority was, of course, vested in the employer, who often issued instructions, both specific and general; but in translating his wishes into action upper servants commonly enjoyed a free hand. They gave orders, supervised routine work, and in general regulated the operation of the house. Their autonomy was most complete in the larger families, as Giles Jacob suggests. In order to insure 'A Good Oeconomy in a large Family,' he writes, the 'superior Servants ought to have the Powers belonging to their Posts and Inferiors [ought] to be kept in due Subjection. . . .'[4] But even in the smaller households, such an important power as the right to discipline the lower staff was often delegated to upper servants by the employer. It was because of this that Thomas Gisborne, although he strongly urged masters to

[1] Heasel, *Servants Book of Knowledge*, p. 69.
[2] See chap. VI.   [3] See chap. VI.
[4] Jacob, *Country Gentleman's Vademecum*, p. 44.

uphold 'the proper authority of the higher servants', felt it necessary to declare that they ought not to 'permit the existence of a domineering aristocracy below stairs'.[1] Lastly, the dependence of the lower servants on such upper servants as the house steward and the housekeeper was considerable; for those officials usually had the power to hire and discharge whomever they pleased.

[1] Thomas Gisborne, *An Enquiry into the Duties of Men*, 1797, 4th ed., II. 497.

Chapter Three

THE RELATIONSHIP OF MASTER AND SERVANT

THE evolution of service from a system based upon fixed status to one that is almost entirely contractual has taken over five hundred years. In the eighteenth century the transformation was far from complete. The relationship of master and servant still retained much of the old medieval order. But the independent attitude of the servant class that contributed so heavily to the elimination of what remained was already highly developed.

I

The theory of the relationship of master and servant current in the eighteenth century was in some ways inconsistent. In part the product of post-medieval society with its flourishing individualism, it acknowledged the relationship to be basically contractual. In part an inheritance from the Middle Ages, when status was fixed and involved recognized rights and duties, it conceived of the relationship as essentially a family one.

Master and servant were in reality united by contract, the motive on both sides in almost every instance being the purest self-interest. This, of course, could not be ignored. Thus the learned Mrs. Elizabeth Carter, in a letter in which she calls servants 'one of the most independent classes of our community', opined to Mrs. Montagu: 'Their covenant is founded on a reciprocation of benefit. . . .'[1] Similarly, Lord Chesterfield called attention to the contractual nature of the relationship in a letter to his godson: 'Service is a mutual contract; the master hires and pays his servant,

---

[1] *Letters from Mrs. Elizabeth Carter*, I. 373.

the servant is to do his master's business. . . .'[1] And in one of Jonas Hanway's moralistic tracts a father, who serves as the author's mouthpiece, says to his daughter, a young girl about to go into service: 'The connexion between thy mistress and thee is a solemn contract for mutual benefit which ought to be held sacred. . . .'[2]

The nature of the actual contract was limited and impersonal enough. On accepting a place the servant undertook to perform a certain type of work; in return the master engaged to maintain him as well as to give him a stipulated wage and other emoluments.

But according to the theory of the day, both parties were more completely involved in the relationship thus established than the terms of the contract suggested. The master was understood to have assumed far-reaching obligations; the servant was seen as having placed his whole energy at the disposal of his employer.

All the servant's time, from the moment he was engaged, was supposed to belong to his master; he was expected to abandon all thought of maintaining a private life. Addressing the servant in one of his sermons, the Rev. Patrick Delany reminds him of this:

> . . . your time and strength are no longer your own, when you are hired; they are your master's, and to be employed in his service; and consequently you cannot employ them as you please, but as he directs: nor can you misemploy them, or with-hold them from him without manifest fraud and injustice.[3]

In the course of advising his servant-readers Thomas Broughton makes the same point: 'When you hired yourselves, you sold all your time to your masters; except what GOD and Nature more immediately require to be reserved.'[4]

The strictest obedience, moreover, was expected of the servant; only if ordered to do something contrary to the dictates of the law of God or the law of the state was he justified in recalcitrance. This submission, explains the Rev. Delany,

---

[1] *Letters of . . . Chesterfield*, VI. 2890. Cf. *London Chronicle*, 1762, XI. 164a.
[2] Hanway, *Domestic Happiness*, p. 78. Cf. Hanway, *Reflections, Essays and Meditations*, I. 242.
[3] [Patrick Delany,] *Twenty Sermons upon Social Duties and Their Opposite Vices*, 1750, p. 192. Cf. *A Present for Servants*, 1768, 8th ed., p. 35; *Midwife*, 1751, II. 9; *London Chronicle*, 1760, VII. 347a.
[4] Thomas Broughton, *Serious Advice and Warning to Servants*, 1763, 4th ed., pp. 24–5. Cf. *A Present for Servants*, p. 35.

necessarily arises from the nature of servitude; for the very condition of that compact is, that one man shall submit his will and actions to the discretion and direction of another: and therefore a servant is supposed to have no will of his own, where his master is concerned; but to submit himself intirely to the will of his master, and obey all his lawful commands.[1]

A similar declaration occurs in an essay of a periodical series entitled *Advice to a Sister*. Although lashing out in a remarkably liberal spirit against those employers who felt 'that servants very thoughts, as well as their abilities, ought to be entirely at their disposal and controul', the author asserts that 'A master is a master . . . though it were but a broomstick; and so long as a servant receives his wages, he ought to be subservient to his will, in every thing just and reasonable. . . .'[2] And the publisher Dodsley expresses the identical view in his poem *Servitude*, written during the years he lived as a footman:

> NEXT, as we're Servants, Masters at our Hands
> Expect Obedience to all just Commands;
> Which, if we rightly think is but their Due,
> Nor more than we in Reason ought to do.
> Purchas'd by annual Wages, Cloaths and Meat,
> Theirs is our Time, our Hands, our Head, our Feet:
> We think, design and act at their Command,
> And, as their Pleasure varies, walk or stand;
> Whilst we receive the covenanted Hire,
> Active Obedience justly they require. . . .[3]

The servant was also expected to know his place and under all circumstances to maintain a deferential manner, whatever his private thoughts. In those contemporary tracts indited especially for his edification he is reminded of the desirability of such qualities as 'Humility and Lowliness', 'Meakness and Gentleness', good temper and fearfulness, respectfulness and submissiveness.[4] Thus Eliza Haywood praises timidity, calling it 'an Indication of your Respect for those you serve';[5] and Jonas Hanway commends

---

[1] Delany, *Twenty Sermons*, p. 182.
[2] *Town and Country Magazine*, 1772, IV. 373.
[3] [Robert Dodsley,] *Servitude*, 1728, p. 18.
[4] Thomas Seaton, *The Conduct of Servants in Great Families*, 1720, pp. 183-96; *A Present for Servants*, p. 73; Anne Barker, *The Complete Servant Maid*, n.d., pp. 5-6, 7-8; *Gentleman's Magazine*, 1771, XLVII. 470.
[5] Eliza Haywood, *A Present for a Servant-Maid*, Dublin, 1743, p. 8.

humility, remarking that 'A proud servant, of all God's creatures, is the strangest inconsistency'.[1] The same conception of what constituted the proper bearing of a domestic appears in Dodsley's *Servitude*. Styling submission

> The humble Liv'ry of a Servant's Mind;
> By which we ought to be distinguish'd more
> Than by the Liveries on our Bodies wore,

Dodsley, speaking as a footman, goes on to conclude:

> For Haughtiness and Pride but ill agrees
> With one whose Duty tis to serve and please.[2]

Thus, despite the contractual foundation of the relationship, the dominion exercised by the master was regarded as almost unlimited, the bounds of the servant's obligation as all but undefined. The servant was looked upon as having temporarily relinquished his freedom. In considering 'the Condition of a *Servant*', Guy Miege observes 'how by going to Service he devests [*sic*] himself of what is dearest to Mankind, his Liberty. . . .'[3]

The harshness of this state was presumed to be greatly mitigated by the emotional or sentimental tie binding master and servant; for it was supposed that what was in the first instance a contract would develop into a truly family bond, characterized by mutual devotion. Indeed, the servant was thought of as becoming an integral part of the family, as the contemporary practice of referring to a man's domestics as his 'family' clearly indicates.

This concept, the origins of which lay far back in the Middle Ages, provided a second sanction for investing the master with complete control. As head of the family, he was seen entitled to the obedience of all its members. He might properly chastise them for dereliction of duty, for insubordination, for impudence, or for almost anything else he chose to interpret as misconduct. In a word, the authority he exercised over his servants was viewed as the equivalent in scope and character to that which he exercised over his children.

Moreover, according to this concept, the master might expect

---

[1] Hanway, *Domestic Happiness*, p. 85.
[2] Dodsley, *Servitude*, p. 20.
[3] [Guy Miege,] *The New State of England under Our Sovereign Queen Anne*, 1703, pt. II. 288. Cf. Defoe, *Law of Subordination*, p. 30; Huntingford, *Laws of Masters and Servants*, p. 119.

fidelity and attachment from his domestics no less than from the other members of his family. They were supposed to guard his secrets, defend his good name against calumny and hostile criticism, and in general make his interests their own. In fact, their indentification was supposed to become so complete that they would remain for years in his service. Heasel leaves no doubt about what their attitude ought to be. 'When your family visits at any other house,' he writes in his instructions for footmen,

> never tell the servants there what is done in your master's family, ... for when a servant keeps tattling up and down every occurrence in the family, it often brings dishonour on his master.... It is also a very great sin, and one of the breaches of the fifth commandment; for as we are commanded to honour our parents, so it is necessarily implied that we also honour and respect all those who have authority over us.[1]

And outlining the duties of the valet, Heasel advises him that he ought to enter the lists should other servants reflect on his master's conduct: '... make it your business to vindicate his character, and if possible convince them that the accusation is not founded on truth.'[2]

But if as a member of the family the servant was regarded as owing loyalty and obedience to its head, he was also seen as having the right to such treatment as a child ought to receive from its father. This view is implicit in much that was written during the century on the relationship of master and servant; it is set forth in unmistakable terms by William Darrell, who, in one of those guides to right living so popular with readers of the period, tells the gentleman with a household to manage: 'Your care must not stop at your Children, let it reach your menial Servants; though you are their Master, you are also their Father.'[3] The care thus recommended was extremely comprehensive. It included moral guidance,

---

[1] Heasel, *Servants Book of Knowledge*, p. 72. Cf. *The Servant's Friend*, n.d., p. 5; *Gentleman's Magazine*, 1771, XLVII; Defoe, *The Maid-Servant's Modest Defence*, pp. 32–3.

[2] Heasel, *Servants Book of Knowledge*, p. 75. Cf. Haywood, *A Present for a Servant-Maid*, p. 33; Barker, *Complete Servant Maid*, p. 9.

[3] [William Darrell,] *The Gentleman Instructed, in the Conduct of a Virtuous and Happy Life*, 1727, 9th ed., pt. I. 87. Cf. *Post Angel*, 1701, II. 18; *Lady's Magazine*, 1785, XVI. 128; *Gentleman's Magazine*, 1787, LVII. 128.

for in his paternal role the master was considered accountable for the moral behaviour of his servants. Hanway writes: 'That masters and mistresses are responsible for the conduct of their servants, is as evident as that God has given them the command. . . .'[1] Secondly, it included religious direction. *'Every Master is a Priest in his own Family'*; runs *A Present for Servants*, *'and I have often thought his Obligation to teach and govern his Servants is much greater than that of a Minister to any particular Family in his charge.'*[2] Thirdly, it included care for the servants' material welfare. The master was supposed to see to it that his servants were well-treated and adequately maintained when in good health, and properly cared for when they fell ill.[3] He was expected to intervene on their behalf when they were beset by trouble or danger. By so doing he was said to provide them with 'protection'—a survival of feudal terminology that recalls the medieval origin of this concept of the family. Finally, he was supposed to make provision for those of his domestics who became superannuated in his employ and for those who by virtue of their fidelity and diligence had earned the right to retire from service at an earlier age. '. . . it is the duty of a master,' writes Patrick Delany,

> to remember a good servant in his last will: to make the best provision he can for him, against that time when it will be no longer in his power, either to reward his fidelity, or relieve his wants: and therefore I would have a dutiful and conscientious servant always considered in the next degree to a dutiful child. . . .[4]

Delany emphasizes the importance of making a testamentary provision as a precaution, but it is clear that he felt a master was under obligation to provide for his domestics while he was still alive. A writer in 1760 stated this obligation in vigorous terms:

> To encourage servants to do well, and to reward them for having done it, is right. The former of these is to be done by good treatment, and a fair indulgence of hope. The latter not in supplying them with the means of indulging continual luxury and vice, but, . . . in doing them some essential service; which it must be in the

---

[1] Hanway, *Domestic Happiness*, p. xiii. Cf. *Prater*, 1757, 2nd ed., p. 131; *Letters from Mrs. Elizabeth Carter*, I. 380; Hanway, *Reflections, Essays and Meditations*, I. 52; *Gentleman's Magazine*, 1787, LVII. 128.
[2] *A Present for Servants*, p. vi.
[3] *London Chronicle*, 1762, XI. 164a; Delany, *Twenty Sermons*, p. 233.
[4] Delany, *Twenty Sermons*, p. 232.

power, one way or other, of every one to do who keeps servants; or, at worst, by a compassionate support of them in old age, in return for their good services in youth.[1]

II

No such harmony as characterized the relationship in theory existed in fact. The chorus of complaint raised against domestics throughout the period makes it abundantly clear that the eighteenth century was no golden age of service.

The friction between master and servant stemmed from a fundamental conflict. The master sought to impose the extensive control and exact the perfect allegiance to which in theory he was entitled; the servant, on the other hand, sought to limit his obligations and preserve an independence that accorded ill with what was expected of him. This conflict had its inception in medieval times, and it has continued to exist to the present day. Generally speaking, it grew stronger as the basis of service became increasingly contractual. Over the years, however, it waxed and waned with changing conditions. In the eighteenth century it was particularly acute.

There were several causes for such discord. Perhaps most important was the increasingly dynamic character that English society assumed during the period. As the expansion of commerce and industry raised more and more men in the economic and social scale, the impulse to rise became widely diffused. Few domestics remained untouched by it, and naturally those who succumbed became both restless and self-seeking. 'They see others in full ascent, which makes them uneasy and ready to do whatever they can for themselves,' remarked an astute contemporary observer.[2] The dynamic character of society also contributed to the acuteness of the conflict between master and servant in another way. The growth of the middle classes greatly increased the demand for servants.[3] This multiplication of the opportunities for employment inevitably endowed the servant with greater independence. Competition for his services increased his bargaining power and encour-

[1] *Gentleman's Magazine,* 1760, xxx. 76. Cf. Haywood, *A Present for a Servant-Maid,* p. 50; Huntingford, *Laws of Masters and Servants,* pp. 116–17.
[2] James Hughes, *Observations on the Labouring Poor,* 1785, p. 10.
[3] Elizabeth W. Gilboy, *Wages in Eighteenth Century England,* Cambridge (Mass.), 1934, p. 34.

aged him to move from one establishment to another; it fostered in him what one writer termed a 'roving disposition'.[1] Moreover, lessened fear of dismissal made him careless to please and impatient of control.[2] The liberal gratuities he received from visitors and tradesmen likewise augmented his independence, for by freeing him from complete reliance on his master's bounty they permitted him to be less mindful of his master's wishes.

Thus conditions obtained that encouraged servants to assert themselves, and they did so in an aggressive fashion. Even when allowance is made for the inevitable exaggeration, the barrage of criticism directed at them by employers leaves the impression that as a group servants were highly insubordinate and very far from identifying their interests with those of their masters. The spirit of the class is well revealed by a note written in 1745 to the Rev. Richard Lardner by an irate domestic:

> Sir, I shall take your warning from this day; I think it is proper to speak to those who dress your victuals, and not to them as have nothing to do with it. I see there is no such thing as pleasing you, I knew what business was before I came to you and more than what you have to do, and though I cant please you, I dont doubt but I shall please other people very well, I never had the uneasiness anywhere, as I have here, & I hope never shall again; for you are never easy [MS. torn] let one do never so much for you, and you can get Mrs. Buck or any body else as may do your work better for I will not stay with you, to be found fault with for nothing; when I am in fault, I desire to be told of it, but not to be told of other peoples, Betty is too good a servant for you, you neve [*sic*] had a better, nor will have again; she understands business, better than you can teach her; and I expect to be paid for the half year I have been without cloaths. . . .[3]

The insubordination of domestics showed itself in numerous ways; the catalogue of grievances voiced against them on this score was long. But their restiveness is more strikingly demonstrated by their refusal to submit to physical correction than by anything else. According to the prevalent theory, an essential part of the master's

---

[1] *Oxford Magazine*, 1771, VI. 84. Cf. Grey, *Apology for the Servants*, p. 14.

[2] Hughes, *Observations on the Labouring Poor*, p. 11.

[3] Mary Lady Jennings, *A Kentish Country House; or the Records of Hall House, Hawkhurst*, Guildford, 1894, p. 73.

THE RELATIONSHIP OF MASTER AND SERVANT

prerogative was the right to enforce discipline by the rod; and servants of both sexes were liberally caned, cuffed, and slapped. Swift's treatment of his footman Patrick is a case in point. On one occasion in 1711, for instance, he 'went up, shut the chamber door, and gave him two or three swinging cuffs on the ear. . . .'[1] The law countenanced such chastisement. Writing in 1703, Guy Miege declares: 'As for stubborn and unruly *Servants*, the Law of *England* gives Masters and Mistresses power to correct them; and resistance in a *Servant* is punished with severe Penalty.'[2] But even though the Master's authority to administer corrective blows was grounded on both law and custom, many servants rebelled against it. Menial servants, says an account of England supposedly written by a Portuguese traveller, 'are become the general plague of the nation, both in town and country; they are not to be corrected, or even spoken to, but they immediately threaten to leave their service. . . .'[3] Their resistance was by no means always confined to threats; in some instances they carried their complaints to the courts. Accustomed to the arbitrary privileges of the upper classes of the continent, Archenholz noticed this with a certain amount of astonishment. 'The first man in the kingdom', he writes in commenting on English social structure, 'is cautious of striking his domestics; for they . . . may . . . commence an action in a court of justice: in such a case, a pecuniary recompense, and many disagreeable circumstances are sure to follow.'[4] A typical instance of a servant aroused by a thrashing to institute such proceedings is detailed by the Rev. William Cole in his diary. One of Cole's neighbours, Dr. Pettingal, 'on calling his Maid, & her not coming so soon as he expected, went out & beat her very severely. . . .' The maid thereupon applied to the local justice for a warrant for her master's arrest, and failing to secure one, betook herself to London 'with a design to put him in the crown office'.[5]

As Archenholz states, such an action was often successful. For, although the law sustained the master in the exercise of his

---
[1] Swift, *Journal to Stella*, p. 307.
[2] Miege, *New State of England*, 1703, pt. II. 288. Cf. [Salomon] Bolton, *The Present State of Great Britain*, 1758, pt. I. 173.
[3] 'The Voyage of Don Manoel Gonzalez to . . . England and Scotland', John Pinkerton, *A General Collection of the Best and Most Interesting Voyages to All Parts of the World*, 1808–14, II. 95.
[4] Archenholz, *Picture of England*, p. 206.
[5] *Blecheley Diary*, p. 253.

traditional right, it set limits to the punishment he might inflict with impunity.[1] Hence damages were often granted by the courts on the grounds that the beating had been excessive or that it had caused permanent injury. A case tried at the Buckingham Assizes in 1760, for example, resulted in an award of ten guineas to the plaintiff, a servant girl whose master had beaten her;[2] John Baker mentions a similar case in his diary, the victim in this instance receiving as damages between thirty and forty pounds.[3]

The insubordinate spirit that prompted domestics to bring suit in this manner was supposed to be less highly developed in country servants than in those of the Metropolis, and it was partly for this reason that many employers preferred to have them in their homes. But there is much evidence to indicate that, on the whole, the conduct of country servants fell far short of the complete submissiveness expected by the employer class. A master was likely to have to reckon with insubordination regardless of the provenance of his domestics.

Hand in hand with insubordination went the pursuit of self-interest: servants tended to exploit their places to the full. The Abbé Le Blanc writes in his discussion of them: 'Les Domestiques Anglois, ont un . . . défaut si général, qu'il fait une partie de leur caractère; c'est d' être extrêment intéressés.'[4] To this bent may be traced many of the malpractices of which masters complained most bitterly: the purloining of provisions, the padding of tradesmen's bills to increase the commissions, the neglect and ill-treatment of guests who failed to give generously. From the employer's point of view, however, the greatest of the attendant evils was the stifling of fidelity and devotion in the servant; for genuine attachment seems to have been the exception rather than the rule. Writing as an Italian visitor to England in 1755, Dr. Shebbeare reported to his pretended correspondent at Rome that 'the servants have very little attachment to those they serve; . . . self is the sole motive. . . .'[5] And in 1786 the Rev. John Trusler declared cynically:

---

[1] William Blackstone, *Commentaries on the Laws of England*, Oxford, 1768, 3rd ed., I. 428. Cf. *Laws Concerning Masters and Servants*, [1768,] 2nd ed., p. 126.
[2] *London Chronicle*, 1760, VIII. 95b.
[3] *Diary of John Baker*, p. 423.
[4] Jean B. Le Blanc, *Lettres d'un François*, La Haye, 1745, I. 148.
[5] Battista Angeloni [John Shebbeare,] *Letters on the English Nation*, 1755, II. 39.

THE RELATIONSHIP OF MASTER AND SERVANT

'To expect attachment from a servant is idle, and betrays an ignorance of the world. Servants will now and then affect it, in order to gain the confidence of their employers; but if we suppose them in our interest, it is because we do not know them.'[1]

This lack of devotion gave rise to a multitude of petty annoyances from which few employers were entirely immune. Not the least harassing of these was the propensity of servants to retail their masters' business. Defoe takes notice of this, admonishing female domestics to 'add to your other Virtues PIETY, which will teach you the Prudence of *Keeping Family-Secrets*; the Want of which is a great Complaint. . . .'[2]

But the principal inconvenience springing from the absence of attachment in servants and the one most persistently deplored was 'their instability of continuing in their places'.[3] Defoe describes them as 'quitting Service for every idle Disgust'.[4] And according to Eliza Haywood, they generally adopted the attitude that *'There are more Places than Parish Churches*, and on the least Occasion presently [gave] Warning'.[5] No doubt, as these contemporaries suggest, caprice was often responsible for their leaving their places. But in many instances it was a very real desire to advance their material interests that kept them on the move. Commenting on the attitude of the average footman, Bernard Mandeville remarked:

> . . . tho' you had taken him from the Dunghill, out of an Hospital, or a Prison, you shall never keep him longer than he can make his Place what in his Estimation of himself he thinks he deserves; nay the best and most civiliz'd, that never were Saucy and Impertinent, will leave the most indulgent Master, and to get handsomely away, frame fifty Excuses, and tell downright Lies as soon as they can mend themselves.[6]

And the case was precisely the same with other types of servants. Complaining of domestics in general, 'Philanthropus' declared in 1760 that they no longer regard their places as inheritances, 'but as

---

[1] Trusler, *London Adviser*, p. 47.
[2] Defoe, *The Maid-Servant's Modest Defence*, p. 35.
[3] *London Chronicle*, 1791, LXIX. 165b. Cf. *Post Angel*, 1701, II. 134; *Oxford Magazine*, 1771, VI. 84; *Gentleman's Magazine*, 1793, LXIII. 229, 331.
[4] Defoe, *Augusta Triumphans*, p. 25.
[5] Haywood, *A Present for a Servant-Maid*, p. 7. Cf. *Town and Country Magazine*, 1772, IV. 373.
[6] Bernard Mandeville, *The Fable of the Bees*, 1724, 3rd ed., p. 347.

situations in which ... they are to make the most that they every way can for themselves.' And he went on to observe that 'they are ever ready to quit them on the smallest view of present advantage'.[1]

There were, of course, domestics who passed long years in the service of a single employer, just as there were others who conformed to the ideal of subservience held by the employer class. A man-cook who served the Leghs remained with them from 1693 until his death in 1757, a period of sixty-four years.[2] A female domestic of Mrs. Boscawen's died in her service in 1786, having lived with her for thirty-six years.[3] Smith, Mrs. Delany's lady's maid, continued in her employ for thirty-four years, from 1745 to 1779.[4] When Caroline Powys visited the Jacksons of Wesenham Hall in 1756, she found that the housekeeper had been with them for fifty-one years, the butler for thirty-two or -three, and Miss Jackson's maid for twenty-four.[5] Lady Hertford informed Lady Luxborough in 1752 that her house steward had been with her for nineteen years and the man who had care of the stables 'and everything without' for ten.[6]

Such instances of long service were exceptional. This is clearly indicated by the advertisements that servants placed in the London papers. Most of these state the length of time the advertiser spent in his last situation, and between three and four years appears to have been the average period. Moreover, other evidence points to the same conclusion. An account book kept by Henry Purefoy and his mother lists the names of some thirty servants who passed through their relatively small household during a span of ten years.[7] The diaries of Anthony Stapley, John Baker, and the Rev. Woodforde reveal a similar turnover. And further corroboration is to be found in John Macdonald's *Travels*. During a career of thirty-nine years of service Macdonald had twenty-eight different masters.[8] He seldom remained in the same place longer than two years; in 1773-4 he changed employers eleven times.[9]

---

[1] *London Chronicle*, 1760, VII. 164ab; *Gentleman's Magazine*, 1760, XXX. 77.
[2] [Evelyn] Newton, *The House of Lyme*, 1917, p. 381.
[3] *Autobiography and Correspondence of ... Mrs. Delany*, Second Series, III. 417.
[4] *Ibid.*, II. 456.   [5] *Diaries of Mrs. Philip Lybbe Powys*, p. 4.
[6] Hughes, *The Gentle Hertford*, p. 409.   [7] *Purefoy Letters*, I. 126.
[8] *Memoirs of an Eighteenth-Century Footman*, introd., pp. xvii–xviii.
[9] *Ibid.*

THE RELATIONSHIP OF MASTER AND SERVANT

There was one device that could be used to restrain this roving as well as to coerce domestics in other respects. A servant's chances of obtaining a situation depended in no small measure on the character given by his last employer; hence a master, by threatening to give a poor one or not to give one at all, could hold a club over his servant's head.[1]

The effectiveness of this weapon was seriously undermined by the employer class itself. Many masters, out of kindness, were reluctant to give bad recommendations, even when they were richly deserved. How widespread this reluctance must have been is apparent from the criticism to which it was subjected. In a forthright passage Sir John Fielding attributes '*Most of the Inconveniencies arising in Families from the Misconduct of Servants . . . to the partial and unjust Characters given of them by their Masters and Mistresses. . . .*'[2] His brother Henry appears to have seen the matter in the same light. A letter to the editor of the *Covent Garden Journal* denounces 'the unjust Characters given of Servants; an Order of People, who are moved out of one Station into another, and are admitted into Places of Trust according to their Recommendations'. It then recounts how the correspondent, having taken a maid who had been recommended 'in the strongest manner imaginable', found her anything but the sort of person she was supposed to be. And it concludes:

> . . . by the Stories I have heard from My Friends since my own Accident, one would imagine that half of the Masters and Mistresses of this Kingdom, by the Characters they give their Servants, live in fear of, and are dependent upon them. I declare for the Future, that whoever acts in my Family in the Capacity of Servant shall, when he or she leaves it, have that Character from me which their Behaviour intitles them to, be it good, bad or indifferent, and I wish from my Soul you would set forth the Consequences of the contrary in such a light, as may deter every Gentleman and Lady from saying more or less of any Servant than they deserve; as this will prevent the greatest Irregularities in decent Families. . . .[3]

---

[1] *Gentleman's Magazine*, 1791, LXI. 1172–3; *Laws Relating to Masters and Servants*, 1755, p. 9n.; Archenholz, *Picture of England*, pp. 206—7; Austin, *Letters from London*, p. 89.
[2] Fielding, *Penal Laws*, p. 142. Cf. Hanway, *Virtue in Humble Life*, 1774, I. 350.
[3] *Covent Garden Journal*, ed. Gerard Jansen, New Haven, 1915, II. 103–4.

An essayist in the *World* likewise censures employers for their lenity in granting characters. 'It is to this mistaken compassion,' he writes, 'that the disorderly behaviour of servants is, perhaps, principally owing. . . .' And he goes on to advise 'all heads of families to give *honest* characters before they . . . exclaim against *dishonest* servants'.[1] Huntingford's remarks on the subject have a similar tenor. Inveighing against what he considered the misplaced 'tenderness' of masters, he maintains that whoever hides the faults of a servant 'acts in a manner disingenuous in itself, inimical to society, and productive of serious evils in its consequences'. He ends by wishing 'that masters would pay the strictest attention to CHARACTER in the recommending and receiving servants, as from neglect in this particular arises no inconsiderable share of the evils attending the servile system'.[2] Domestics were naturally well aware that they could count on the leniency these writers so vigorously decried. As a consequence, in many cases threats of withholding a character or of giving a bad one lost their force.

They also lost their force for other reasons. In London a servant whose master refused him a satisfactory recommendation could easily procure a counterfeit testimonial; for there were people who, 'taking upon themselves false names and pretended stations', made a profitable business of supplying such references.[3] Huntingford cites an instance of one impostor who made upwards of a hundred pounds a year.[4] And a newspaper account that appeared in 1792 relates how 'a woman with some address and education, who keeps a house of intrigue in the environs of town, clears her rent and taxes by giving false characters of female servants that lodge with her, when out of place'.[5] Sometimes the references that were sold were written out; in other cases they were verbal, the pretended ex-master meeting the prospective employer personally in order to discuss the servant's merits. An instance of a false character given verbally occurs in the testimony heard by a committee of

[1] *World*, III. 152–3. Cf. *Public Advertiser*, 1768, No. 10534, Aug. 3, 4d.
[2] Huntingford, *Laws of Masters and Servants*, p. 98.
[3] *Ibid.* Cf. Henry Fielding, *An Enquiry into the Cause of the Late Increase of Robbers, &c.*, 1751, 2nd ed., p. 202; *London Chronicle*, 1791, LXIX. 165b.
[4] Huntingford, *Laws of Masters and Servants*, p. 99. Cf. [Jonas Hanway,] *Eight Letters to His Grace —— Duke of ——, on the Custom of Vails-Giving*, 1760, p. 39.
[5] *London Chronicle*, 1792, LXXI. 350a.

the House of Commons in 1791. James Free told how on engaging a coachman, he had interviewed a man supposed to be his former master. Later on, however, the coachman confessed that the fellow who had impersonated his master 'was a Man notoriously in the Habit of giving false Characters to Servants out of Place, and that for what he had said of him he had paid him one Guinea. . . .' The man who had given the false character, Free testified, was found to have rented his lodgings for a few weeks, passing himself off as a country squire out of Gloucestershire.[1] Besides being able to purchase a recommendation from such professional vendors, a servant could get one of his own friends to give him a character. Recourse was often had to this subterfuge. Writing of livery servants in 1784, an anonymous pamphleteer states that 'the insolence to which they are at present arrived, is such as to laugh at dismission from their place, and even at refusal of character, as they write fictitious ones for one another. . . .'[2]

This collusion displays in yet another form the assertiveness of servants. At the same time it reveals the spirit that led them to make a collective stand against employers.

For servants, especially in London, where great numbers of them were concentrated in a relatively small area and where the rate of interaction amongst them was high, were animated by a strong sense of solidarity or group loyalty. This is well brought out in Steele's play *The Lying Lover* (1703). Simon says to Latine: 'I'll stand your friend as much as one servant can to another, against all masters and mistresses whatever.'[3] The existence of this propensity is also stresssed in Townley's farce *High Life Below Stairs*. Freeman says of his servant Robert: '. . . though he is a very honest Fellow, yet he is so much of a Servant, that he'll never tell anything to the Disadvantage of another.' And later on in the play Robert remarks: 'Sir, I am but a Servant myself, and it would not become me to speak ill of a Brother Servant.'[4]

The existence of such a spirit inevitably led to active combination for the purpose of defending and advancing common interests. Writing under one of his numerous pseudonyms in 1725, Defoe

---

[1] *Journal of the House of Commons*, 1791, XLVI. 472.
[2] *The Heads of a Plan for the Raising the Money for Maintaining Paupers by a New Method*, 1784, pp. 36-7n.
[3] *Steele's Plays*, p. 157.
[4] Townley, *High Life Below Stairs*, pp. 5, 8.

denounces the 'Insolence and Intrigues of our Servant Wenches, who, by their caballing together, have made their Party so considerable, that Every-body cries out against them. . . .'[1] What Defoe refers to here was probably an informal association. But there were also well-organized groups that functioned both as friendly societies and as something resembling the modern trade-union. Excoriating 'common menial servants' as 'the plague of almost every house in town', the pseudo-traveller Gonzalez observes that 'they form themselves into societies or rather confederacies, contributing to the maintenance of each other, when out of places. . . .'[2] Bernard Mandeville, who, like Defoe, was scandalized at the independent attitude of the servant class, gives a detailed account of the manner in which one of these groups operated. 'I am credibly inform'd,' he writes,

> that a parcel of Footmen are arriv'd to that Height of Insolence as to have enter'd into a Society together, and made Laws by which they oblige themselves not to serve for less than such a Sum, nor carry Burdens or any Bundle or Parcel above a certain Weight, not exceeding Two or Three Pounds, with other Regulations directly opposite to the Interest of those they Serve, and altogether destructive to the Use they were design'd for. If any of them be turn'd away for strictly adhering to the Orders of this Honourable Corporation, he is taken care of till another Service is provided for him, and there is no Money wanting at any time to commence and maintain a Law-suit against any Master that shall pretend to strike or offer any other Injury to his Gentleman Footman, contrary to the Statutes of their Society.[3]

Towards the end of the period Joseph Farington, the artist, noted in his diary the existence of another group with the same design: 'Footmen by combining together now make a stand for conditions. The Plan is by subscribing each a certain sum weekly, those who are out of place receive from this fund a weekly allowance till they are engaged upon prescribed conditions.'[4]

Groups of this kind undoubtedly organized much of the opposi-

[1] [Daniel Defoe,] *Everybody's Business is Nobody's Business*, 1767, p. 4. Cf. *Heads of a Plan*, p. 47; Defoe, *The Maid-Servant's Modest Defence*, p. 7.
[2] 'Voyage of . . . Gonzalez', Pinkerton, *Voyages*, II. 95.
[3] Mandeville, *Fable of the Bees*, p. 350.
[4] *The Farington Diary*, ed. James Greig, 1922–8, I. 192.

tion to the campaign against vails-giving that employers waged in the early 1760's. It is very likely that they also gave direction to the agitation that arose in 1744 and 1795 against the employment of French servants.[1] Representing an aggressive minority, they seem to have adopted a course of militant action whenever the welfare of the occupational group appeared to be threatened.

Thus not only did employers have to contend with individual servants who were insubordinate and motivated entirely by self-interest, but with organized groups as well. That this was so is eloquent testimony to the acuteness of the conflict between master and servant.

III

The employer class did not wholly despair of rendering servants tractable and instilling into them a greater attachment to their masters. Rather unrealistically, it relied a good deal upon suasion; but it also considered, and in one or two instances embraced, more radical means of effecting their amendment.

A favourite device for indoctrinating them with proper principles was the circulation of tracts. *A Present for Servants*, distributed by the Society for Promoting Christian Knowledge; Thomas Broughton's *Serious Advice and Warning to Servants*, published under the auspices of the same organization; Eliza Haywood's *A Present for a Servant-Maid*; and Sarah Trimmer's *The Servant's Friend* are typical of these productions. Setting forth the traditional view of the relationship of master and servant, they sought to inspire in their readers a deportment that coincided with the ideal pattern.

Satire, too, was counted on to have a corrective effect. The diverting ironies of Jonathan Swift's *Directions for Servants* were intended to shame the class out of its misconduct. Writing to Faulkner in 1739, Swift speaks of the piece as being 'very useful as well as humorous'.[2] The mordant satire of James Townley's *High Life Below Stairs* was also meant to bring them into line.[3]

[1] See Hecht, 'Continental and Colonial Servants', *Smith College Studies in History*, XL. 19.
[2] *Correspondence of Jonathan Swift*, VI. 145.
[3] For contemporary appraisals of the play see Hanway, *Sentiments and Advice of Thomas Trueman*, p. 33; Thomas Ruggles, *History of the Poor*,

In an advertisement attached to the printed play Townley avers that 'It was a real desire to do good amongst a very large and useful Body of People, that gave rise to this little piece'. This declaration rings true. It is more than the usual repetition of the neo-classical formula that the author's purpose is to instruct as well as to amuse.

While some supposed that persuasion and ridicule could induce servants to alter their attitude and reform their ways, others were less sanguine. There were a good many demands for remedial action and more than a few suggestions as to what the nature of such action should be.

Many of these suggestions naturally dealt with the problem of insubordination. Christopher Tancred, writing in 1724, demanded that servants be made the subject of legislation that would, among other things, provide 'a Penalty sufficient to deter them from committing such irregular Practices, as render their Services insupportable'.[1] Defoe, too, in a pamphlet published in 1725, called for an Act of Parliament giving the magistracy power to discipline them. '. . . if Servants misbehave themselves,' he declared, 'they ought to be amerced or punished.'[2] Similarly, an anonymous author, writing in 1784, proposed 'making them liable to punishment for misbehaviour instead of being dismissed their service. . . .' According to his plan, servants who transgressed would 'be liable at the discretion of two justices, to be confined in the penitentiary house. . . .' A record of their offences would be kept there, so that later employees could readily check on their pasts. Only after a probationary period during which their conduct proved satisfactory would their names be expunged from the register.[3] A somewhat less drastic proposal was made by Patrick Colquhoun in 1795. Calling attention to the fact that servants in husbandry were 'punishable by Justices in a summary way', he recommended extending the same laws that governed them to domestic servants. Masters, he held, would be protected against the 'errors and improprieties, as well as crimes' that the 'ill-regulated passions' of

1793–4, II. 248; *The Bee and Other Essays by Oliver Goldsmith*, 1914, pp. 61–2; Fred[erick] A. Wendeborn, *A View of England towards the Close of the Eighteenth Century*, 1791, I. 283; Richard B. Peake, *Memoirs of the Colman Family*, [1841,] I. 267.

[1] Christopher Tancred, *A Scheme for an Act of Parliament for the Better Regulating Servants, and Ascertaining Their Wages*, 1724, p. vii.
[2] Defoe, *Everybody's Business*, p. 23.
[3] *Heads of a Plan*, pp. 46, 35–6, 37.

domestics often led them into, 'if examples could occasionally be made, by inflicting slight punishments upon them; in the same manner as upon other servants for breaches of moral contracts.'[1] In the following year an anonymous writer also advocated legislative action along the same lines. Addressing William Wilberforce, who was both a member of Parliament and one of the moving spirits of a recently formed organization for the encouragement of good servants, he suggested that the reformer introduce legislation that would enable justices to fine servants who were insolent or abusive to their employers.[2]

At least one proposal for dealing with the problem of insubordination did not call for the intervention of Parliament. In 1786 a newspaper correspondent signing himself 'B. X.' put forward the idea that employers ought not contract with their domestics for 'large wages *certain*', but rather 'let all servants be their own *Security*, by having so much wages only *certain*, and more if they behave well, and give satisfaction at the year's end'.[3]

Along with these schemes for reducing domestics to a state of proper subordination, mention must be made of the suggestions that Parliament might endow the local justices with authority to regulate wages, as they fixed those of farm servants; for, although these suggestions arose in part from the very natural desire of employers to halt the advance of wages, they also stemmed from the widespread belief that too much money made domestics refractory. As 'B. X.' put it: 'High wages ruin all servants, and often make them insolent, impertinent, and saucy. . . .'[4]

The proposals for the abolition of vails-giving made prior to the suppression of the practice in the 1760's also proceeded from concern over insubordination. Vails-giving, it was rightly believed, weakened the master's authority by decreasing the servant's dependence upon him. The domestic who received large sums as vails, declared Hanway, was 'not much awed by his Master's *frowns*, nor afraid of his Resentments'.[5] The same line of reasoning

---

[1] Colquhoun, *Police of the Metropolis*, p. 438.
[2] The pamphlet was entitled 'A Letter to William Wilberforce, Esq. M.P., Member of the British Society for the Encouragement of Good Servants'. See *Gentleman's Magazine*, 1796, LXVI. 51.
[3] *London Chronicle*, 1768, XXIII. 55a.
[4] Ibid. Cf. Mandeville, *Fable of the Bees*, p. 349.
[5] Hanway, *Eight Letters*, p. 39. Cf. Mandeville, *Fable of the Bees*, p. 349.

also produced proposals for the elimination of other gratuities, such as card money and Christmas boxes.

But insubordination was not the only major problem of behaviour that inspired corrective proposals. Projects for reducing the frequency with which servants changed their places were set forth from time to time.

Writing in 1727, Defoe recommended a thorough revision of the system under which they were hired. According to his plan, the prevailing practice of engaging domestics on the basis of a month's warning or a month's wages would be entirely discarded; all servants would be obliged to bind themselves for a fixed period of time, the contract being made and duly recorded before a justice of the peace. No breach of contract on the part of the servant would be tolerated, except, of course, in the event that he had been mistreated; so that it would be impossible for him to leave his place until the agreed term had expired.[1] Thus essentially the same system under which servants in husbandry and many menials in the country were hired would be applied universally to domestics, the only difference being that, whereas farm servants bound themselves for but one year at a time, Defoe's scheme allowed for longer terms of service.

In 1728 Defoe again suggested that the 'roving temper' of domestics could be effectively curbed by altering the basis on which they were engaged. Denouncing the 'foolish old Custom call'd Warning', he urged that all domestics be hired by the year without the option of leaving their employ during that period. 'No servant', he wrote, 'should quit a Place, where they are well fed and paid, without assigning a good Reason before a Magistrate.' This proposal, like the earlier one, could have been implemented only through the enactment of new legislation; and Defoe called upon Parliament to take up the matter. 'If this be not worthy the Consideration of a Legislature,' he declared, 'I would fain know what is.'[2]

But Defoe did not regard legislative action as the sole possible remedy. When making his earlier proposal, he argued that much could be done by private initiative. Calling attention to a charity in the parish of St. Clement Danes that bestowed ten pounds on

---

[1] Defoe, *Everybody's Business*, p. 23.
[2] Defoe, *Augusta Triumphans*, p. 25.

THE RELATIONSHIP OF MASTER AND SERVANT

every maid who had lived ten years in one place, he stated that if such institutions were set up in other parishes, the results would be highly beneficial to employers.[1]

A plan on this same general order, although more comprehensive and more completely worked out, was offered to the public by an anonymous author in 1752. It provided that a fund be established by subscription for the payment of premiums to 'Servants that have lived long in a Place'. Every servant, male or female, who remained in a family for a full year was to receive one pound, for two years three pounds and so on up in the same proportion. Each of the beneficiaries was to be nominated by a subscriber and then approved by a managing committee. The plan was to be put into operation throughout the Metropolitan area. One half of the fund was to be reserved for disbursal within the bills of mortality, the other half to be distributed to servants in the out-parishes. Similar funds, the author suggested, might be set up in other towns.[2]

Another such plan was propounded in 1771. It called for the creation of a governing body 'under the title of the benevolent society, in every parish, who should raise a fund for bestowing premiums on all servants who have lived seven years in any one place'. The premiums were 'to be classed according to the ranks of the servants, and not less than five guineas to be given to the lowest'. Every housekeeper to subscribe a shilling a year to maintain the fund from which the premiums were to come.[3]

Entirely different in character was a proposal made in 1784. Like Defoe in 1728, the anonymous author prescribed as a nostrum an act of Parliament that would force all domestics to bind themselves for a fixed period of one year. '... I would,' he wrote,

> oblige every master to take, and every servant to hire himself for one year certain; to this I can see no possible objection, (it is customary now in many counties) as if the master misbehaves in any shameful manner to the servant by cruelty, or withholding legal wages, I trust in this free country justice may always be obtained by the meanest....[4]

But the idea of encouraging long service by the contribution of monetary rewards had by no means died out. In his *History of the*

[1] Defoe, *Everybody's Business*, pp. 14–15. Cf. *Post Angel*, 1701, II. 17–18.
[2] *A Proposal for the Amendment and Encouragement of Servants*, 1752, passim.
[3] *Oxford Magazine*, 1771, VI. 84.   [4] *Heads of a Plan*, p. 35.

Poor, which was published in 1793–4, Thomas Ruggles recommended that Parliament authorize a system of special payments, whereby a servant, after his first three years in a place, would receive a percentage of all wages he drew, in addition to his regular stipend.[1]

At the same time that proposals such as these were being offered as remedies for the inconstancy of servants, suggestions were made as to how the giving of characters could be transformed into a more effective instrument of control. Christopher Tancred in 1724, for instance, advised that a general register of servants be established and their testimonials kept continually on file so that employers and the magistrates could readily investigate their records. He also wished to see Parliament make it punishable by fine to engage a domestic who did not have a written character from his last employer. '... every Person,' he wrote, 'retaining any Servant without such a Testimonial, shall forfeit Five Pounds for every Day such Servant shall be retain'd in their Service....' Moreover, he advocated that the use of a false character be made subject to a heavy penalty:

> ... every Servant producing any counterfeit Testimonial, shall, upon Conviction, by Confession, or Oath of one Witness, before Justices of Peace ... be committed to the House of Correction there to be kept to hard Labour for one whole Year, and shall stand in the Pillory one Hour upon the next Market-Day, after Expiration of such a Year, at the next Market-Town to the Place where the Conviction shall be.[2]

A suggestion made in 1753 by Saunders Welch, the magistrate, bore a strong resemblance to Tancred's idea of a general registration of servants. In an open letter to the Duke of Newcastle Welch declared that a law ought to be passed to prevent a servant from leaving his place of residence or the parish where he had a legal settlement without a certificate from the local authorities, stating that he had 'behaved with Honesty and Industry'.[3] Presumably his former employer was to supply the necessary information. Had such a scheme been put into effect, almost all domestics would in time have become the bearers of labour passports; and as a

[1] Ruggles, *History of the Poor*, II. 257.
[2] Tancred, *Scheme for an Act of Parliament*, pp. 19–20.
[3] *London Chronicle*, 1758, III. 50c.

THE RELATIONSHIP OF MASTER AND SERVANT

result, characters would have been standardized and the possibility of false recommendations would have been greatly reduced. This idea of a labour passport was put forward again in 1767 by an anonymous writer. He proposed the registration of all types of working people who left the country to seek a livelihood in the Metropolis; each was to receive and carry with him a certificate testifying to his previous good conduct. If servants 'went without such a certificate', he wrote, 'it would be at their peril'. And he supplied a sample of the paper they would be obliged to carry:

Parish of B—— in the county of S——.

John Smith, aged 19, a single man, is permitted to go to service as a footman to Mrs. Johnston, who does now reside in London, and we testify to the best of our knowledge that he has behaved himself well and honestly.

A. B. Rector or Curate
M. H. and R. B. Church Wardens, or Overseers

Vestry, Oct. 27, 1766.[1]

Still another approach to the problem was recommended by Sir John Fielding in 1768. He was convinced

that if a Register-Office, founded on the same Principles, and executed by the same Methods as that in the Strand, so long carried on by Mr. Fielding and Co. were to be under Parliamentary Sanction, to have all Imitators suppressed, to be executed by Commissioners, and the Profits arising to go to the Government, it would be a great Blessing to Mankind; as it would open a fair Channel for Preferment for every faithful, industrious and diligent Servant, and would effectually prevent dissolute Servants from Admission into quiet, worthy Families.[2]

Evidently Fielding assumed that government control of the enterprise would make it possible to investigate in a really thorough fashion the written characters that servants presented. He also seems to have imagined that the office would gradually supersede all other means of recruitment in London and the surrounding region.

A certain similarity exists between Fielding's project and a plan conceived and put into effect some twenty years later. About 1789 an organization variously styled the Society for the Encouragement

[1] *Considerations on the Dearness of Corn and Provisions*, pp. 17–18.
[2] Fielding, *Penal Laws*, p. 141.

of Good Servants,[1] the Society for the Encrease and Encouragement of Good Servants,[2] and the British Society for Rewarding Servants [3] was founded in London, although it may not have begun to function until 1792.[4] It sought to promote constancy and fidelity in servants by raising a fund for the relief of those who because of illness or infirmity could no longer work. 'Long and approved service in the family of a subscriber, or two or more subscribers successively' was to entitle a servant to a substantial measure of support.[5] But the chief objective of the Society was 'to distinguish the deserving from the unworthy among servants';[6] and its plan, like Fielding's earlier, relied upon a register office to perform the screening process. '. . . it is proposed', explained one of the proponents of the scheme in 1789,

> to engage some *creditable* person to keep an office under the inspection of the society, at which such servants only are to be registered as obtain certificates of their merit from a member.
> The basis of the plan is 'a settled form of a servant's character'. When any member of the society has occasion to hire a servant, he shall require the one who offers himself to obtain from the last person he served a certificate of his character filled up agreeably to . . . such . . . printed form as may hereafter be settled by the society.[7]

Although it was realized that few could participate in the benefits offered by the Society, it was expected that the hope of participating would 'have an influence on the generality of servants'. It was presumed that 'The very name of such a Society' would 'bind them, as it were, to their good behaviour, without the terrors of the law'.[8]

In 1790 James Huntingford, who was secretary of the Society and one of its principal promoters, suggested that the efforts of the organization be supplemented by extensive legislation. He counselled, like others before him, that the servant in the country

---

[1] *Gentleman's Magazine*, 1789, LIX, p. iv.
[2] Huntingford, *Laws of Masters and Servants*, p. 109.
[3] Highmore, *Pietas Londinensis*, p. 953; *Gentleman's Magazine*, 1796, LXVI. 51.
[4] Highmore, *Pietas Londinensis*, p. 953.
[5] Huntingford, *Laws of Masters and Servants*, p. 110.
[6] *Gentleman's Magazine*, 1789, LIX, p. iv.   [7] Ibid.
[8] Huntingford, *Laws of Masters and Servants*, p. 112.

be restrained by law from leaving his home parish without 'a real certificate of character from his last employer', showing that he had conducted himself well. Such an act, Huntingford argued, 'might in time produce an effectual reformation in the behaviour of servants', since they would be likely to mend their ways rather than suffer 'a kind of imprisonment in their own particular parish'. It would also, he felt, 'effectually prevent dissolute servants from admission into quiet and respectable families....'[1]

Huntingford likewise asked that the impersonation of an employer for the purpose of giving a character, the forging of a certificate of recommendation and the falsification of the time a servant had been employed be made penal offences by Parliament. Moreover, he wanted a law to compel employers to give all recommendations in writing, forbid the hiring of servants without a written character and punish with imprisonment those who presumed to offer themselves without the proper testimonials.[2]

Some of these demands were met in 1791. In that year a group of householders presented a petition to the House of Commons, calling attention to the frequency with which characters were forged and employers impersonated, and requesting the enactment of a law 'to put a Stop to such pernicious Evils'. Accordingly, the petition was referred to a committee set up to consider the matter. Among those who testified before the committee were Huntingford and the popular physician Dr. Richard Brocklesby. As a result of the testimony, Sir Adam Ferguson and Hawkins Browne were given leave to bring in a bill dealing with the problem of false characters.[3] The bill passed without difficulty. It provided that a fine of twenty pounds be imposed on anyone who impersonated an employer, gave a false or forged character, or supplied misinformation in a character. It further provided that the same penalty be imposed on those who falsified their past record of service.[4] It was not all that Huntingford had asked, but from his viewpoint it was a step in the right direction.

The various proposals put forward from the time of Defoe to

[1] Huntingford, *Laws of Masters and Servants*, p. 101.
[2] *Ibid.*, p. 122.
[3] *Journal of the House of Commons*, 1791, XLVI. 299, 392, 471–2.
[4] Ruggles, *History of the Poor*, II. 250–1. For convictions under the act see *Lloyd's Evening Post*, 1793, LXXII. 467c; LXXVIII. 1619a; *Sun*, 1795, No. 851, June 19, 3d.

that of Huntingford for making servants more subservient, more constant, and more dependent on the recommendations of employers represent more than the opinions of their authors. Taken together, they are a fairly accurate measure of the dissatisfaction of the employer class.

IV

Not all employers accepted the obligations and played the role that theory assigned to them. There were some who, far from treating their servants as part of the family, ignored them as persons and were wholly indifferent to their welfare. There were others whose bearing towards their servants was uniformly haughty and disdainful. Propriety demanded that employers maintain a certain amount of reserve, the degree varying with the servant's nominal rank.[1] But some assumed an attitude that went well beyond the dictates of propriety. Eliza Haywood suggests that such hauteur was not uncommon when she says to her servant-readers: 'But supposing they are a little harsh in their Expressions, use you with Haughtiness, and keep you at the greatest Distance. . . .'[2] And John Macdonald gives an actual example. He relates how John Crauford of Errol, who had been his master, 'was so proud that he would not let a servant ride in the chaise with him, [while travelling] but would rather be at the expense of a horse'.[3]

But such employers were probably greatly outnumbered by those whose attitude was in some degree considerate and paternal, and there were many who felt a more than superficial concern for the well-being of their servants. Lady Mary Coke, for example, wrote in 1767: 'Heard but a bad account of a Servant that was ill in my house: it made me uneasy.' And a day or two later she declared: '. . . I was really quite melancholy . . . from the very bad account they gave me of the poor sick servant.'[4] Similarly, Horace Walpole, writing to Lady Ossory in 1785, voiced a genuine concern over the state of his 'poor honest servant, David', who

---

[1] Hanway, *Eight Letters*, p. 44; [Elizabeth Bonhote,] *The Parental Monitor*, 1788, II. 158–9.

[2] Haywood, *A Present for a Servant-Maid*, p. 32.

[3] *Memoirs of an Eighteenth-Century Footman*, p. 85.

[4] *The Letters and Journals of Lady Mary Coke*, ed. James A. Hume, Edinburgh, 1889–96, I. 134, 136.

had been dying of a dropsy for seven or eight months and had 'suffered dreadfully'.¹ Mrs. Piozzi expressed herself in the same vein when her coachman fell ill in 1792: 'Jacob's sore throat and fever has been a great addition to my agony, but he will live, poor fellow, I thank God. . . .'²

The solicitude of employers showed itself in deeds as well as words: sick servants often received the good care and attention that theory held to be their due. When a servant employed by Lady Cave was taken ill in 1719, for instance, she 'sent for Dr. Farrar to him'.³ In the 1720's the Duke of Chandos had a Dr. Donelli regularly attend the staff at Cannons.⁴ When Price, Lady Luxborough's servant, was stricken with palsy in 1752, he was made as comfortable as possible in the guest room, a Dr. Wall was called in, and someone was always kept 'ready at hand to assist him, and turn him'.⁵ When Robin, a servant retained by John Dawson, was taken ill in 1761 a Dr. Doubleday was summoned for him.⁶ Lady Mary Coke had Sir William Duncan, one of the best London physicians, attend her house steward in 1769.⁷ Horace Walpole had Sir John Elliott, another fashionable London practitioner, treat one of his maids in 1785.⁸ And when the Rev. Woodforde's maid was ill in 1794, he sent her over to consult a Dr. Thorne.⁹

When stricken with illness, servants were usually taken care of at home. Sometimes, however, they were treated outside. After the first small-pox hospital was founded in 1746, the fourth Duke of Bedford, one of the subscribers, regularly sent his servants there to be inoculated. This practice was designed to prevent contagion, not to save expense; for the cost of maintaining a servant in the hospital was borne by the employer. When a footman was sent there from Bedford House in 1761, for example, the Duke supplied meat, milk, vegetables, bread, and other provisions for him; and

---

¹ *Letters of Horace Walpole*, XIII. 340, 345.
² *Intimate Letters of Hester Piozzi*, p. 65.
³ *Verney Letters*, II. 64.
⁴ Baker, *James Brydges First Duke of Chandos*, p. 182.
⁵ *Letters Written by the Late Right Honourable Lady Luxborough to William Shenstone, Esq.*, [ed. John Hodgetts,] 1775, p. 315.
⁶ 'Diary of John Dawson of Brunton', ('North Country Diaries', II), *Surtees Society Publications*, CXXIV. 262.
⁷ *Letters and Journals of Lady Mary Coke*, III. 39.
⁸ *Letters of Horace Walpole*, XIII. 248.
⁹ *Diary of a Country Parson*, IV. 85.

he also paid the nurse.¹ Although, unlike the Duke, John Baker had his domestics inoculated at home, he took the precaution of sending them out of the house afterwards. An entry made in his diary in 1774 reads: 'between 9 and 10 tonight came Mr. Reid and inoculated in Servants hall William Wisdom and his daughter Jenny, Becky, Betty laundry, Betty dairy, Nany Peters and the boy Ned Clarke.'² And two weeks later he wrote: 'walked over between 5 and 6 to Dr Linfield's, and saw all the small pox folks . . . sent them at night two bottles of punch, with jellies mixt in them . . . for them to heat and drink going to bed.'³ When his postilion was run over by a chaise in 1775, he had him brought into the house, intending to keep him there, and summoned Dr. Hill and Mr. Martin, a surgeon. But when Mr. Martin 'said it might be a long business and advised to send him to St Thomas's Hospital', Baker did so.⁴

Sometimes, through the connivance of friends on the governing boards, employers placed servants in public hospitals instead of in private ones, thereby lessening the expense. When Greenwich Hospital was purged in 1742 of eight hundred patients who were found to have no right there, many domestics were included in the number.⁵ An ironical reference to the hospital made in 1775 intimated that the situation then was much the same as it had been earlier. So many old sailors have lately been admitted, declared a London newspaper, 'that it is now scarce possible to accommodate a Nobleman's Groom, Footman, or Postillion in a Manner suitable to the Dignity of his Profession, and the original Design of the Foundation.'⁶

It can hardly be doubted that the kindliness so evident in the care given to sick servants influenced the provision made for their ordinary bodily needs. Employers who were willing to go to the trouble and expense of having their servants properly looked after in time of illness could scarcely have been indifferent to the way they were fed, clothed, and housed.

But the material requirements of domestics were not the only ones that evoked fatherly concern. Some employers, in conformity

---

¹ Thomson, *The Russells*, p. 240.
² *Diary of John Baker*, p. 279. Cf. *Diary of a Country Parson*, I. 190.
³ *Diary of John Baker*, p. 281. ⁴ *Ibid.*, p. 311.
⁵ *Annual Register*, 1772, XV. 123.
⁶ *St. James's Chronicle*, 1775, No. 2245, July 4–6, 2b.

with their theoretical obligation, provided also for their servants' spiritual needs. Claver Morris, a country doctor, for instance, remarks in his diary: 'I read to my Servants, in the Causes of the Decay of Christian Piety.'[1] Like Morris, Lady Fermanagh also exposed her domestics to religious literature, although she seems to have let them do their own reading. Writing to her husband in London, she asks him to send down four copies of *A Week's Preparation to the Sacrament.* 'They are for the servants,' she says.[2]

In some houses prayers were read regularly, the whole establishment attending. Thomas Hearne, the antiquary, noted in 1731 that Lord Coleraine read 'Prayers in his own House constantly night and morning', and that all his servants gathered for the occasion.[3] The practice was also maintained at Lady Hertford's somewhat later. According to John Cowslade, who knew the house well, every morning 'At ten, the minister of the parish . . . or his curate, came and read prayers, (all the servants in general being assembled at the foot of the stairs at the lobby for that purpose). . . .'[4] And there were prayers in the evening as well. Mary Hamilton found a similar routine established at Sir Robert Gunning's when she visited there in 1783; at Lady Dartrey's where she visited in 1784, prayers were read to the servants and the children of the family every day at noon.[5]

The education of domestics, too, might receive the attention of employers. The Rev. William Cole, for example, sent his footboy 'to Schole to Wm. Chenils for Writing & Accounts' in 1766; and the following year he 'spoke to the Schole Master, Mr Spain, for both . . . Servants to learn of him'.[6] The footboy attended from nine to twelve in the morning and again from three to four in the afternoon; the footman went from six to eight in the evening. Similarly, in 1776 the Rev. Woodforde arranged to have his footman taught to read and write, agreeing to pay for the lessons at the rate of 4s. 6d. per quarter.[7] The interest and indulgence shown by Cole and Woodforde were not characteristic of clergymen alone. John Baker, a lawyer, undertook to teach one of his maids himself.

---

[1] *The Diary of a West Country Physician*, ed. Edmund Hobhouse, 1934, p. 120.
[2] *Verney Letters*, II. 59.   [3] Hearne, *Collections*, x. 424.
[4] Hughes, *The Gentle Hertford*, p. 96.
[5] Anson, *Mary Hamilton*, pp. 134, 239.
[6] *Blecheley Diary*, pp. 159, 300.   [7] *Diary of a Country Parson*, I. 194.

It was his practice to have her read aloud to him in the evening; and, by way of encouragement, he gave her small sums whenever her performance was particularly good.[1] But it was probably more usual to entrust the task of instruction to professional teachers. Dr. Claver Morris sent one of his maids to the local dame school to learn to read.[2] Lady Harriet Wentworth, who eloped with her footman in 1764, was said to have had him taught mathematics, writing, and music while he was still in her employ.[3] Edward Coke likewise had a teacher for his footmen.[4] And 'a young lady of fortune', who in 1777 accused her coachman of having assaulted her, had engaged a teacher to instruct him in reading and writing.[5]

There is evidence that many masters and mistresses took seriously the obligation to act as protector, using their influence and financial resources to help their domestics out of difficulties. Lady Mary Coke gave her house steward twenty guineas in 1771, so that he might rid himself of some of the debts he had accumulated.[6] A like generosity was displayed by Sir Robert Bedingfeld in 1789, when he secured the discharge of his gardener's son 'from ye Regiment he had inlisted in', defraying half of the expense, which amounted to twenty guineas.[7] An example of assistance of another kind is an appeal Elizabeth Purefoy made to a neighbour on behalf of one of her former servants:

> Poor old Ned May who served mee as a Coachman fourteen years & was with you & your late spouse sometime in the same service, ... has desired mee to let you know that he has been with Mr. Withers about such wages as are in arrear & due to him, who sais it is not in his power to pay him; and as Ned May informs mee you was so good as to make him a promise to see him paid I hope you will stand his freind in the affair. . . .[8]

There is also much evidence that employers often fulfilled the duty of providing for those who had given long and faithful service.

[1] *Diary of John Baker*, pp. 298, 301, 321, 335–6, 388.
[2] *Diary of a West Country Physician*, p. 32.
[3] *The Diaries of a Duchess*, ed. James Greig, 1926, p. 59.
[4] Charles W. James, *Chief Justice Coke His Family and Descendants at Holkham*, [1929,] p. 148.
[5] *Gentleman's Magazine*, 1777, XLVII. 503.
[6] *Letters and Journals of Lady Mary Coke*, IV. 241.
[7] 'Bedingfeld Papers', *Catholic Record Society Publications*, VII. 206. Cf. *Diary of a Country Parson*, I. 247.
[8] *Purefoy Letters*, I. 155.

THE RELATIONSHIP OF MASTER AND SERVANT

Sometimes they left legacies; sometimes they bestowed pensions.[1] And there were still other ways in which they rewarded fidelity.[2] The spirit that induced this beneficence is disclosed by Horace Walpole when he says: 'I know . . . how pleasant it is to have laid up a little for those I love, for those that depend on me, and for old servants.'[3]

Thus it is clear that the medieval tradition of family feeling retained a certain amount of vitality. A good servant was as likely as not to receive more from his master than was called for by actual contract.

[1] See chap. VI.   [2] See chap. VII.
[3] *Letters of Horace Walpole*, XIII. 149.

Chapter Four

THE CONDITIONS OF SERVICE: HOUSING, DIET, CLOTHING

WHEN an employer took a servant into his family he incurred the obligation of providing maintenance: shelter, board, and, in many cases, clothing. Paternalism must often have influenced the manner in which this obligation was discharged. As a rule, however, the employer's concern with his own reputability probably influenced it more.

I

In place, size, and equipment the living quarters provided for servants were far from uniform. They varied with the wealth of the employer and the type of dwelling; they also varied with the nominal rank of the servant.

As a rule, the two main categories of domestics were lodged in different parts of the house. Moreover, the quarters of upper domestics were commonly nearer their master's apartments than were those of lower domestics. Thus the architect Isaac Ware proposes as the ideal plan that upper domestics be lodged within the house proper and that lower domestics be relegated to the semi-detached wings, and he declares: 'This is the conduct of reason; the house-keeper, the clerk of the kitchen, and other domestics of the like rank will . . . be separated from the rabble of the kitchen; they will be at quiet to discharge their several duties, and they will be ready to attend the master or lady.'[1]

It is, of course, the three-part Palladian structure of the eighteenth century that Ware has in mind, and such houses sometimes incorporated this scheme. At Thorndon, Lord Petre's seat, for

---

[1] Ware, *Complete Body of Architecture*, p. 413.

THE CONDITIONS OF SERVICE

example, the house steward, housekeeper, and butler were quartered in the basement of the central block, while the lower servants had their rooms in the attic storey of the wings.[1] But even in houses of this type, the arrangement advocated by Ware was far from universal; and in houses of medieval or Tudor origin it was seldom found.

There were other arrangements that embodied the same principles and presumably achieved the same objectives. At Kedleston, Lord Scarsdale's seat, the basement of the central block included the quarters of the housekeeper and butler, the chamber floor of the north-east wing, except for the master suite, was 'wholly applied to the servants waiting upon the Lord and Lady', and the north-west wing contained 'lodging rooms for the servants belonging to the kitchen, &c.'[2] Again, at Axwell Park, the seat of Sir Thomas Clavering, the mezzanine floor included 'six good lodging rooms for the upper servants of the family', while the lower staff undoubtedly occupied three of the bedrooms in the attic storey.[3]

But the strict segregation of upper and lower servants was by no means to be found in every house. At Rushbrook Hall, the home of Sir Robert Davers, the housekeeper slept in a garret not far from those occupied by the housemaid and the dairy maid; and the steward and the bailiff had their bedrooms on the ground floor of an outbuilding along with those of the groom, park-keeper, and coachman.[4]

This sort of promiscuous arrangement most commonly existed in the smaller house, where the available space might be so limited as to confine the whole staff to a single floor. Yet even in such a house, upper and lower servants were sometimes lodged in widely separated quarters. Thus an advertiser who sought a cottage in 1781 stipulated that it must contain a room on the chamber floor 'for a Lady's Maid, with a Garret for common Servants'.[5]

Regardless of the size of the house, the attic storey was generally favoured for lower servants. Upper servants, on the other hand, were usually quartered on the various floors below. No storey

---

[1] James Paine, *Plans, Elevations and Sections of Noblemen and Gentlemen's Houses*, 1767–83, II. 6, 7.
[2] *Ibid.*, II. 12, 13. [3] *Ibid.*, I. 14.
[4] *Rushbrook Parish Registers*, Woodbridge, 1909, pp. 408, 414.
[5] *Lloyd's Evening Post*, 1781, XLVIII. 603b.

seems to have been especially preferred for this purpose. The butler and the housekeeper might live on the principal floor, as at Woodhall Park;[1] in the basement, as at Lord Melbourne's seat, Brocket Hall;[2] or in the mezzanine, as at Blenheim, where that floor contained 'an incredible quantity of Rooms for upper servts'.[3] Personal attendants formed something of an exception. Since they were frequently lodged close by their employers, they were most often to be found on the principal and chamber floors. The arrangement of servants' rooms at Worksop Manor House, one of the Duke of Norfolk's seats, was representative in this respect. The whole east side of the chamber floor was 'occupied by their Graces and their attendants'.[4] Some of the arrangements that occur in the designs of Robert Adam are also characteristic. For instance, in the plan of the principal storey of Great Saxham House, which he drew for Hutchinson Mure in 1779, the lady's maid is placed between Mrs. Mure's bedroom and dressing-room. Again, in his sketches for the principal floor of Harewood House, the seat of the Lascelles family, a servant's room, obviously intended for the valet, is located directly opposite Lord Harewood's bedchamber.[5]

Certain servants were normally domiciled outside the house. The porter usually lived in a lodge situated at the entrance of the estate; the gardener, the park-keeper, and the gamekeeper occupied cottages elsewhere in the grounds.

Although the large London house possessed nothing comparable with these cottages, the disposition of the servants' quarters was essentially similar to its rural counterpart. At Bedford House the main rooms for lower servants were on the attic floor of the central block and over the offices and stables in the wings. On the other hand, the ground floor contained the rooms of such servants as the house steward, housekeeper, clerk of the kitchen, man-cook, and butler.[6]

In contrast to this generous allocation of space for servants were

[1] H. Avray Tipping, *English Homes*, 1920–8, Period VI, I. 223.
[2] Paine, *Noblemen and Gentlemen's Houses*, II. 15.
[3] *Diaries of a Duchess*, p. 5.
[4] Paine, *Noblemen and Gentlemen's Houses*, II. 13.
[5] Arthur T. Bolton, *The Architecture of Robert and James Adam*, 1922, I. 42, 160–2.
[6] Thomson, *The Russells*, pp. 223, 231, 232.

the cramped quarters characteristic of the smaller London house. In such a house the whole staff was often packed into a single storey. Frequently that storey was the attic. Ware, discussing what he terms 'the common London house', advises that the attic 'be divided into a larger number [of rooms] than the floors below, for the reception of beds for servants'.[1] Quite as often the staff was consigned to the basement, which was made habitable by the use of an area, a device introduced early in the century. Saussure, who visited London soon after the accession of George I, writes: 'In all the newly-built quarters the houses have one floor made in the earth, containing the kitchens, offices, and servants' rooms.'[2] And Archenholz, who travelled in England about 1780, observes that the new houses raised in the West End 'have each of them two stories under ground, to which light is communicated by means of a forecourt. The servants are lodged, and the kitchen, store-rooms &c. are placed there, so the rest of the house is entirely at the disposal of the master.'[3]

In many houses, of course, the staff was not concentrated in one place. Sometimes both attic and basement included rooms for servants; sometimes in addition to the regular quarters a cubicle for a maid or valet was tucked into the first or second floor. Entresols were also occasionally used to augment the space available for the staff. Lord Derby's house in Grosvenor Square contained one devoted to this purpose.[4] Additional space was sometimes secured outside the house proper. The stable, whether an annexe attached to the rear or an outbuilding located a short distance from it, often contained rooms for domestics. At Lord Derby's an extension at the back containing the stable and coach-house included quarters above for the groom; at Sir Watkin Williams Wynn's in St. James's Square a similar extension included two bedchambers for servants.[5]

But whatever the arrangement of the quarters for the staff, the

[1] Ware, *Complete Body of Architecture*, p. 346.
[2] Ceasar de Saussure, *A Foreign View of England in the Reigns of George I. & George II.*, trans. and ed. Madame van Muyden, 1902, p. 69.
[3] Archenholz, *Picture of England*, p. 81. Cf. Sophie von la Roche, *Sophie in London 1786*, trans. and ed. Clare Williams, 1933, p. 87.
[4] Robert and James Adam, *The Works in Architecture of Robert and James Adam*, 1822, II. No. i, pl. i.
[5] *Ibid.*, II. No. i, pl. i; II. No. ii, pl. II.

conditions under which servants lived in the smaller London house were generally inferior to those in the large London house as well as to those in the country. In the country house, whether large or small, two, three, or even four lower domestics often shared a single room. If it were in the attic or basement, it might not be particularly well-lighted; but its size was usually such as to permit the occupants to move about freely. Moreover, some lower servants were better lodged than the rest. Since the cottages of the porter, gardener, park-keeper, and gamekeeper were regarded as ornamental features of the estate and were sometimes even designed in the Gothic or Chinese styles, which represented the advanced taste of the period,[1] they were well-built and well-maintained. Writing in his diary after visiting the gardener's house at Hackfall in 1792, Byng comments on what 'a nice cottage it is' and refers approvingly to its 'snug parlour'.[2] In some respects such quarters often compared favourably with those of upper servants; but, on the whole, upper servants were much more comfortably lodged than their subordinates. At the least each normally had his own room, and many had what almost amounted to a flat. At the disposal of the house steward there might be an office, a sitting-room, and a bedroom, all connected or at any rate grouped together; the housekeeper might have a combination sitting- and dining-room and an adjoining bedchamber; and other household officials might also have suites of rooms. At Althorp, Lord Spencer's seat, for instance, the butler's apartment consisted of three rooms, two of which were connected.[3] Very similar accommodation was provided in the large London house. At Bedford House, for example, three or four housemaids shared two rooms and four kitchen-maids one. Among the upper servants the clerk of the kitchen and the English man-cook each had his own room, while the butler had two, and the house steward and the housekeeper three a piece: a bedchamber, a breakfast-room, and a closet that was really a small sitting-room.[4] There were no such suites in the small London house; indeed, although each upper servant usually had his own room, it was often very small. Lower servants fared

---

[1] George J. Parkyns, *Six Designs for Improving and Embellishing Grounds*, 1793, *passim*.
[2] *The Torrington Diaries*, ed. C. Bruyn Andrews, 1934–8, III. 52.
[3] Tipping, *English Homes*, Period VI, I. 300.
[4] Thomson, *The Russells*, pp. 224, 231, 232.

even worse. Their rooms might be dark, damp, or cold, but not necessarily more so than those provided for upper servants. The inferiority of their quarters consisted rather in the smallness of the rooms in relation to the numbers crowded into them. A news item of 1758 revealingly mentions 'Three men servants at a gentleman's house in Monument yard, who lay in a small garret. . . .'[1] And their lot may well have been typical. Often the servants' quarters were so crowded that part of the staff had to be lodged elsewhere in the house. It was a common expedient for 'a bed for one man or two maid-servants [to be] contrived to let down in the kitchen'.[2] And such devices were also sometimes installed in other rooms. Mathew Henderson, a footman who murdered his mistress in 1746, mentioned in his confession that 'he went up into the back-parlour where he used to lie, and let down his bed. . . .'[3] Where these crowded conditions were at their worst, they caused even the master and mistress of the household to be severely cramped. Archenholz observes that 'Many families who have twenty thousand a year, have but a few apartments in town, and, as they keep a prodigious train of servants, are of course confined in regard to room'.[4]

Superfluous furniture probably seldom contributed to the congestion, for everywhere the quarters provided for domestics tended to be simply equipped. An inventory of the furnishings of Cannons drawn up in 1725 lists for the footmen's room only a bedstead, feather bed and bedding. More complete though certainly far from lavish equipment is listed for the housemaids' room: two bedsteads, with feather beds and bedding; a wainscot chest of drawers; two wainscot chairs; an inlaid table.[5] The same simplicity reigned in the quarters of the lower servants at Bedford House. Each room had one or at most two bedsteads, each equipped with a feather bed, hangings, and bedding; it also contained one or more chairs, a dressing-glass, and sometimes a small table or a cupboard.[6] The furnishings of a 'Maids' Garret' at Shardeloes, the seat of the Drake family, were much more

---

[1] *Gentleman's Magazine*, 1758, XXVIII. 608.
[2] Ware, *Complete Body of Architecture*, pp. 346–7.
[3] *Gentleman's Magazine*, 1746, XVI. 174.
[4] Archenholz, *Picture of England*, p. 80.
[5] Baker, *James Brydges First Duke of Chandos*, pp. 162–3.
[6] Thomson, *The Russells*, p. 232.

scanty: a bedstead, bedding, and hangings.[1] As a rule the quarters of upper domestics were fitted up more elaborately than those of their subordinates. Sometimes they even contained handsome pieces of furniture that formerly had been used in other parts of the house. Yet they were in no sense pretentious. An inventory of Rushbrook Hall made in 1759 lists the contents of the house steward's bedroom as 'A bedstead and blue camblet furniture, stove grate etc., an old writing desk with drawers'; and it describes the valet's room as containing 'A bedstead and old stuff furniture etc.'[2] The quarters assigned to upper servants at Bedford House seem to have been better equipped. One of the house steward's two workrooms was supplied with 'walnut-tree splat back chairs' with black leather seats, a wainscot table, two painted cupboards with folding doors, a reading desk, and a nest of drawers; the clerk of the kitchen's room had a bedstead, bed and bedding, five beech matted chairs, an elbow chair, a mahogany banister back chair upholstered in black leather, a painted press with folding doors, two wainscot chamber tables, a walnut bureau, a pier glass in a walnut frame, and fire utensils; the housekeeper's breakfast-room contained eight beech matted chairs, a round mahogany pillar and claw table, a wainscot oval dining table, a wicker fire-screen, a dressing-glass in a mahogany frame, an old Persian rug, a clock made by Tompion, and fire utensils.[3]

Although domestics were not lodged in luxury, employers probably sought to provide the best accommodation circumstances would permit. For the conditions under which the staff of a house lived suggested the extent of the master's resources; and while such conditions were visible to relatively few, they inevitably became more generally known by report.

The quarters that employers provided must be appraised in contemporary terms. From that point of view it would seem that upper servants had little cause for complaint. The same cannot be said of lower servants. There were those whose discomfort was sufficiently great to make them 'fret and fume' at being 'laid in some cold Out-house'.[4] Yet much that in retrospect seems

---

[1] *Shardeloes Papers of the 17th and 18th Centuries*, ed. G[eorge] Eland, 1947, p. 13.
[2] *Rushbrook Parish Registers*, pp. 411, 414.
[3] Thomson, *The Russells*, pp. 224, 231, 232.
[4] *A Present for Servants*, p. 57.

HOUSING, DIET, CLOTHING

highly objectionable was a matter of indifference to servants at the time. The explanation of this indifference is simple. The servant's room was quite literally a dormitory; ordinarily he did little there besides sleep. His leisure hours were spent in the kitchen, the servants' hall, or outside the house. Moreover, even when he lacked all privacy, when he had to share his bed, when his room was overcrowded, the situation was often no worse than what he had known at home; and sometimes it was decidedly better. When these considerations are taken into account, it is impossible not to conclude that, on the whole, domestics were well housed.

II

Variations corresponding more or less directly to those in living quarters existed in the diet of servants. It differed from house to house, largely in accordance with the income of the master. An important discrepancy also existed between the diet of upper and lower domestics. In the simpler homes, where the staff was relatively small, all dined together in the kitchen or servants' hall, those of superior rank merely enjoying the distinction of sitting at the head of the table. The food was usually much the same as that prepared for the master; the remains from his table constituted its staples. In the more elaborate establishments, however, the upper domestics took their meals in the steward or housekeeper's room, at what was termed the second table, while their inferiors ate in the servants' hall. The meals provided in such households for upper domestics, as a rule, surpassed in quality those served to the lower staff. The former were based on the cuisine of the first table; the latter were specially cooked plain fare to which were added the leftovers from the second. Recording her impressions in 1786, Sophie von la Roche writes that 'England knows nothing of separate cooking for servants, who partake of all the courses sampled by the masters, the latter having first choice and the servants what remains. . . .'[1] In the main, of course, she was right; but she evidently failed to distinguish the differences between what was served in the steward's room of great houses and what was sent in to the servants' hall. Thomas Whitehead, who

[1] la Roche, *Sophie in England*, pp. 207-8.

had been valet to the Duke of Kingston, testifies to how good the food in the steward's room could be. At Thoresby, the Duke of Kingston's seat, he says, 'this table would not disgrace a gentleman of ten thousand a year'; and he goes on to relate that 'If any gentleman called while the Duke was out a-sporting, if the steward's room dinner was ready, they dined with us.'[1] It is doubtful whether the fare provided for lower servants was as good as that in any house.

The disparity in diet that existed between the steward's or housekeeper's room and the servants' hall is vividly depicted by a pamphleteer, supposedly a servant, who excoriates upper domestics as a class. Among other charges, he accuses them of starving their subordinates both in order to gorge themselves and to have food to give friends and relatives. They were responsible, he claims, for 'half cold Meals, and not a sufficiency of them', and for 'Want of . . . proper Small-beer to quench your Thirst'. He speaks of 'coarse, unwholesome Diet', inquiring: 'Does your real Lord know, that you are debarred of a vegetable Support necessary to dilute the acrimonious particles of Flesh. I mean Greens, Potatoes, and Roots of all kinds?' And as a curative he proposes that in great houses the whole staff dine together, with the English cook acting as a sort of supervisor:

> . . . Let him and the House-keeper sit at the upper-end of the Table, with the rest of the Servants, they will then see, that they cut fair, and eat all, as the old Roast-beef saying was, and if the Lord has a charitable heart, let the Remainder be given to the real necessitous poor, and not set by . . . (as is now the case) or kept for an expected entertainment 'till it is unwholesome, and given to the lower Servants to eat. By this means every one will have his Meal hot, decent, and in good time to set about his Business again; not to have to wait two Hours after his Lord has dined, for his Dinner; by which time his Lord wants him, and then he is forced to go without one.[2]

These complaints were certainly not groundless. Nancy Woodforde describes how the upper servants of the local squire half-starved the lower staff in order to have extra food for their own purposes. The butler and the housekeeper, she says, 'kept so much company

[1] Whitehead, *Original Anecdotes*, p. 137.
[2] *Treatise on the Use and Abuse of the Second . . . Table*, pp. 29–30. 66.

that the other Servants were kept short of every thing that they aught to have and which Mrs Tooke [the housekeeper] saved from them to entertain her Company.'[1] Equally cogent evidence is a petition for ale presented to a duke by seventeen of his lower servants:

> We Your Graces Servants whose Names are here inclos'd beg leave to petition for Ale; not for our selves particular, but for the Servants of Your Grace's friends, which we have been frequently refus'd by Mr. Martin, Your Grace's Butler, without giving any reason for the same, but in saying I am Master and you shall have none. . . .[2]

And it is possible to cite still other instances of lower servants being denied proper rations by their superiors. In 1768 a news item reported how a nobleman's lower servants, having consistently received 'short allowance', investigated the cause and found that the French cook had been selling for his own profit the provisions intended for their table.[3] Similarly, in 1775 a news item disclosed that a French cook in a noble household had been caught with a large stock of victuals that 'he had withdrawn from the liberality of the family, to the no small mortification and disappointment of the half-starved English servants'.[4] But although upper domestics were inclined to look out for themselves at the expense of their subordinates, it seems improbable that lower domestics were everywhere systematically stinted. From the extreme violence of the pamphleteer quoted above it may be inferred that he overstates the case: the inequality between the second and third tables cannot always have been as great as he suggests.

Since meat was the staple of their masters' diet, it was prominent in the diet of both upper and lower servants, a fact of no little significance when it is considered what a large segment of the population tasted it only occasionally. According to Hanway, in some houses servants had meat three times a day.[5] And another writer cites as one of the causes for the high price of meat in 1785 'the enormous quantity of animal food servants in great families

---

[1] *Woodforde Diaries and Papers*, ed. Dorothy Woodforde, 1932, p. 74.
[2] Turberville, *History of Welbeck Abbey*, II. 59–60.
[3] *London Chronicle*, 1768, XXIV. 495a.
[4] Ibid., 1775, XXXVII. 258c.
[5] Hanway, *Letters on . . . the Rising Generation*, II. 191.

wantonly eat, perhaps five times as much as nature really requires. . . .'¹ Indeed, if the meals served at the Duke of Chandos' seat can be considered representative, the portions were certainly generous. At Cannons for dinner each servant had 21 ounces of beef on Tuesday, Thursday, and Sunday; 21 ounces of mutton on Monday and Friday; and 14 ounces of pork on Wednesday and Saturday.²

Sweets—'pastries, jellies, tarts, and all good things prized by the master'—also figured prominently in the diet of domestics. And they had fruit, too, 'in the greatest profusion'.³

Most domestics, in fact, insisted on sharing all the delicacies enjoyed by their employers; only those who in large families ate at the third table made no such claims. A clear intimation of the attitude of the majority is supplied by Eliza Haywood when she warns them against being too demanding: 'I do not deny but you have the same Appetites with your Superiors, and a good Mistress will doubtless allow her Servants a taste of every Thing in Season; but then you are not to expect it as often, or in as full Proportion as she has it herself. . . .'⁴

More often than not it was as leftovers that delicacies reached the tables of grateful servants, but other culinary remnants were by no means always so well received. Thus in 1767 'Oliver Tiridates', who characterized the servants of the well-to-do as not only voracious in their appetite for meat, but finicking as well, complained: 'In general, servants won't eat cold meat, so that there is a fresh joint bought two days in the week at least oftener than is necessary. . . .'⁵

On the whole, however, domestics were more concerned with quantity than quality; and in consequence, regular meals were sometimes augmented, sometimes supplemented, by irregular practices. To swell their rations, for instance, footmen made certain that the leftovers would be substantial by discouraging guests from eating too heartily. '. . . if any one, they think, eats too much of any one particular dish,' runs a contemporary account of the practice,

---

¹ *A Political Enquiry into the Consequences of Enclosing Waste Lands*, 1785, p. 68.
² Baker, *James Brydges First Duke of Chandos*, p. 177.
³ *Servants Pocket-Book*, p. 3.
⁴ Haywood, *A Present for a Servant-Maid*, pp. 31-2.
⁵ *Public Advertiser*, 1767, No. 10338, Dec. 18, 1d.

lest there should be none left for themselves, though the person should not have half done, yet if he chance to place his knife and fork across, away flies the plate, and is immediately replaced with a clean one, a plain hint for him to chuse something else.[1]

A more direct method was used by servants to secure extra rations: they simply pillaged the larder. The depredations suffered by the Earl of Bristol in 1721 are a case in point. The housekeeper, he wrote at the time, 'comes daily to me with complaints of the servants hideing more meat (showing me vaste quantities of her finding out) than woud suffice as many more as we now have. . . .'[2] It was to forestall such thievery that the Earl of Nottingham instructed his clerk of the kitchen not to 'suffer any person whatsoever domestick or stranger to come wtin ye kitchen office on any pretense wtsoever. . . .'[3]

In addition to large amounts of food, servants required a generous supply of liquor. Beer and ale were the beverages usually provided. In one country house, which probably was typical, the menservants were given ale at breakfast and beer at dinner and supper; moreover, jugs of ale were placed in their rooms, so that they could quench their thirst between meals.[4] Some notion of the quantities consumed may be gained from the figures for Cannons. A gallon of ale a day was furnished for each of the two tables of upper domestics, while six gallons a day were supplied for the servants' hall.[5] Perhaps even more revealing is Mordant's statement that for the average servant a quart of beer a day was a far from adequate ration.[6] But malt liquors were not the only drink provided. At Cannons, for instance, both cider and wine were sometimes served.[7] At Thoresby, the Duke of Kingston's seat, the upper servants drank wine regularly.[8] No doubt where wine was provided, the amount was usually moderate, the type usually less than the best. There may have been some houses, however, in which good wine flowed freely. 'Numa,' writing in 1777, asks:

[1] *The Fortunate Blue-coat Boy*, 1770, I. 97–8.
[2] *Letter Books of John Hervey*, II. 185.
[3] Finch, *History of Burley*, I. 231.
[4] Stirling, *Annals of a Yorkshire House*, II. p. 59n.
[5] Baker, *James Brydges First Duke of Chandos*, pp. 176, 181.
[6] Mordant, *Complete Steward*, I. 225.
[7] Baker, *James Brydges First Duke of Chandos*, p. 176.
[8] Whitehead, *Original Anecdotes*, p. 114.

'How then can a man of twenty thousand a year be ruined without gaming? . . .' And he answers: 'His servants, instead of being limited to fifty or sixty pounds a year for maintenance, are unlimited and drink out twice that sum in Tokay and Champaign.'[1]

Although few, if any, employers went so far as to supply tokay and champagne, most were more or less actively concerned with how their servants were fed. It was to their advantage. For as vicarious consumers domestics effectively put in evidence their master's pecuniary capacity; and the better the fare he provided for them the greater the reputability he derived from their eating at his expense. The relationship between the servant's diet and the master's prestige is well brought out in Shenstone's poem *The Price of an Equipage*:

> Bless me, said I, where can it end?
> What madness has possess'd my friend?
> Four power'd slaves, and those the tallest,
> Their stomachs doubtless not the smallest!
> Can *Damon's* revenue maintain
> In lace and food, so large a train?[2]

The diet of domestics was, of course, visible to few beyond the immediate family; but word of the quantity and quality of the food and drink supplied inevitably got abroad. It is revealing in this connexion that the servants whose petition for ale is quoted above, after calling attention to how they had been deprived of their regular ration, express the hope that their master will 'redress this Grievance before it gets to the Ears of the Publick. . . .'[3]

If contemporary opinion can be trusted, few employers had need to be apprehensive because how they fed their domestics became known outside the house. It was generally agreed that the diet of the servant class left little to be desired. '. . . servants,' declared the French traveller La Rochefoucauld, 'constitute the main part of the employers' expenses; they are boarded according to general custom and the food required is immense—they never leave the table and there is a supply of cold meat, tea and punch from morning till night.'[4] And English observers heartily concurred.[5]

---

[1] *Morning Post*, 1777, No. 1413, May 1, 4b.
[2] *The Works in Verse and Prose of William Shenstone*, 1764, I. 219.
[3] Turberville, *History of Welbeck Abbey*, II. 60.
[4] Marchand, *Frenchman in England*, pp. 25–6.
[5] See, for instance, Jonas Hanway, *An Earnest Appeal for Mercy to*

Very likely, however, it was chiefly the servants of the nobility and gentry that these observers had in mind; and it is important to recall that the shopkeeper's maid and the apothecary's footman fared less well. They received no large servings of beef and mutton, like those at Cannons; nor did they have the opportunity to taste the delicacies generally enjoyed by the domestics of the upper classes.

Yet, since they shared their masters' diet, even the servants of the lower middle class must have been comparatively well fed. Certainly they ate more and better food than such folk as weavers, soldiers, sailors, and agricultural workers. The contrast in diet evidently struck a correspondent who addressed the editor of a London newspaper in 1800: 'The poor labourer in your fields toils throughout the day, upon his slender pittance of bread and cheese, often upon dry bread; while the "pampered menial" fares sumptuously every day.'[1]

III

The dress of the servant class was even farther from uniformity than either its living quarters or its diet. A variety of factors contributed to make this so.

Only livery servants were entitled to clothing as part of their regular maintenance. But custom, contract, and the combined generosity and self-interest of employers caused a great many others to be provided with all or part of what they wore.

When servants were engaged, they were frequently granted the right to the 'cast clothes' of the master or mistress as a regular perquisite. Thus the Duke of Kingston's valet at one time received 'his wardrobe regularly the Saturday before Easter Newmarket-meeting and the Saturday before October meeting....'[2] Such arrangements were sometimes made contingent on the servant's satisfactory performance of his duties. '... I shall give you my old clothes if you please me,' John Macdonald was told when one employer engaged him.[3] But even when there had

---

the *Children of the Poor*, 1766, p. 90; *Public Advertiser*, 1767, No. 10301, Nov. 6, 2a.

[1] *London Chronicle*, 1800, LXXXIII. 47c.
[2] Whitehead, *Original Anecdotes*, p. 156. Cf. Newton, *Lyme Letters*, p. 318; Hanway, *Eight Letters*, p. 38.
[3] *Memoirs of an Eighteenth-Century Footman*, p. 93.

been no specific agreement, employers customarily turned over their discarded garments to their servants. Occasionally these gifts were bestowed as special rewards. When Macdonald served Coutts, the banker, he performed his duties so well that he was given 'several presents of clothes'.[1] More often, however, such donations were made as a matter of course. Body servants were the most frequent recipients, but others were also sometimes favoured; and it was not uncommon for several servants to share an employer's discarded outfits.

Besides giving his 'cast clothes' during his lifetime, an employer was likely to bequeath to one or more domestics whatever remained at his death. Sir Francis Page left his footman all his 'Robes, Gowns and Wearing Apparel'.[2] The poet Gray willed his servant all his 'wearing-apparel & linen'.[3] Sarah, Duchess of Marlborough, directed in her will that her wardrobe be divided between her lady's maid and two other maidservants.[4]

Even when there was no such testamentary bequest, the heirs of the deceased usually presented his clothing to some favourite servant, since custom decreed that to be the proper course. Thus in 1741, shortly after his wife's death, Lord Bristol commended his son for having promptly turned over Lady Bristol's personal effects to her maid: 'I am glad to find you have delivered to Williams all the things which were your poor mother's, & which by a customary sort of right are now become due to every common servant in her place. . . .'[5]

But the clothing domestics received from their employers was not always second-hand. The Rev. Woodforde's diary contains the note: 'Before breakfast walked to Lewis' shop and there bought 6 yds. of printed linen for my under Maid. . . .'[6] And Timothy Burrell records having bought one of his maids three shifts and the material for a dress as well as having paid the mantua-maker.[7]

---

[1] *Memoirs of an Eighteenth-Century Footman*, p. 186.
[2] Charles C. Brooks, *The History of Steeple Ashton and Middle Ashton*, Longhampton, 1929, p. 231.
[3] *Correspondence of Thomas Grey*, ed. Paget Toynbee and Leonard Whibley, Oxford, 1935, III. 1284.
[4] Colville, *Duchess Sarah*, p. 373.
[5] *Letter Books of John Hervey*, III. 272-3.
[6] *Diary of a Country Parson*, I. 335.
[7] 'Extracts from the Journal and Account-Book of Timothy Burrell', *Sussex Archaeological Collections*, III. 137.

These were incidental gifts; but livery servants, as a rule, were provided with new clothes regularly. What a livery servant was to receive was agreed upon at the time he took service. The general nature of such agreements may be judged from a letter Lady Strafford's gamekeeper sent her in 1740:

> I humbly beg your ladyship will be pleased to consider my clothing for with walking about the park and woods I am got as ragged as a sheep; its upwards of two years since I had any and my lord was pleased to be so good as tell me I should have a frock every year and a plush coat every tow [sic] years, and a laced hatt as other noblemen's keepers had.[1]

The usual allowance of clothing included at least one or two livery suits, a hat, a greatcoat, and a set of work clothes. The correspondence Squire Purefoy and his mother carried on with various tradesmen perfectly illustrates the purchase of these items. When his tailor fails to put in an appearance, he writes plaintively: 'I hoped to have seen you here before now, and my mother having a new footman you may now take measure of him as well as ye coachman....' At another time he hopes the tailor will soon be in the country, because he needs a coat and a pair of breeches and 'because the Servants Liveries are also wanting....' He orders work clothes as well as livery suits, on one occasion desiring 'Linnen washing frocks for the 3 men servants', on another instructing the tailor to 'bring the Coachman a linnen frock to put over his cloaths when hee rubs his horses down'. The squire's mother orders hats. 'I desire you will send mee two Caroline Hatts', she writes, 'of a fashionable size for the Servants.' She likewise orders material for the servants' waistcoats.[2] The diary of the Rev. William Cole contains a record of similar purchases. Cole notes one year: 'the Taylors here making Tom's Livery'; he writes the following year: 'Two Taylors ... making Tom a new Livery....' Under various dates he also mentions their 'making a Fustian Frock for Tom', their 'making a Great Coat for Tom' and their 'making Tom 2 Waistcoats'.[3]

Some employers supplied more complete outfits. At Bedford House in the time of the fourth Duke the work clothes given to

---

[1] Wilkinson, *Worthies, Families and Celebrities of Barnsley*, p. 440.
[2] *Purefoy Letters*, II. 307, 309, 315, 318, 321.
[3] *Blecheley Diary*, pp. 70 159, 187, 201, 263.

footmen included worsted stockings, heavy shoes, coarse shirts, and leather or cloth breeches.[1] At Cannons all the liverymen of the first Duke of Chandos were given dress stockings in addition to the usual items of apparel; the gamekeepers, along with their breeches, frocks, and coats, received boots.[2]

More often than not the cost of such accessories as linen shirts, neckwear, peruques, dress shoes, and fancy hose were borne by the servant. An itemized account of an average footman's expenses that appeared in a London newspaper in 1760 included disbursements for shoes, stockings, shirts, wigs, and neckcloths.[3] Virtually the same list was presented again in 1768 by a newspaper correspondent who called attention to the fact that footmen were obliged to supply part of their clothing.[4]

Even the clothes that the employer did supply were not necessarily the personal property of the servant. Indeed, either the agreement concluded when the servant was engaged or notice served upon him subsequently might expressly deny him rights in the outfit with which he was provided. When the Rev. Woodforde purchased a new livery and greatcoat for his footman in 1785, for instance, he was careful to explain that they remained his property. 'I told Briton that I gave neither to him,' he remarks in his diary, 'but only to wear them during his Service with me.'[5] Whether or not his master's ownership had been made explicit by such a declaration, the servant who carried off a livery suit or other apparel was likely to find himself in difficulties. If he refused to part with it, a legal action might be brought against him; if he pawned or sold it, he might be faced with criminal prosecution.

Although the outfit provided did not automatically become the property of the servant, it might ultimately fall to him anyway. The frequency with which new clothing was to be furnished was agreed on when the servant was hired; and often the terms of the agreement also included the proviso that when the new clothes were purchased the master would relinquish his rights in the old, leaving the servant free to sell them or to alter them for wear when off duty. John Baker evidently had made such an agreement with his servant Charles, for on one occasion he entered in his accounts:

[1] Thomson, *The Russells*, p. 229.
[2] Baker, *James Brydges First Duke of Chandos*, p. 200.
[3] *London Chronicle*, 1760, III. 187c.
[4] *Ibid.*, 1768, XXIII. 143a.   [5] *Diary of a Country Parson*, II. 212.

HOUSING, DIET, CLOTHING

'To Charles in consideration wearing on his old livery and for what he might have sold it for . . . 1 1 0.'[1]

The livery worn by servants like John Baker's Charles distinguished them from upper menservants, who always wore mufti. The distinction, of course, corresponded to those differences in living quarters and diet that marked the division of the servant hierarchy into its two major categories.

Nothing comparable with the livery suit distinguished lower from upper maidservants. From time to time suggestions were advanced that a uniform or some other clear-cut badge of servitude be introduced. Defoe wished 'Servant-maids to wear Liveries as our Footmen do'.[2] In 1771 another writer advocated the revival of an earlier plan for a system of insignia—a plan he attributed to Queen Caroline. 'The Good Queen', he explained, 'proposed a law to oblige all women servants to wear a kind of badge or mark made of coloured worsted on the sleeve of their gowns, to distinguish them from citizens' wives and daughters'.[3] And towards the end of the century 'A Country Friend' reported that there was again much talk 'of female servants being likely to wear liveries'. But although many employers felt strongly on the subject, none of the various suggestions put forward was ever given a trial: the maidservant remained free to follow the fashion.

She followed it as closely as possible. No doubt the superior resources of those who held the higher posts enabled them to surpass their less fortunate sisters; but as a group, maidservants seem to have presented a highly attractive appearance. Even the poorest of them, writes Moritz, the German traveller, 'is careful to be in the fashion'.[4] Archenholz, too, was greatly impressed by the attractiveness of their costume:

> The appearance of the female domestics will perhaps, astonish a foreign visitor more than anything in London. They are in general handsome and well clothed: their dress has the appearance of some taste. . . . They are usually clad in gowns well adjusted to their shapes, and hats adorned with ribbands. There are some who even wear silk and sattin, when they are dressed.[5]

[1] *Diary of John Baker*, p. 378.   [2] Defoe, *Everybody's Business*, p. 15.
[3] *Oxford Magazine*, 1771, VI. 84. Cf. *H. M. C. Egmont Diary*, I. 11.
[4] *Travels of Carl Philip Moritz in England in 1782*, ed. P[ercy] E. Matheson, 1924, p. 159.
[5] Archenholz, *Picture of England*, p. 207.

Menservants were no less interested in the subject. The liveryman whose master clothed him in splendid style was likely to feel proud of his outfit. Recollecting his days of service with a certain master, John Macdonald boasts: 'Our livery was the genteelest in London, richly trimmed with silver....'[1] When in search of employment, such a servant often preferred one place to another merely because of the prospect of wearing a finer livery. He was no less interested in his appearance when, being off duty or unemployed, he wore mufti. Macdonald relates how in such circumstances, 'Having good clothes, with rich vests,' he dressed in the height of fashion.[2] Upper servants almost always dressed that way. Their appearance rivalled that of their masters.

Employers were in no small measure responsible for the way servants dressed. They supplied much of the clothing, which was, on the whole, of high quality; moreover, many of them gave their retainers every encouragement to make a good appearance. The clothing worn by servants was, after all, more visible than either their living quarters or their diet; in consequence it was even more crucial for the repute of an employer that his servants be well dressed than that they be well housed and well fed.

The appearance of liverymen was of particular concern, and with good reason. For one thing, their duties kept them more in evidence than did those of other servants. Then, too, the outfit they wore was especially effective in contributing to the prestige of those they served. Designed to advertise the affluence of the master by its cut and quality, the livery suit also achieved that end by proclaiming the relative idleness of the servant. For by indicating his remoteness from productive labour, it suggested that his master had wealth enough to maintain a man who brought no economic return.

Since employers fully appreciated the importance of the livery suit as part of the equipment of display, they sought to dress their lower menservants in the richest manner possible. One vied with another to have his liveries more elaborate and more striking, and the London newspapers reported the success of the principal competitors in such items as: 'Lord Derby's coachman, and footmen, with their red feathers, and flame-coloured silk stockings, looked like so many figurantes taken from behind the scenes of the Opera

---

[1] *Memoirs of an Eighteenth-Century Footman*, p. 95.
[2] *Ibid.*, p. 236.

HOUSING, DIET, CLOTHING

House.'[1] This matching of liveries led in the course of the period to a general increase in the extravagance of the outfits. Contrasting past decades with 1767, Hanway declares:

> It was a rare thing in my memory to see any gold or silver lace on the clothes of a domestic servant in livery: lace of wool, cotton or with a mixture of silk contented us. Now we behold rich vestments, besilvered and begilded like the servants of sovereign princes.[2]

Colour as well as ornament was exploited to the full. Traditionally a livery was made up in the inherited colours of the family.[3] But the use of inherited colours tended to be abandoned, since the upper classes were obliged to meet the splendour of the wealthy parvenus who, being unrestricted by tradition, frequently selected the most blatant shades. How this competitive struggle impressed a sensitive outsider is apparent in the description of a royal birthday written by an American soon after the close of the century:

> The livery of the footmen was also gaudy and fantastical to the last degree. They wore lace not only on the borders, but on all the seams of their garments, and their large cocked hats were surrounded with broad fringes of silver or gold. On such occasions as these, it is a point of great ambition to display the finest equipage. . . .[4]

Conscious of the prestige derived from being served by men and women who dressed like members of the upper classes, many employers insisted on having only such attendants about their persons. '. . . pride,' observes Soame Jenyns,

> has put it into our heads, that it is most honourable to be waited on by gentlemen and ladies; and all, who are really such by birth or education, having also too much of the same pride, however

---

[1] *Morning Post*, 1777, No. 1443, June 5, 2b. For an insight into the competitive role of the livery suit see *Spectator*, I. 66; *Female Tatler*, 1709, No. 71, Dec. 16–19, 1a; *Directions to Lords and Ladies*, 1766, p. 15; Gisborne, *Duties of the Female Sex*, p. 88; *The Memoirs of Susan Sibbald, 1783–1812*, ed. Francis P. Hett, New York, 1926, p. 42; [Susannah M. Gunning,] *Barford Abbey*, 1771, 2nd ed., I. 156; Clara Reeve, *The Two Mentors*, 1803, 3rd ed., p. 39.
[2] Hanway, *Letters on . . . the Rising Generation*, II. 173.
[3] *Notes and Queries*, Seventh Series, 1891, XII. 32.
[4] Silliman, *Journal of Travels*, I. 219. Cf. *Public Advertiser*, 1767, No. 10301, Nov. 6, 2a.

necessitous, to submit to any servitude, however easy, we are obliged to take the lowest of the people, and convert them by our own ingenuity into the genteel personages we think proper should attend us. Hence . . . the valet de chambre cannot be distinguished from his master, but by being better drest; and Joan, who used to be but *as good as my lady in the dark* is now by no means inferior to her in the day-light.[1]

It is the nobility and the gentry that Jenyns is describing here; but another essayist suggests that the same attitude was characteristic of the lowest stratum of employers, those who kept only a single maid. 'My wife,' he writes, '. . . prides herself on having the smartest servants in the neighbourhood. Mrs. Becky, let me tell you, does some credit to her taste; who would think she was a *servant* of all work?'[2]

All sorts of devices were used by employers to insure the maintenance of a high standard of personal appearance among their servants. Slovenliness was rebuked, fastidiousness rewarded. Clothing purchased by the servant was carefully scrutinized to make certain it was in good taste. Gifts of apparel were often given with the proviso that the servant wear them himself. Employers in some instances went so far as to insist that the candidate for such a post as lady's maid have a sumptuous wardrobe of her own. '. . . there are *Ladies* and *Mistresses*,' asserts Defoe

> who will not take into their *Service* for *Waiting Women*, or *Chamber-Maids*, those who have not *Cloathing* suitable to the *Families* into which they are hir'd. And it is no unusual Thing for Those who hire Servants for *Great Families* to ask questions relating thereunto. . . .[3]

The desire to be served by splendidly accoutred servants ran counter, of course, to the widely entertained notion that servants ought to dress in strict accordance with their social status. The conflict is amusingly illustrated by an experience of John Macdonald's. Going to be interviewed for a place, he put on 'a gold-laced vest and other things in form' and was rejected for being 'more like a gentleman than a servant'. Hoping to remedy the defect, he sought the next place 'dressed plain without lace', but

---

[1] *World*, IV. 11–12. Cf. *London Chronicle*, 1765, XVII. 300a.
[2] *Lady's Magazine*, 1785, XVI. 126.
[3] Defoe, *The Maid-Servant's Modest Defence*, pp. 11–12.

again met with rejection, the footman of the prospective employer later explaining: 'I am sorry I did not tell you to dress yourself finer, for Sir Francis is very nice.'[1]

The prejudice Macdonald encountered in the first instance had a threefold origin. It stemmed from the conviction that 'servants in silk stockings, ruffles, and other appurtenances of dress highly unbecoming their station' tended greatly 'to destroy all distinction among the different orders of society'.[2] It also arose from the belief that fine clothes encouraged the wearers in unjustifiable pretensions and acts of insubordination. And in addition it drew some strength from the mercantilist fear that well-dressed servants meant a greater consumption of foreign silks and laces.

But though deeply rooted as well as widely held, the belief that servants ought to be restricted to the drab, the coarse, and the sleazy exerted little influence on what they actually wore. As a group, they remained extremely well dressed throughout the period.

IV

When it is considered that the servant was fed, housed, and often clothed by the employer, it appears that a life of service could be a relatively sheltered existence. The servant could be thrown on his own resources through dismissal, either merited or undeserved, or through the voluntary abandonment of his place. But as long as his master wanted his services and as long as he chose to give them, he was sure of most of the basic necessities. Moreover, changing economic conditions affected him little, if at all. A rise in the price of food, of rent, of sea coals, or of candles left him untouched. The cost of living was his master's problem, not his. So, too, in the case of most taxes, the burden did not rest on his shoulders.

The relative security of the servant's position did not escape the notice of contemporaries. Appealing to maidservants to be contented with their lot, Eliza Haywood stresses the fact that service shields them against the impact of economic forces:

> Whatever Changes happen in public Affairs, your Circumstances are unaffected by them. Whether Provisions are dear or cheap is

[1] *Memoirs of an Eighteenth-Century Footman*, pp. 179–80. Cf. *Rambler*, 1793, I. 70.
[2] *Heads of a Plan*, p. 48.

the same Thing to you. Secure of having all your real Necessities supplied, you rise without Anxiety, and go to Bed without Danger of having your Repose disturbed.[1]

Again, in 1758 an open letter from an advocate of a servant tax to the Chancellor of the Exchequer emphasized the immunity of domestics from the economic buffets felt by almost every other group:

> ... if times are good or bad, the markets high or low, they of all people feel no difference; in all seasons, under all circumstances during service, they have not only no others, in general, but not so much as themselves, it may properly be said, to provide for; for have they not meat and drink, and lodging and cloathing (the male part of them at least) all provided for them without the trouble even of a thought on their parts?[2]

This security was one of the attractions of service as an occupation. The employer's obligation to provide his servants with most of the basic necessities made service a refuge, especially for women; the way in which the obligation was generally discharged caused service to be widely regarded as a comfortable mode of life.

[1] Haywood, *A Present for a Servant-Maid*, p. 32.
[2] *London Chronicle*, 1758, III. 476a. Cf. *ibid.*, 1800, LXXXVIII. 47c.

Chapter Five

THE CONDITIONS OF SERVICE: RECREATION

ALTHOUGH in theory the servant ceded all his waking hours to his master, in practice his bondage to the routine of his post was not nearly so complete. Making due allowance for the exaggerations that portray the servant class as engaged in a perpetual bacchanal, discounting at least in part the testimony of those critics who depict domestics as continually running in pursuit of pleasure, there is much evidence to indicate that service permitted a considerable amount of recreation.

I

Life in the family of which the servant was a part often provided diversion. The male servant, for instance, frequently accompanied his master on the chase; and sometimes whole days and even weeks were passed in this way. Referring in her *Memoirs* to a certain Yorkshire town, Mrs. Harrison Cappe identifies it as a place 'where the Duke of Cleveland, and afterwards Lord Darlington, with their grooms and footmen, used sometimes to spend whole weeks, for the purpose of fox-hunting. . . .'[1] Similar evidence is supplied by Sir Gilbert Elliot, who, discussing the habits of the fifth Duke of Bedford, says that His Grace usually took 'but two, or three, or four servants out with him hunting. . . .'[2] And John Macdonald relates in his *Travels* how, when he was in the service of Keith Stewart, brother of the Earl of Galloway, he and

---

[1] *Memoirs of . . . Mrs. Catherine Cappe*, p. 106.
[2] Countess of Minto, [Emma Kynymound] *The Life and Letters of Sir Gilbert Elliot*, 1874, I. 301. Cf. Stirling, *Annals of a Yorkshire House*, I. 159.

his master dashed around from one hunt to another: 'We went to Oxfordshire, to Blenheim, to Lord Foley's, Lord Thanet's, Stow-in-the-Hole, Cheltenham in Gloucestershire, Hampshire and Bedfordshire.'[1]

Servants also participated in other sports. Observing that when in the country Englishmen of the upper classes often engaged in 'jeux d'exercise, la plupart très violens', the French traveller Le Blanc remarks: 'Celui pour lequel ils paroissent avoir le plus goût, en est un où ils jouent avec tous leurs Valets. . . .'[2] The game referred to was probably cricket; at any rate cricket matches in which servants took part were sometimes held. Jane Edwards informed her son of such a contest in 1732. It was originally intended, she wrote, 'that my brother and his servants should attack the townspeople of Exton, but it is now settled for them to play promiscuously, servants and townspeople on both sides. . . .'[3]

Less strenuous amusements gave the women a chance as well as the men. The Rev. Benjamin Rogers describes a harvest festival held in 1729 at which domestics of both sexes were present.[4] Mrs. Harris tells her son in 1774 about an amateur theatrical at which 'The ladies acted . . . to all their servants. . . .'[5] Fanny Burney mentions in her diary a similar performance for which servants were allowed to make up the audience.[6] And when Mrs. Montagu's nephew and his wife were visiting her in 1785, she wrote to a friend: 'The young Couple and the Men Servants out of Livery and several of my Maids dance in the Drawing room from the time we have drunk our tea till Supper. . . .'[7]

On occasions of rejoicing, public or private, servants were customarily included in the festivities. National and religious holidays, political victories, weddings, and birthdays all brought them a share of the feasting and merriment. In order to celebrate Nelson's triumph at the Nile, for instance, one master regaled his servants with roast beef, plum pudding, and punch in the servants'

---

[1] *Memoirs of an Eighteenth-Century Footman*, p. 95.
[2] Le Blanc, *Lettres d'un François*, II. 19.
[3] Noel, *Letters and Records of the Noel Family*, p. 81.
[4] 'The Diary of Benjamin Rogers', ed. C. D. Linnell, *Publications of the Bedfordshire Historical Record Society*, 1950, XXX. 11.
[5] *Letters of the First Earl of Malmesbury*, I. 283.
[6] *The Early Diary of Frances Burney, 1768–1778*, ed. Annie R. Ellis, 1889, I. 123.
[7] Mrs. Montagu, 'Queen of the Blues', II. 198–9.

hall, and afterwards allowed them to hold a dance in the barn.[1] A party held at Stowe in 1800 bore a strong resemblance to this affair, and at the time a visitor noted in her journal: 'Dancing again in the evening for the Servants, the Ladies danced a great deal with them.'[2] And a celebration of the same kind was held at Sheffield Place in 1792 on the birthday of Maria Holroyd's aunt.[3]

In some families such affairs were held regularly on the anniversary of some particular event. The Earl of Egmont's servants always made merry on his birthday with a masquerade ball.[4] On the twin birthdays of Dr. Johnson and 'Queeny' Thrale, Mrs. Piozzi 'made a little dance and supper' for the servants every year, 'putting the summerhouse into their hands for the two evenings. . . .'[5] And towards the end of the century the same sort of thing was done annually at Stowe in celebration of the birthday of young George Grenville.[6]

II

In much of this, servants were either the beneficiaries of a condescending patronage or the accessories of their masters' pleasure. But they also frequently had a well-developed social life of their own.

Some employers disapproved of their servants entertaining at home. In 1725 Dr. Claver Morris noted in his diary: 'Betty Biggs . . . having been told by Will Clark that I would allow no Sweet-hart to come to a Maid-Servant in my House, came to me & said, Though she could very easily do the Work of my House, . . . she could not be settled in it. . . .'[7] Morris may merely have been prudish about the improprieties that a maidservant might commit under his roof, but Horace Walpole would not even permit a manservant to receive male acquaintances. When looking for a steward-butler in 1762, he wrote to his business agent: 'One material condition will be, that he is not to have friends coming

[1] Bamford, *Dear Miss Heber*, pp. 185–6.
[2] *The Wynne Diaries*, ed. Anne Freemantle, 1935–40, III. 25.
[3] Jane H. Adeane, *The Girlhood of Maria Josepha Holroyd*, 1897, 2nd ed., p. 118.
[4] *H. M. C. Egmont Diary*, I. 390; II. 186, 290; III. 78.
[5] Hester L. Piozzi, *Anecdotes of the Late Samuel Johnson LLD*, 1786, 4th ed., p. 211.
[6] *Wynne Diaries*, III. 12, 26.
[7] *Diary of a West Country Physician*, p. 126.

THE CONDITIONS OF SERVICE

to my house after him.'¹ That this attitude was very common is evident from the great frequency with which advertisements for servants included a stipulation that they would not be permitted to receive visits. An advertiser who needed a cook in 1777, for example, stated: 'No person need apply who has followers.'² An employer in want of a footman in 1780 made it clear that a satisfactory candidate had to be 'single, and have no followers'.³ An employer who sought a cook in 1795 stated firmly: 'no followers will be permitted.'⁴ This evidence is corroborated by a passage in Heasel's manual for servants. Outlining the responsibilities of the housekeeper, he mentions as part of her task the duty of seeing that those under her direction have as few callers as possible.⁵

Nevertheless, in many houses servants were permitted to receive calls from their friends and relations. Thus, referring to his footman, the Rev. William Cole records in his diary that he 'gave Tom leave to ask his particular Acquaintance to sup & play at Cards in the kitchen, as they could not come last week. . . .' In another passage he writes: 'Mrs. Troutbeck's & Mrs. Locock's Maids drank Tea with mine, with Tom Watts & Tom Allen.' Again, he notes: 'Jonathan Tansley, my Gardener's Brother, all the Afternoon & Evening in the Kitchen with my Cook, whom he Courts.' And in yet another entry he writes: 'My Cook's Brother from Crawley in Bedfordshire, Tansley & his Wife, Wm & Tom Wood & Tom Holden dined in the Kitchen'.⁶ Such visits were also frequent occurrences in the home of the Rev. Woodforde, whose diary depicts him as extremely generous in the time he allowed his servants to enjoy themselves. In one typical entry he writes: 'Mrs Bodham's steward Willm. Ward, and her Housekeeper, Mrs Spooner, came to our House this Morning to spend the Day with our Folks and to go and see Weston House [a neighbouring seat] which they did and afterwards dined with our Folks.' In another he notes: 'Mrs Reeves of Ringland drank Tea with our Maids, this Afternoon in the Kitchen. . . .' Still another

---

¹ *Letters of Horace Walpole*, v. 246.
² *Morning Post*, 1777, No. 1321, Jan. 14, 2d.
³ *General Advertiser*, 1780, No. 1062, Mar. 23, 3d.
⁴ *Morning Chronicle*, 1795, No. 7918, Feb. 28, 3d.
⁵ Heasel, *Servants Book of Knowledge*, p. 56. Cf. *Batchelor's Monitor*, p. 66.
⁶ *Blecheley Diary*, pp. 174, 48, 6, 58–9.

entry chronicles the fact that 'Billy Bidewell stayed & supped and spent the Evening with our Folks in the Kitchen'. And he duly records the visit of a large party of domestics from the household of the local squire: 'Mr. Custance's servants George, Harry, Haylett the Gardener with the Cook Maid, Betty and Sukey Chamber-Maids all supped and spent the evening with our Folks in kitchen.'[1] John Baker's diary indicates that his domestics entertained in the same way. An illustrative passage recounts the visit of 'Mr Walter the exciseman and his wife and daughter'. Making their call about seven in the evening, they first drank tea and played cards with the housekeeper; and then, after she had retired, they 'supt with the servants', taking their departure at about a quarter after eleven.[2] On another occasion Mr. Copley's maid came to dine with the housekeeper, and at yet another time a Mr. Fleet visited her.[3] Still further evidence of how commonly domestics had guests at their masters' homes occurs in the *Travels* of John Macdonald. Having been forced to confess to his master that he had frequently given wine to several servants who had visited him, Macdonald related the incident to a friend who was a butler and received the sage advice: 'Never give a glass of wine to any person. If anyone comes to see you, treat them with a pot of porter or two. . . .'[4] Quite clearly he was expected to have callers and to entertain them as well.

But by no means all the entertaining done by domestics was of this impromptu variety. In the absence of their masters and mistresses they sometimes held large parties of a sort that must have required a certain amount of planning and preparation: the gambols portrayed in Townley's *High Life Below Stairs* were often enacted in reality. '. . . at home [they] have their routs and their gaming tables,' declares Soame Jenyns.[5] And a letter addressed to the editor of a London newspaper describes how 'As the day advances, Mrs Housekeeper takes the lead, struts to market, makes appointments for the Evening with a snug party, who are conveyed thro' the area after night closes in, to "eat a bit of supper

---

[1] *Diary of a Country Parson*, IV. 316; V. 262; IV. 259; II. 113.
[2] *Diary of John Baker*, p. 367.
[3] *Ibid.*, pp. 344, 358. Cf. 'Diary of Benjamin Rogers', *Publications of the Bedfordshire Historical Record Society*, XXX. 54.
[4] *Memoirs of an Eighteenth-Century Footman*, p. 75.
[5] *World*, IV. 12.

and play at cards." . . .'¹ Since the pressure of social life took the nobility and gentry out of their homes far more often than it did middle-class employers, this sort of merry-making was most common in upper-class houses. But that lavish parties were no monopoly of any section of the servant class is evident from some satirical instructions for domestics written in 1780. Along with other advice on how to spend the Christmas holidays when their masters were away from home, the author counselled them to entertain on a grand scale: 'In the evening, if you have any gentility, you will provide card tables, and give a dance—two fiddlers will be much better than one, and a pipe and a tabor you will have of course. . . .'² Significantly, these instructions were directed 'to Servants at both Ends of Town'—or, in other words, to those of the nobility and gentry, and to those of the middle classes. It was not only in the Metropolis, however, that domestics in middle-class homes staged surreptitious kitchen frolics. Recalling in her autobiography the impressions of her childhood, Elizabeth Ham, the daughter of a country brewer, describes how she witnessed one held by her father's servants some time in the 1790's. '. . . they drank strong beer, and played cards,' she writes, 'and sang songs, and were all very merry. . . .'³

III

Although a good deal of social life centred in the home, much recreation was also taken outside it. Visits to friends and relatives appear to have been a routine diversion; jaunts and expeditions of various kinds were far from being exceptional events. Several passages in the diary of the Rev. William Cole reveal the scope of this activity in the country. Cole's footman Tom is mentioned as having 'engaged himself to go with Mrs Willis's Servants & others to Dinner at a Cricket Match. . . .' He goes 'to Will Grace's to play at Cards to meet some young People'. And with two fellow-servants he is given 'leave to go to see the Mountabank' at a nearby town, Cole presenting 'each of them with . . . something to try their Luck at the Lottery'.⁴ The picture presented by the

---

¹ *St. James's Chronicle*, 1771, No. 1713, Feb. 13-15, 2a.
² *London Chronicle*, 1780, XLVIII. 605a.
³ *Elizabeth Ham by Herself 1783-1820*, ed. Eric Gillett, [1945,] p. 31.
⁴ *Blecheley Diary*, pp. 143, 173, 179.

RECREATION

Rev. Woodforde's diary is substantially the same. Will, his footman, visits the home of the neighbouring squire, where the servants make 'him too welcome by making him rather merry'.[1] Betty, Woodforde's upper maid, gets 'leave to go and see her Brother at S^r· W^m· Jernegans' and to remain there for two or three days.[2] Both of Woodforde's maids attend a 'Rafling for a Gown' held 'at the Heart'. His maid Winifred goes one morning to a nearby fair and returns in the afternoon of the following day. And on the birthday anniversary of the local squire's son, when there is 'a frolic given to the servants &c at Weston House', his maid Betty stays at the party from five in the afternoon until eleven at night.[3]

Public houses do not seem to have absorbed an inordinately large share of the leisure time allowed the servants of Cole and Woodforde, but as the most important centres of social life in the average rural community they undoubtedly counted many servants among their regular patrons. A writer, who in 1759 described the opportunities they provided for petty gambling, states:

> In the village where I live we have five public-houses, two of which have Nine-pin grounds and shuffleboards; . . . our livery servants neglect their household and other services, to spend their time at those houses: I myself experienced this with a servant for whom I had a particular regard, but who being expert at those games could not be kept from these houses.[4]

And an open letter that 'Philanthropist' addressed to the pious Lord Dartmouth in 1775 relates how on May Day domestics 'sally forth, and with their lasses in their hands, ramble the fields in loose festivity, and pass some three or four hours in drinking, swearing, and ribaldry, at the public houses declaredly open for their reception.'[5]

In the Metropolis such establishments assumed a greater significance in the social life of the servant class than they did in the country. Certain public houses in London were frequented almost exclusively by domestics, who found in them places of reunion and conviviality on the one hand, and headquarters where common

---
[1] *Diary of a Country Parson*, II. 45.
[2] Ibid., II. 56. Cf. *Diary of a West Country Physician*, p. 57.
[3] *Diary of a Country Parson*, III. 358, 359, 350.
[4] *Grand Magazine of Magazines*, 1759, II. 20.
[5] *London Packet*, 1775, No. 865, May 5–8, 4a.

interests could be discussed, vacancies could be heard of and meetings could be held on the other. In this dual role they played host to different groups. Some of these groups were clubs possessing various degrees of formal organization; others were merely cliques that met in a casual fashion at particular houses. As a rule, the haunts of upper domestics were distinct from those generally favoured by lower domestics, but there were some taverns that attracted habitués from all ranks of the class.[1]

It was when off duty, when out of place, and when eating out under the system of board wages that servants usually visited these houses. But livery servants also frequented them a good deal while waiting for their employers to come from the opera, the theatre or some other place of amusement.[2]

Refreshments and the pleasures of fraternization were the principal attractions. The strong appeal held by the latter is suggested by John Macdonald when he writes: 'I . . . went over to the public-house, to have something to drink. I had enough at home, but I did not care a farthing for it, as there was no company.'[3] Anthony Heasel likewise intimates that the opportunity for companionship, the chance to meet old friends and make new, drew servants to public houses. Maintaining that 'Public houses are not places for footmen to be seen in', he warns that 'if they make a practice of doing so by keeping too much company, it will turn into a habit, and the expense run to more than they can afford'.[4]

But good liquor and good company were not the only allurements. Yet another inviting feature of public houses was the opportunity they provided for play. 'The footmen of persons of fortune', says Hanway, 'amuse themselves with cards at alehouses. . . .'[5] And on special occasions there was also dancing.

The special occasions were routs and assemblies, sometimes given by a group of servants, sometimes by individuals. One of these affairs is pictured in Steele's *The Gentleman*: Tom takes Sir Harry to an alehouse where a party of servants are holding a masquerade.[6] Mention of an actual gathering of this kind occurred

---

[1] *Servants Pocket-Book*, p. 15.
[2] Hanway, *Virtue in Humble Life*, 1774, I. 419.
[3] *Memoirs of an Eighteenth-Century Footman*, p. 72.
[4] Heasel, *Servants Book of Knowledge*, p. 72.
[5] Hanway, *Defects of Police*, p. 25. Cf. *London Chronicle*, 1787, LXI. 590b.
[6] *Steele's Plays*, pp. 401–6.

in a London newspaper in 1725. A group of servants, it was reported, 'had met in Masquerade in a great Room the upper End of Beau Street, *Covent Garden*'.¹ Very little different is the scene described by John Macdonald, the footman, when he tells of 'a supper and ball' given by a gentleman's servant turned publican. After remarking that a total of thirty men and twenty-two women made up the assembled guests, he goes on to say:

> I was one of the company, which was very genteel, from noblemen and gentlemen's houses. . . . The evening was spent very agreeably by the company at country dances, cards and drinking. Supper was at eleven o'clock. After supper the company came into the drawing-room and began again.²

Not all such parties were confined to servants; there were affairs at which they mingled with the members of other occupational groups. 'The sixpenny hop', wrote an essayist of the mid-century, 'is crouded with ladies and gentlemen from the kitchen. . . .'³ A more detailed picture is supplied by Lichtenberg, a German traveller who was in England in 1774. He mentions in his diary a club of servants, journeymen, and apprentices that gave entertainments regularly once a week: 'On these evenings every member laid down fourpence, for which he had music and a female gratis; anything else had to be paid for separately.'⁴ A news item that appeared in 1777 describes an actual occasion of this sort. It relates how 'Last Friday night upwards of a hundred low tradesmen, gentlemen's servants, their wives and mistresses, assembled at Mason's hall Great Queen street, to *kick up a dance*. . . .'⁵

Since the gatherings held by servants were unauthorized by the magistracy, they were regarded as illegal; and all possible measures were taken to discover and suppress them. Thus in 1758 Sir John Fielding solicited the co-operation of the employer class, pointing out that by means of anonymous letters 'the most delicate Lady' might 'with Safety give Notice to the Justices of any Hop, Gaming-House, &c. where her Servants waste their Time, lose their Money,

---

¹ *Weekly Journal*, 1725, No. 337, Apr. 10, 2093–4.
² *Memoirs of an Eighteenth-Century Footman*, p. 237. Cf. *ibid.*, p. 182.
³ *Connoisseur*, Oxford, 1774, 6th ed., II. 97.
⁴ *Lichtenberg's Visits to England*, ed. Margaret M. Mare and W[illiam] H. Quarrell, Oxford, 1938, p. 118.
⁵ *Morning Post*, 1777, No. 1344, Feb. 10, 2d.

and debauch their Morals'.¹ Intelligence of this kind was extremely difficult to obtain because of the general reluctance to play the informer. But from time to time the existence of an unlawful assembly was brought to the attention of the authorities, who thereupon proceeded to suppress it. In 1764, for example, a ball of 250 persons, 'most of them apprentice boys and servant girls', was surprised and broken up.² A similar dispersal occurred in 1792:

> Some men and women servants, to the number of 40 and upwards, having assembled in the evening at the Pitt's head, Little Stanhope-street, May Fair, on the invitation of the publican, to make merry by a dance on the King's birth-night, information was given of it to Justice Hyde, who, headed by fifty or more constables, and the patroles from Hyde park, went to the house, and took up every servant found in it.³

The tavern life of which these functions constituted the high point was but one of the many recreational possibilities the Metropolis had to offer. Some of the others were identical in form with the diversions to be found in the country; some were unique.

Like the servants in the country, those in London naturally paid visits to friends. John Macdonald, for example, tells how on one occasion, while his employers were dining, he made the rounds: 'I went to the St. James's end of town with Mr Duff's servant. We called at different houses and drank several liquors....'⁴ And elsewhere in his *Travels* he speaks of going 'to Mr Grant's one day to see the servants' and of going 'to see Mr Bogle's servants'.⁵

In addition to paying ordinary calls servants also attended parties. A pamphleteer who savagely attacked upper servants for their luxurious way of life gives a graphic account of the way in which such affairs were arranged for them by tradesmen who sought their custom. One of their favourite diversions, he writes,

> is, the hurrying Junkets at the House of the several Tradesmen to the respective Families. They run thither without any Ceremony; drink a Dish of Chocolate, and away; at last, with a little Persuasion,

---

¹ Fielding, *Origin and Effects of a Plan of Police*, p. 31.
² *London Chronicle*, 1764, XV. 182c.
³ *Gentleman's Magazine*, 1792, LXVI. 570. Cf. *Annual Register*, 1792, XXXIV. 23.
⁴ *Memoirs of an Eighteenth-Century Footman*, p. 77.
⁵ *Ibid.*, pp. 76, 79.

RECREATION

a Time is fixed on to spend the Evening, with a pressing Request, that they will invite any Acquaintance of proper Rank. This is carried so far, that a House-full of these Gentry is easily got together. I once counted above twenty Chairs that carried Company of this Sort from a certain Blockhead's in *Bond-Street*. This Invitation goes quite round, and each Tradesman endeavours to excel in the Elegance of his Entertainment. . . .[1]

Domestics in London supplemented such social intercourse with an extensive patronage of the amusement world. Eliza Haywood testifies to this when, advising maid-servants against attending 'publick Shews', she says: 'It is those expensive ones . . . which drain your Purse, as well as waste your Time: such as Plays, the Wells and Gardens and other publick Shews and Entertainments. . . .'[2] Among the places frequented by servants were the fashionable pleasure gardens. James Northcote, writing in 1771 from Sir Joshua Reynolds', where he was a resident student, tells how 'This evening Miss Reynolds was out on a visit with the men servants, and the maids she gave leave to go to Vauxhall. . . .'[3] On occasion servants were also to be found at Carlisle House. In 1763, for example, Mrs. Cornelys, the proprietress, gave a ball to 'the upper servants of persons of fashion'. The gathering 'consisted of 220 persons, who made up fourscore couple in country dances' and a number of tables at cards.[4] Less modish places, such as Bagnigge Wells, Marylebone Gardens, and White Conduit House, were likewise visited by servants.[5] While in London in 1776, John Baker's valet, housemaid, and cook, for instance, went to Sadler's Wells.[6] In fact, the clientele of almost all the principal resorts of pleasure included domestics, who seem to have spent their money liberally in this direction. Thus on his visit to the Metropolis Matt Bramble found 'the gayest places of public entertainment' filled with 'serving men, and Abigails disguised like their betters'.[7]

---

[1] *Treatise on the Use and Abuse of the Second . . . Table*, pp. 15–16.
[2] Haywood, *A Present for a Servant-Maid*, p. 41.
[3] William T. Whitley, *Artists and Their Friends in England, 1700–1800*, London and Boston, 1928, II. 282.
[4] [T. Mackinlay,] *Mrs. Cornely's Entertainments*, [Bradford, 1840,] p. 4.
[5] *A Sunday Ramble . . . in and about the Cities of London and Westminster*, n.d., 3rd ed., p. 50; Seaton, *Conduct of Servants*, p. 162.
[6] *Diary of John Baker*, p. 354.
[7] Smollett, 'Humphry Clinker', *Works*, VII. 109.

Even the exhibitions held by the Society of Arts in 1760, 1761, and 1762 were crowded with maids and footmen, whose numbers seem to have caused no little inconvenience to the connoisseurs and virtuosi. A newspaper correspondent gave a complaining account of their presence in 1762:

> While I was waiting the other day for an opportunity to squeeze through the crowd at the door, one of those gentlemen who, like Joseph, wear coats of many colours, was attempting to introduce some of the ladies who twirl the mop so invitingly on a Saturday morning. The men, however, who held the staff of authority at the door stopped him short. 'Sir, I cannot admit you in that coat.'—'Why', says he, 'I have got a ticket.'—'If you had ten tickets you should not go in unless you change your coat.'—'Well, if you will not let me go in you will not refuse the ladies?'—'No Sir! by no means!' exclaimed the sweet girls. 'If you will not let the gentleman in we will not go in without him.' How the dispute ended I do not know, but I suppose the gentleman went home and put on his thickset coat, or borrowed one from a fellow servant and then saw the show.[1]

Perhaps the centres of amusement at which domestics figured most prominently were the theatres. Hanway's exemplary footman Thomas Trueman is made to remark, when reminiscing, that 'once or twice in a year' his fellow-servants 'used to gratify themselves in the sight of a play'.[2] But Soame Jenyns is probably much nearer the truth when he refers to their play-going as though it were an every-day affair.[3] Sometimes domestics accompanied their masters to the theatre. One of the fourth Duke of Bedford's servants, whose special duty it was to squire the young Marquess of Tavistock, included in his expense account such items as: 'November 30, 1751. Paid at the playhouse with Lord Tavistock 10s. 0d.'[4] Sometimes, on the other hand, domestics were sent alone. Writing to her husband in 1758, Mrs. Montagu mentions the fatigued state in which their gardener had arrived in London and then adds: '. . . . so I thought you would not dislike his recreating himself and resting his horse a little. I have sent him to the play to-night.'[5] As a rule, however, the price of admission

---

[1] Quoted in Whitley, *Artists and Their Friends*, I. 178.
[2] Hanway, *Virtue in Humble Life*, 1774, I. 411.
[3] *World*, IV. 12.   [4] Thomson, *The Russells*, p. 199.
[5] *Elizabeth Montagu*, II. 151.

probably came out of their own pocket, although during a good part of the century many attended without either paying or being paid for.

From the period of the Restoration the footmen of those who occupied the boxes were admitted without charge to the upper gallery at the conclusion of the fourth act. In 1696, however, the manager of the Theatre Royal (Drury Lane), thinking to offset what he imagined to be the greater popularity of the rival house, allowed them to enter at the beginning of the performance.[1] His lead was followed in time by the other theatres, and what had been at first extended as a privilege became in due course a prescriptive right.

How much they prized the right was demonstrated by the footmen in 1737 when, having created a considerable disturbance at Drury Lane, they were barred from the gallery by the manager. Gathering in a body three hundred strong on the following night, they broke into the theatre and fought their way to the stage door.[2] There they were finally stopped, but only after twenty-five persons had been seriously injured. Although three of the ring-leaders were subsequently sent to Newgate, the footmen did not allow the matter to rest. Determined to regain their former place at any cost, they threatened Charles Fleetwood, the manager, in a letter, which read:

> *We are willing to admonish you before we attempt our Design; and Provide you use us Civil, and admit us into our gallery, which is our Property, according to Formalities; and if you think proper to Come to a Composition this way, you'll hear no further, and if not, our Intention is to combine in a Body in Cognito, And Reduce the play house to the ground, Valuing no Detection we are Indemnified.*[3]

As a precaution a guard of fifty soldiers was posted at the theatre for several nights after this letter was received, but the footmen made no attempt to carry out their threat. The management, meanwhile, reversed its stand; and the footmen were again allowed to take possession of the gallery.

---

[1] Colley Cibber, *An Apology for the Life of Mr. Colley Cibber*, 1740, 2nd ed., p. 190.
[2] *Gentlemen's Magazine*, 1737, VII. 186; *London Magazine*, 1737, VI. 163; *Autobiography and Correspondence of . . . Mrs. Delany*, First Series, I. 598.
[3] *Gentlemen's Magazine*, 1737, VII. 186.

It was closed to them permanently, however, in 1759. When Townley's *High Life Below Stairs* was produced in that year

> The whole race of the domestic gentry ... were in a ferment of rage at what they conceived would be their ruin; and from the upper gallery ... came hisses and groans, and even many a handful of half-pence was flung on the stage at Philip and my Lord Duke and Sir Harry, &c.[1]

Garrick, who was then manager of Drury Lane, took the occasion of this tumult 'to shut the galleries from the servants, and ever after make it a pay place....'[2] In taking this step he was undoubtedly also greatly influenced by public opinion, which, thoroughly aroused at the time over the vails question, was as unsympathetic towards the servant class as it ever became during the century. Ultimately the other theatres followed Garrick's example, so that the domestics of the Metropolis lost what had been a constant source of free entertainment.

There seems to have been no marked diminution, however, in the number of servants who attended the theatre. Those who formerly would have been admitted free now paid, as many had always done. Thomas Mortimer, writing in 1786, asserted that one could 'find the first gallery crouded every night with livery servants and chambermaids, the former occupiers of the second....'[3] And a decade later a newspaper correspondent complained that they had even invaded the pit:

> ... the Negligence of the Managers, or their Servants at the Pit door, bit fair to destroy this part of the audience, by admitting Footmen in Liveries to take their Seat among the Company if they drop their Three Shillings at the Door. Last Night was not the first Time This Winter I have sat Cheek and Jole with a Neighbour's Footman.[4]

Some servants continued to gain admission without paying. Throughout the period and well into the nineteenth century, footmen were admitted to the boxes without charge so that they could keep desirable places for their employers. This practice enabled a good many to see at least part of the performance since

---

[1] *Life of John O'Keeffe*, II. 161–2.   [2] *Ibid.*, II. 162.
[3] Thomas Mortimer, *The National Debt No National Grievance*, 1768, p. 116.
[4] *St. James's Chronicle*, 1778, No. 2659, Apr. 21–3, 4b.

often they were not obliged to relinquish their seats before the beginning of the third act. In Henry Fielding's *Miss Lucy in Town* (1735) Tawdry explains that fashionable ladies 'take a Stage-Box where they let the Footman sit the first two Acts to shew his Livery. . . .'[1] Sometimes such a footman was fortunate enough to be able to retain his place through the better part of the play. A newspaper correspondent, who in 1769 advocated the introduction of reserved seats, cites as typical an instance in which 'the third act was well nigh finished, before the gentlemen arrived' to relieve the servants who were keeping places for them.[2] The practice of sending footmen on ahead to occupy choice seats was roundly condemned in the press on several occasions. A news item in 1766, which reported, falsely as it turned out, that the managers of the theatres had decided to introduce reserved seats, concluded with the remark: 'This will prevent the indecency of a dirty servant sitting by a lady elegantly dressed, which has been so often complained of.'[3] But no move was ever made to alter the system.

IV

Thus the amusements enjoyed by servants ranged from simple visits to the most sophisticated entertainments of the Capital. In the light of the evidence the only warrantable conclusion is that domestics as a class were given a good deal of time off. A distinction must be made, of course, between the almost unlimited freedom enjoyed by many upper servants and the more restricted liberty granted lower servants, between the opportunities for social life and diversion open to the servants in large establishments and those possessed by the servants of the lower middle class. Yet, on the whole, it would appear that service was far from being all drudgery. Contemporaries were well aware that this was so. Thomas Trueman, the fictitious footman in one of Hanway's moral tracts, says in his pedantic way: 'There are times for the relaxation of walking abroad; and in general, liberty enough is given; and as far as the line properly extends, domestics having the same passions and inclinations as other people, seem to gratify

---

[1] Henry Fielding, *Miss Lucy in Town*, 1742, p. 7.
[2] *London Chronicle*, 1769, XXVI. 452b.
[3] *Ibid.*, 1766, XIX. 86c.

them in much the same way'.[1] Eliza Haywood, who advances the conventional view that when a servant is idle he is stealing what rightfully belongs to his employer, admits that 'The Condition of a Servant would be too severe, were they not allowed some Time which they may call their own. . . .'[2] And another writer declares that employers are entirely too indulgent in allowing domestics to have their own social life: '. . . they begin to stand in need of amusement, of idle time, of visiting seasons, and of days of pleasure as well as yourselves, and you permit them to have such'.[3]

[1] Hanway, *Virtue in Humble Life*, 1774, I. 411.
[2] Haywood, *A Present for a Servant-Maid*, p. 39.
[3] *Universal Magazine*, 1796, XCVIII. 237.

Chapter Six

THE REWARDS OF SERVICE: PECUNIARY PROFITS

Domestics received compensation for their services in several different forms. There were regular payments and there were incidental fees. Moreover, quite apart from the ordinary revenues of his place, the deserving servant might receive some kind of special reward from an appreciative master.

I

Wages were, of course, the basic form of compensation. They were usually paid quarterly, although arrangements providing for monthly and even weekly payments were not unknown.

Advertisements, diaries, letters, and account books furnish wage figures for most levels of the hierarchy. It is therefore possible to reconstruct the scale of payment in some detail. The essential data are set forth below, each figure representing the wages of a single servant for the designated year:[1]

[1] Most of these figures are taken from advertisements in the *Daily Advertiser*, 1742–95. A few come from advertisements in other papers: *London Chronicle*, 1760, VII. 307b; *Morning Post*, 1777, No. 1318, Jan. 10, 3a, No. 1320, Jan. 13, 3a, No. 1336, Jan. 31, 3a; *Morning Chronicle*, 1795, No. 7958, Apr. 16, 2a, 1796, No. 8251, Mar. 19, 1c, 1797, No. 8595, Apr. 27, 4b, 1798, No. 8938, Jan. 16, 1b. The remainder are taken from Adeane, *Girlhood of Maria Josepha Holroyd*, p. 331; Jane H. Adeane, *The Early Married Life of Maria Josepha Holroyd*, 1889, p. 125; *Autobiography and Correspondence of . . . Mrs. Delany*, Second Series, II. 96; Baker, *James Brydges First Duke of Chandos*, pp. 172–7, 179–80; Bamford, *Dear Miss Heber*, p. 133; *Barnard Letters 1778–1824*, ed. Anthony Powell, 1928, p. 55; *Diary of a Country Parson*, I. 63, 68, 74, 182, 186, 357, II. 2, 3, 55, 84, 114, 168, 295, III. 2, 78, 164, 241, 328, IV. 2, 89, 164, 165, 256, V. 4, 94, 160, 161, 234, 295, 360; *Diary of John Baker*, pp. 53, 299–300, 314, 335–8,

THE REWARDS OF SERVICE

1. *Land Steward*

1713	£50
1722	30
1722	70
1722	100
1723	30
1727	100
1732	40
1732–71	700
1760–75	200
1772	30 gns.

2. *House Steward*

1708	50
1710	50
1712–42	40
1724	50
1732	80
1734	50
1770	100
1771	40
1772	50 gns.

3. *House Steward-Valet*

1757	25
1763	25

4. *House Steward-Butler*

1770	30
1771	35

5. *Clerk of the Kitchen*

1702	£30
1720	32
1734	50
1760 *ca.*	100

6. *Clerk of the Stables*

1734	50

7. *Man-Cook*

1700–32	30–35
1729	40
1750 *ca.*	60
1760	30
1770	20
1770 *ca.*	52 gns.
1779	90 gns.
1792	55–60 gns.
1795	30 gns.

8. *Confectioner*

1700	20
1734	60
1749	30
1750–71	52 10s.

9. *Bailiff*

1721	25
1727	30
1733	25
1734	25

345–6, 358, 378–82, 423, 430, 457; *Diary of John Hervey*, pp. 183–5; Doughty, *The Betts*, pp. 193, 214, 232, 244; 'Extracts from the Journal and Account Books of Timothy Burrell', *Sussex Archaeological Collections*, III. 137, 142, 145, 147, 150, 157; Finch, *History of Burley*, I. 278; *Gentleman's Magazine*, 1791, LXI. 199; *H. M. C. Egmont Diary*, I. 76, 192; *H. M. C. Verulam*, p. 146; James, *Chief Justice Coke*, p. 282; John H. Jesse, *George Selwyn and His Contemporaries*, New York, 1882, IV. 298; Longe, *Martha Lady Giffard*, pp. 252, 355–6; March, *A Duke and His Friends*, II. 682; 'Marchant Diary', *Sussex Archaeological Collections*, XXV. 188, 193; Newton, *Lyme Letters*, p. 317; *Notes and Queries*, Second Series, 1860, X. 286; Nulle, *Duke of Newcastle*, pp. 184–5; Frederica St. J. Orlebar, *The Orlebar Chronicles . . . 1553–1733*, 1930, I. 209, 243, 252; *Pembroke Papers*, ed. Lord Herbert, 1950, p. 32; *Purefoy Letters*, I. 127, 142, 145, 146, 153; Sitwell, *The Hurts*, p. 257; 'Stapley Diaries', *Sussex Archaeological Collections*, XXIII. 49; Thomson, *The Russells*, pp. 224–30, 233, 237, 239, 277; *Verney Letters*, I. 232.

PECUNIARY PROFITS

10. *Valet*

1701	£ 4
1714–42	10
1725	20
1729	20
1731	16
1748	6
1755	8
1768	14
1770	12 gns.
1770	14
1770	15
1771	30
1774	15 gns.
1774	25
1777	18 gns.
1784	30 gns.
1788	25

11. *Butler*

1705	6
1708	15
1712	10
1727–41	10
1732	57 10s.
1760	10
1760	20
1769	20
1770	10
1770	30 gns.
1771	20
1787	18
1796	30 gns.
1797	35

12. *Gardener*

1705	20
1721	12
1732	30
1748	9
1755	18
1756	16
1756	16
1758	16
1760	22
1761	16
1762	20
1762	£ 25
1764	11
1767	12 gns.
1770	12
1770	25
1771	12 gns.
1771	25
1772	14
1772	20
1772	30
1774–7	26
1774	35
1785	16
1785	20 gns.
1788	12 gns.
1789	16 gns.
1790	10
1792	16 gns.
1792	18 gns.
1795	12

13. *Gardener-Bailiff*

1769	20
1769	20
1769	25

14. *Groom of the Chambers*

1708	12
1732–71	16

15. *Coachman*

1708	6
1721	8
1722	7
1732	12
1734	10
1749	10
1750	10
1751	10
1753	10
1756	12
1756	12
1756	16
1758	10
1760	10
1760	10
1761	20
1766	8

THE REWARDS OF SERVICE

15. *Coachman—(cont.)*

		1762	£ 8
1766	£ 15	1762	8
1770	11	1763	9
1770	15 gns.	1764	7
1770	20 gns.	1765	9
1771	26 6s.	1765	9
1773	14 gns.	1765	17
1774–7	21	1766	3
1775	20	1766	12 gns.
1784	16	1766	12 gns.
1786	16 gns.	1767	10
1789	14 gns.	1767	12
1789	20	1767	12
1792	14 gns.	1768	12
1792	18 gns.	1769	10 gns.
1792	20	1770	6
1793	20	1770	10
1795	18	1771	10 gns.
		1771	14 gns.
		1771	14 gns.

16. *Footman*

		1771	17 gns.
1702	6	1772	14
1704	2 10s.	1772	14 gns.
1704	4	1773	12 gns.
1713	6	1774	12–14
1718	5	1774	12 gns.
1720	5	1775	12
1730 *ca.*	5–6	1775	12 gns.
1735	5 15s.	1775	16
1736	7 gns.	1776	14
1738	7	1782	4 gns.
1740	2 15s.	1784	14
1742	7	1784	14 gns.
1745	7–8	1785	12
1746	5	1785	14
1748	6	1785	16 gns.
1748	7	1786	20
1748	9	1787	8
1750 *ca.*	6–8	1787	13–15 gns.
1750	10	1787	16
1755	7	1789	10
1757	10	1789	14
1758	8	1792	12–14
1760	8	1792	14 gns.
1760	8	1792	14–20 gns.
1760	12 gns.	1792	15 gns.
1761	12	1792	16 gns.
1762	8	1792	18 gns.

PECUNIARY PROFITS

1792	20 gns.	1760	£ 9
1792	20 gns.	1763	12
1793	14 gns.	1770	14
1793	16 gns.	1771	15
1794	10 gns.		
1794	14 gns.	22. *Under-Coachman*	
1795	£ 15	1708	8
1795	16	1732–71	9–10
1795	16		
1795	16 gns.	23. *Porter*	
1795	17	1770	8
1795	18 gns.	1771	8
		1792	14–16 gns.

17. *Footman-Valet*

1760	8	24. *Postilion*	
1760	8 gns.	1700–42	5
1762	14 gns.	1732–53	6
1772	15	1734	6
1788	13 gns.	1753–71	11
1789	20	1763	6
1790	15	1770	10–12
1794	18	1774	10 gns.
		1775	12

18. *Footman-Gardener*

		1776	15 gns.
1749	10	1776	6 gns.
1762	10–12	1777	7 gns.
1784	10 gns.		
		25. *Footboy*	

19. *Footman-Groom*

		1743	2
1756	8	1750	0
1775	20	1753	6
1792	20 gns.	1756	0
1793	14–20 gns.	1757	3
		1760	6

20. *Groom*

		1764	2
1761	10 gns.	1768	2
1763	13	1768	2
1773	15–21	1774–6	4
1774	15–19 gns.	1786	0
1780	12	1792	0
1787	14 gns.	1793	5 gns.
1789	16	1794	5 gns.
1790	12 gns.		
1795	15 gns.	26. *Lady's Maid*	
		1705	6

21. *Under-Butler*

		1708	5
1732	6	1708	10
1734	8	1711	10

D.S.C.—L

THE REWARDS OF SERVICE

26. Lady's Maid—(cont.)

Year	Amount
1720	£ 6
1720	10
1734	10
1760 ca.	8
1760 ca.	20
1764	10 gns.
1765	7
1769	10 gns.
1775	16
1785	14 gns.
1793	10 gns.
1795	18
1797	16

27. Housekeeper

Year	Amount
1719	10
1732–71	12
1734	30
1743	10
1757	10
1759	10
1760	10
1762	12
1766	12
1768	6
1768	9
1769	10
1770	12
1770	14
1770	16
1770	16
1771	15 gns.
1771	16
1773	20
1774–6	16 gns.
1795	16 gns.

28. Housekeeper-Lady's Maid

Year	Amount
1767	10 gns.
1770	15 gns.

29. Cook

Year	Amount
1700–05	6
1703	5 10s.
1732–4	18
1742	15
1743	3–3 10s.

Year	Amount
1744	£ 4
1748	8
1753	8
1753	10
1754	6
1755	7
1756	8
1757	8
1758	7–8
1758	8
1758	15
1759	14
1760	7
1760	9
1760	9
1760	14
1761	6
1761	7
1761	20
1762	8
1762	8
1762	8
1763	7
1763	8
1764	8
1764	10
1765	7
1765	8
1765	10
1765	20 gns.
1765	20 gns.
1767	10
1767	14
1768	7
1768	10 gns.
1769	8
1769	10
1769	10 gns.
1770	5
1770	8 gns.
1770	9
1770	10
1770	10 gns.
1770	12
1770	15 gns.
1771	8
1771	8
1771	8

PECUNIARY PROFITS

1771	£ 9	
1771	9 gns.	
1772	9	
1772	10	
1773	8 gns.	
1773	9 gns.	
1774	10 gns.	
1774–5	12 gns.	
1775	8 gns.	
1775	9 gns.	
1775	10	
1775	10 gns.	
1775	14 gns.	
1777	12 gns.	
1784	10 gns.	
1784	12 gns.	
1784	20	
1785	5	
1785	8 gns.	
1785	8 gns.	
1785	12 gns.	
1786	9	
1786	12 gns.	
1787	13 gns.	
1787	14	
1789	7–8	
1789	8 gns.	
1789	10 gns.	
1790	8	
1790	10	
1790	10	
1790	10 gns.	
1790	12	
1790	15 gns.	
1792	8 gns.	
1792	11 gns.	
1792	12 gns.	
1793	10 gns.	
1795	10–12	
1795	16	
1798	20 gns.	

30. Cook-Housekeeper

1758	10
1759	15
1771	20
1772	20
1786	25

1788	14 gns.
1792	20 gns.
1795	10 gns.

31. Chambermaid

1769	12 gns.
1771	£ 6–7
1773	7
1775	10

32. Housemaid

1702	4
1734	6
1750 ca.	5–6
1751	6
1760	7
1762	7
1762	7
1763	7
1763	7
1767	6
1767	7
1768	6
1769	7
1769	7 gns.
1770	4 10s.
1770	6
1770	7 gns.
1771	6
1771	7 gns.
1771	10
1772	7 gns.
1774	7
1774	8
1774–6	8 gns.
1775	8
1776	6
1776	10 gns.
1777	7
1784	8 gns.
1785	7
1785	7
1785	8 gns.
1790	8 gns.
1792	9
1792	9 gns.
1792	11
1793	8 gns.

THE REWARDS OF SERVICE

33. *Maid of all Work*

Year	Wage	Year	Wage
		1771	7 gns.
1743	£ 3–3 10s.	1771	£ 8
1749	4 10s.–5	1771	10
1749	6	1772	6
1752	5	1772	10
1755	5	1773	6
1755	6	1773	6
1756	4	1773	7
1756	6	1773	7
1756	8	1774	7
1757	5	1774	8
1757	5	1774	8 gns.
1757	6	1775	6
1757	7	1775	7
1757	7 gns.	1775	7–10
1758	7	1775	7 gns.
1760	4	1775	8
1761	7	1775	9
1762	6	1784	7 gns.
1762	6	1784	8
1762	7	1784	8 gns.
1762	7	1784	8 gns.
1762	7	1784	8 gns.
1762	8	1784	9 gns.
1763	6	1784	9 gns.
1763	7	1785	8 gns.
1763	7	1785	8 gns.
1763	8	1786	6
1763	8	1786	6 gns.
1764	6	1786	8 gns.
1765	6	1786	8 gns.
1766	5–6	1786	9 gns.
1766	7	1786	10 gns.
1767	6	1786	12 gns.
1767	7	1787	7
1767	7	1787	8 gns.
1767	7 gns.	1787	8 gns.
1767	8	1788	8 gns.
1768	6	1788	9 gns.
1768	6 gns.	1788	9 gns.
1768	7	1788	10
1770	4	1788	10
1770	5	1788	10 gns.
1770	6	1789	8 gns.
1770	7	1789	9 gns.
1770	8	1789	9 gns.
1770	8 gns.	1789	10 gns.
1771	6	1789	10 gns.

PECUNIARY PROFITS

1790	8 gns.	1772	£ 7
1791	9–14 gns.	1773	8
1791	£ 10	1774	7 gns.
1792	8	1774	8
1792	8 gns.	1784	7
1792	8 gns.	1785	9 gns.
1792	9 gns.	1788	8 gns.
1792	10	1793	10 gns.
1792	10 gns.	1793	10 gns.
1792	10 gns.		
1793	7 gns.	35. Dairy Maid	
1793	8 gns.	1707	3
1793	9 gns.	1720	5 10s.
1794	10 gns.	1743	2
1795	9 gns.	1770	10
1795	10 gns.	1774–6	5–6 gns.

34. Laundry Maid

		36. Scullery Maid	
1705	2 5s.	1772	6
1732–71	5	1772	7
1732–71	6	1775	7
1734	6	1786	6
1749	6		

Perhaps the most striking aspect of these figures is the variation in the wages of servants of like rank during the same year. In 1772, for instance, one land steward had £30, a second £70, and a third £100; in 1792 one footman was offered £12, another £20.

Such disparities were created by several different variables. These included the degree of skill and competence possessed by the servant, the scope of the duties and responsibilities he assumed, the scheme of payment he agreed with his master, and the location of the place where he was hired.

Very naturally the more skilful and accomplished were compensated at higher rates than those of less ability. Careful distinction was made between different levels of competence. Among gardeners, for example, those who had creative ability as landscapists, who understood such abstruse matters as forcing and the cultivation of exotic fruits, were distinguished from those whose abilities were only just sufficient for the maintenance of a kitchen garden; among cooks the difference between a 'professed cook'—one with a mastery of French cuisine and an ability to turn out the more elaborate native dishes—and a 'good plain cook' was fully recognized. There existed, moreover, a considerable awareness of the gradations of ability between such extremes; and wages were given accordingly. This is demonstrated by advertisements. Seeking a footman-gardener in 1762, an employer gave notice in print that he was willing to pay between £10 and £12; in quest of a porter in 1792 another employer announced that he would give anywhere from 14 guineas to 16 guineas.[1] In each case the advertiser, by mentioning a range of rates, implies the intention of adjusting wages to ability. As a rule the ability to which wages were adjusted comprehended those skills normally requisite for a post. Sometimes it included special skills as well, and these were rewarded at advanced rates. In 1757 an advertiser who sought a footman offered £10 to an ordinary one, £15 to one who could blow the French horn; similarly, in 1787 an advertiser stated that he would give 13 guineas to a footman with the usual complement of skills but 15 guineas to one who could dress hair.[2]

A servant's wages were determined by his duties no less than by his ability. The gardener charged with the maintenance and improvement of extensive grounds, like those of Blenheim or Chatsworth, inevitably earned more than the gardener who tended the diminutive acreage of a seat like the Leasowes; the agent-general of a great territorial magnate like the Duke of Bedford naturally received a higher salary than the steward who looked after the estate of a small squire. A similar discrepancy usually existed between the wages of the servant who discharged duties not ordinarily appurtenant to his post and those of the servant whose activities were confined to the normal routine. When considering a candidate for the place of house steward in 1724, the Duke of Chandos proposed to give him £70 if the collection of rentals—a function usually performed by the land steward—were included in his duties; but he was to have only £50 if he assumed merely the regular routine of the post.[3]

Along with the ability he brought to the task and the duties he was expected to perform, the scheme of payment under which he was hired influenced the servant's wages. Where fees and perquisites ran high, wages were set low and vice versa. This is clearly revealed in advertisements of the period. In 1765 an advertiser,

[1] *Daily Advertiser*, 1762, No. 9884, Sept. 9, 3b; 1792, No. 19926, Oct. 6, 2c.
[2] *Ibid.*, 1757, No. 8186, Apr. 7, 3a; 1787, No. 18401, Nov. 23, 2b.
[3] Baker, *James Brydges First Duke of Chandos*, p. 174.

after naming the very generous figure of £17 as the wage he would give a footman, added in explanation: 'but the Vails are small'; again, in 1793 an employer who advertised for 'a compleat Cook' stated: '... as there are no Perquisites her Wages will be in Proportion.'[1] But it was not only with other revenues that wages were likely to be correlated in the scheme of payment; they might be tied to one or more items provided for the servant's maintenance. Sometimes, for example, the livery servant was given the option of accepting a lower wage and having his shoes and stockings supplied, or a higher wage without shoes and stockings. Occasionally, too, he was given the same choice in regard to his livery suit. Advertising for a lackey in 1762, a City merchant offered £8 a year with a livery and £15 if the man supplied his own.[2] In the case of the gardener the size of the wages depended on the provision made for lodging and food. If he were given a house and the right to eat with the other servants, his wages were lower than if he had 'to find everything for himself'.

Yet another factor that influenced wages was geographical location. As in other occupations, the rates in the country tended to be lower than in the Capital and other urban centres. In 1740 Anthony Stapley, a Sussex gentleman, engaged a footman at £2 15s. a year; at the same time the Duke of Bedford was paying £6 and £8 in London.[3] In 1770 a Lancashire baronet gave his cook £5 a year, while in London advertisements were offering £8 and £9.[4] Too much, however, should not be inferred from these examples. For one thing, a qualitative element may partly explain the difference in wages between town and country. During most of the period London servants were, on the whole, superior in ability to country servants, although with each decade the distinction tended to grow less, until by the close of the century it had almost disappeared. More important is the certainty that whatever the difference between urban and rural rates, there were many families in the country where the former rather than the latter prevailed. Since the servants of the larger country houses were taken up to London from time to time, they naturally were well

[1] *Daily Advertiser*, 1765, No. 10655, Feb. 25, 2c; 1793, No. 20061, Mar. 13, 2c.
[2] *Ibid.*, 1762, No. 9885, Sept. 10, 3c.
[3] 'Stapley Diaries', *Sussex Archaeological Collections*, XXIII. 49.
[4] *Notes and Queries*, Second Series, 1860, x. 286.

THE REWARDS OF SERVICE

informed on the wages paid there and quite as naturally were unwilling to accept less. It was in small homes that rural rates obtained.

This analysis of the major variables indicates how hazardous must be any attempt to compare wage data for servants. What, then, can be said of the course of wages during the century? Very little with certainty. The figures for the footman and the maid of all work, the two posts most heavily represented in the wage data at hand, seem to confirm the belief of contemporaries that the general trend was upwards. Other evidence also appears to support this view. Mordant, in the model list of wage disbursements included in his treatise on stewardship, gives £3—presumably an average figure—as the wage of a postilion in 1757.[1] According to Trusler, in the late 1770's such a servant commanded £12.[2] Similarly, Mordant's list gives £7 as the wage of a head footman in 1757, £5 as the wage of an under footman,[3] but Trusler names £14 as the wage of the average London footman in 1786,[4] and Baert puts the figure at £16 for 1802.[5] Estimates for the housemaid likewise suggest a rise. Illustrating the proper method of recording the payment of servants' wages, Edward Laurence cites as a sample entry the wages of an average housemaid in 1727, £3 15s.[6] Mordant's figures for the same post in 1757 are somewhat higher: £5 for a head housemaid, £4 for an under-housemaid,'[7] and Trusler, writing in 1786, gives £7 to £9 as the rates for 'inferior woman-servants', among whom, of course, housemaids are included.[8] The upward movement that these comparisons suggest seems even more clearly discernible in the increasingly higher rates at which Parson Woodforde paid his footman between 1766 and 1802. The duties of the post, the requisite abilities, and the terms of hire remained constant. Yet, whereas in 1766 Woodforde managed to get a footman for as little as £3, by 1784 he was paying

---

[1] Mordant, *Complete Steward*, II. 36.
[2] Trusler, *Way to Be Rich*, p. 46.
[3] Mordant, *Complete Steward*, II. 36.
[4] Trusler, *London Adviser*, p. 48.
[5] [Charles, Baron de Baert-Duholant,] *Tableau de la Grande Bretagne*, Paris, 1802, p. 176n.
[6] Laurence, *Duty of a Steward*, p. 153.
[7] Mordant, *Complete Steward*, II. 37.
[8] Trusler, *London Adviser*, p. 48.

5 guineas, and by 1787 he was obliged to give £8, which continued to be the rate until his death in 1802.¹

Although, despite this array of evidence, the over-all trend during the period can only be described in terms of probability, it is certain that after 1760 wages were raised voluntarily by a growing number of employers. The advance was given in order to compensate domestics for the loss of certain gratuities known as vails.² Its size varied. In 1765 it was reported that in Devonshire, Cumberland, Westmorland, Northumberland, Lancashire, and Lincoln wages had been increased by one third.³ In London the advance sometimes exceeded, sometimes fell below, that figure. In 1760 an advertisement for a coachman made it clear that the £16 he would receive was £6 more than previously had been given; an advertisement that offered £10 for a footman in 1762 indicated that the wages of the post formerly had been only £8.⁴ There long remained a considerable body of employers who, since their servants continued to receive vails, gave no advance at all. But before the century expired their number had dwindled into insignificance.

Regardless of the course of wages, however, they furnish no real clue to the size of the incomes derived from service. For in almost every instance they formed but a part of the servant's receipts; and often they amounted to relatively little when compared with the yield of allowances, fees, and perquisites.

II

Two allowances employers often gave their servants were board wages and tea money. Both were contracted for at the time of hiring.

Board wages were money payments disbursed on a weekly basis in place of meals. Usually they were given for only a limited period, such as when a servant was taken on the road or when he sojourned with his employer in London or remained behind while the family was not in residence. Sometimes, however, a servant

---

¹ *Diary of a Country Parson*, I. 63; II. 114, 295; III. 2, 78, 164, 241; IV. 2, 89, 164, 256; V. 94, 160, 234, 295, 360.
² See below, pp. 158–60.
³ *Scots Magazine*, Edinburgh, 1763, XXV. 412.
⁴ *Daily Advertiser*, 1760, No. 9288, Oct. 14, 3a; No. 9682, Jan. 16, 3b.

THE REWARDS OF SERVICE

was placed 'on constant board wages', which meant that he always had to find his own food.[1]

The principal object of putting servants on board wages was to curb extravagance. 'By their profusion in house-keeping,' declared Soame Jenyns, 'they have compelled us to allow them board-wages. . . .'[2] But the system also had other advantages from the employer's point of view. It served his convenience and reduced his responsibilities; it lessened the number of potential pilferers to which his household provisions were exposed.

The amounts given as board wages varied appreciably. The figures cited below suggest the range of variation:[3]

1. *Valet*
   - 1731 — 10s. 6d.
   - 1775 — 12
   - 1777 — 10s. 6d.

2. *Coachman*
   - 1734 — 8s.
   - 1789 — 7
   - 1792 — 7
   - 1793 — 7

3. *Gardener*
   - 1758 — 4s.
   - 1767 — 9
   - 1772 — 7
   - 1790 — 7
   - 1795 — 6

4. *Footman*
   - 1730 — 7s.
   - 1736 — 8s. 2d.
   - 1742 — 7s.
   - 1760 — 9
   - 1775 — 10s. 6d.

5. *Postilion*
   - 1734 — 7s.
   - 1775 — 8s. 6d.
   - 1777 — 7

6. *Housemaid*
   - 1767 — 6s.
   - 1785 — 6
   - 1789 — 6

7. *Laundry Maid*
   - 1773 — 5s.
   - 1784 — 6

8. *Maid of All Work*
   - 1770 — 7s.
   - 1774 — 5
   - 1775 — 5

The reasons for the variations that occurred in board wages are not altogether clear. It is certain that the nominal rank of a servant

[1] For examples of 'constant board wages' see *Daily Advertiser*, 1772, No. 6031, May 2, 2c; John T. Smith, *Nollekens and His Times*, 1829, 2nd ed., I. 74; *Letter Books of John Hervey*, III. 210.

[2] *World*, IV. 16.

[3] The principal source of these figures is the advertisements of the *Daily Advertiser*, 1730–95. Some, however, occur in: *Diary of John Baker*, pp. 335–6, 419, 422, 432; H. M. C. Egmont Diary, I. 192; Nulle, *Duke of Newcastle*, p. 185; Sitwell, *The Hurts*, pp. 269, 272.

influenced the amount he received. Trusler, writing in 1786, says that in London 10s. 6d. was the usual rate for upper servants, 7s. for lower;[1] and precisely this differential existed in the board wages John Baker paid in 1777 to his valet on the one hand and his postilion on the other.[2] Very likely the sex of the servant also played a determining role. Judging by the figures cited above, women were usually paid less than men. Society's lower valuation of women was no doubt responsible, but the differential seems to have been rationalized by the assumption that they could get along on a lighter diet.[3] Regional variations in the prices of foodstuffs may have been still another factor that determined board wages. Servants who were expected to provide their own meals in London and other urban centres, where expenses ran high, may have been given more than those who remained in the country.

Whether in London or in the country, astute servants were able to profit by the system. Sometimes they got themselves invited to meals in the servants' hall or housekeeper's room of homes where they had friends; sometimes, as Steele points out, they contrived to 'eat after their Masters' in taverns and inns.[4] By pursuing such a course they could save the money given them as board wages for purposes of their own.

Because by enlarging the financial resources of servants it decreased their dependence, because by multiplying the hours during which they were free of supervision it increased their opportunities to live a life outside the family, the system of board wages was repeatedly subjected to attack. Steele denounced it as an 'Instance of false Oeconomy... sufficient to debauch the whole Nation of Servants' and attributed to it both their insubordination and the 'Licentiousness' that he claimed 'prevailed among them'.[5] A later essayist insisted that it gave them 'a constant excuse to loiter at public-houses' and at the same time put 'money in their pockets to squander there in gaming, drunkenness, and extravagance'.[6] And a writer in 1762 thought it so vicious in its effects that he wished a new method could be devised 'for having servants

---

[1] Trusler, *London Adviser*, p. 48. Cf. Frederick Kielmansegge, *Diary of a Journey to England in the Years 1761–2*, ed. [Sophia] Kielmansegg, 1902, p. 20.
[2] *Diary of John Baker*, pp. 432, 419.
[3] *Servants Pocket-Book*, p. 5.
[4] *Spectator*, II. 33.
[5] *Ibid.*
[6] *World*, IV. 15.

fed without suffering them to finger the money'. Public houses, he suggested, might be required to board them at fixed rates, which presumably would be paid directly by their masters.[1] But despite this criticism, employers never developed any hesitancy about giving board wages.

Just as board wages were given in lieu of meals, tea money was given in lieu of tea and sugar. In many homes maidservants were regularly supplied with these commodities. After stating the wages of the post, advertisements frequently add: 'and tea', or more specifically, 'tea once a day' or 'tea twice a day'.[2] But many employers felt they came off better by substituting a money payment for the allowance in kind.

A pound or a guinea seems to have been the usual payment during the second half of the century. These are the amounts most frequently mentioned by advertisements, as is indicated by the figures below:[3]

1. *Housekeeper*		4. *Maid of All Work*	
1770	42s.	1762	20s.
1795	21	1762	21
2. *Cook*		1762	21
1761	20s.	1764	21
1765	20	1766	21
1769	21	1769	21
		1771	21
3. *Housemaid*		1772	21
1762	21s.	1773	21
1763	20		

But despite the apparent constancy of the allowance, the 2 guineas offered a housekeeper in 1770 were by no means a solitary aberration. Col. Dow gave each of his two maids 2 guineas in 1768;[4] Woodforde gave his upper-maid only 10s. in 1784.[5]

Although Grosley, mindful of these allowances, asserted in 1765 that 'tous les domestiques' had tea 'ou en argent, ou en nature',[6] not every maidservant was in fact given her daily dish or its

[1] *London Chronicle*, 1762, XI. 165a.
[2] See, for example, *Daily Advertiser*, 1762, No. 9946, Nov. 23, 2c; 1763, No. 10219, Oct. 6, 3a; 1771, No. 12603, May 17, 3a.
[3] All these figures are taken from the *Daily Advertiser*, 1730–95.
[4] *Memoirs of an Eighteenth-Century Footman*, p. 93.
[5] *Diary of a Country Parson*, I. 271   [6] Grosley, *Londres*, I. 132.

monetary equivalent. Some advertisements stoutly proclaim: 'no tea'; others intimate, with dubious sincerity, that something will be allowed for tea in the regular wages. A servant who accepted such terms might feel himself deprived, but she usually could indemnify herself with revenues from other sources.

III

In addition to such allowances as board wages, and tea money servants received extra funds from their employers indirectly through the valuable perquisites attached to almost every household post. The butler was permitted to dispose of the candle ends and old bottles; the cook was allowed to sell the 'kitchen stuff': drippings, bones and chunks of fat; the coachman was given the half-worn carriage parts; the gamekeeper had a right to the dogs and firearms he took away from suspected poachers.

The most lucrative perquisites were the used clothes that upper servants received by agreement and the liveries that generally fell to lower servants after they had worn them *'long enough to have New'*.[1] Some of these garments were, of course, used by the servants themselves; but many were promptly sold for high prices to the Jews of Monmouth Street and Rosemary Lane. Clearly it was the loss of profit, not the loss of style, that concerned the Duke of Kingston's valet when he moaned: 'During the sixteen years that I served the Duke, I had but two lots of clothes given me the first amounting to fifty, the second to near ninety pounds. . . .'[2]

There was opportunity for domestics to swell the legitimate yield of their perquisites by unscrupulous practices, and doubtless the less vigilant employers were often sadly defrauded. Eliza Haywood had heard 'that in large Families, were a great Quantity of every Thing was ordered in', cooks were frequently 'base enough to melt whole Pounds of Butter into Oil, on Purpose. . . .'[3] The Rev. Trusler also mentioned this practice along with several others. There are cooks, he warned, who 'strip your meat of its fat, melt more butter than necessary, and convey the ends of candles, &c. into the grease-pot, to increase its weight'. And he

---
[1] Fielding, *Penal Laws*, p. 142.
[2] Whitehead, *Original Anecdotes*, p. 156.
[3] Haywood, *A Present for a Servant-Maid*, p. 31.

added the caveat that coachmen 'often injure the wheels, if they are likely to last too long'.¹

Stewards were particularly rapacious. Because of the nature of their duties, they were more exposed to temptation than other servants; and their resistance seems to have been singularly weak. Among the many sharp practices to which they were given a few stand out as having been especially common. A steward might sacrifice his master's interests by letting the tenants 'hold their Farms at the low *Old Rent*, instead of an Improv'd one'.² Then again, when selling produce from the estate, such as timber or hay, he might take less than the market price in exchange for a rebate from the purchaser. Yet another dodge he might attempt was the illicit manipulation of the funds that passed through his hands. An agent of the first Earl of Bristol's, for instance, took some eight or nine hundred pounds he had collected as rent and instead of paying it to his lordship's banker, 'surreptitiously imployd it in carrying on a malting trade'.³ To be sure, not every steward used such means as these to fill his pockets; but, according to contemporary opinion, the number who did was far from small. '... there is hardly a little town or middling village in England,' declared an observer in 1766, 'where since the revolution of 1688, you do not see some scurvy petty fogger or other, start up and enrich himself at the expence of landed gentlemen by undertaking the management of their affairs.'⁴

IV

For the ranks of the hierarchy that lacked the steward's opportunities, during much of the period the principal supplement to wages was vails. A survival of an ancient form of largess, these fees, collected from the guests of a house, constituted a regular part of a servant's income. Before being engaged he was usually apprised of the amount of vails he could expect. Advertisements frequently included, along with other particulars of the place to be filled, a statement as to their approximate size.⁵ When this was not the

¹ Trusler, *London Adviser*, p. 49.
² Laurence, *Duty of a Steward*, p. 7.
³ *Letter Books of John Hervey*, III. 369.
⁴ V[ivant] d[e] M[ezague], *A General View of England*, 1766, p. 26.
⁵ See, for example, *Daily Advertiser*, 1747, No. 5185, Aug. 26, 3b; 1756, No. 8027, Oct. 4, 3c; 1757, No. 8200, Apr. 23, 3a; 1760, No. 9156,

case, the matter was discussed at the time of hiring, the master making clear how often he saw company and on what scale he entertained, the servant stipulating how much he hoped to realize.[1] Sometimes the master even went so far as to guarantee a certain sum.[2] Usually, however, the servant was content to take his chances as to what he would receive.

The distribution of vails generally took place just before a guest was to depart. The servants ranged themselves in two files flanking the door, and as the guest walked past he gave each of them an appropriate donation. Several considerations regulated the size of these presents. The nominal rank of the servant was taken into account: a steward received more than a butler and a butler more than a footman or groom. The social status of the master was also a determining factor. Vails, explained Baron de Pöllnitz, 'must be proportioned to the Rank of the Master of the House at whose Table you have sat. . . .'[3] And the French traveller Le Blanc wrote:

> ... il faut absolument donner à chaque Domestique, & cela plus ou moins selon son rang & celui de la Personne chez qui l'on est. Ils ont mis tous les Etats à contribution, & l'on pourroit s'y faire si du moins on en avoit le tarif. On sent bien qu'il n'est pas juste de traiter le Sommelier d'un Pair du Royaumme, comme celui du Chérif d'une petite Ville; mais comment apprécier les différences qui doivent s'observer entre ceux d'un Duc, d'un Comte, ou d'un Baron? Ce sont de ces choses qu' apparemment l'on ne peut apprendre que par une grande pratique du monde.[4]

Lastly, the actual service rendered influenced the amounts bestowed by the guests. In some houses, according to Hanway, the servants even adopted a fixed schedule of rates: so much to be paid by the guest for having taken breakfast, so much for having drunk tea, so much for having eaten dinner.[5]

May 13, 2c; 1761, No. 9581, Sept. 21, 3c; 1762, No. 9735, Mar. 19, 3a; 1765, No. 10655, Feb. 25, 2c.
[1] *London Magazine*, 1779, XLVIII. 16; Hanway, *Eight Letters*, p. 47.
[2] See, for example, *Daily Advertiser*, 1756, No. 7813, Jan. 28, 2c; 'Marchant Diary', *Sussex Archaeological Collections*, XXV. 175.
[3] *Memoirs of Charles Lewis, Baron de Pöllnitz*, 1737–8, II. 464.
[4] Le Blanc, *Lettres d'un François*, I. 148–9. Cf. *Gentleman's Magazine*, 1748, XVIII. 456; Hanway, *Eight Letters*, p. 27.
[5] Hanway, *Eight Letters*, p. 28.

There were homes in which only the menservants were entitled to vails, but as a rule all the members of the household shared in the visitors' bounty. Those whose duties kept them in the background usually received a percentage of the takings of those who had access to the guests. In some houses the servants themselves saw to it that each secured his proper share; in others all the vails were pooled, and the employer undertook to effect an equitable distribution. The practice at the second Lord Hardwicke's exemplifies the latter arrangement. 'Lady Grey', says Hutchinson, the American, in describing it, 'calls for all the money that has been left while in the country, and distributes it among the servants in proportion to their rank.'[1]

Even when forced to divide their profits in this way, servants regarded the system of supplementing wages by vails as eminently satisfactory; and their attitude is understandable. Not that the proceeds from vails were always very large. A footman's place advertised in 1762, for instance, paid annual wages of £8 but was worth only £2 in vails.[2] But the yield of vails might be considerable. A coachman's place advertised in 1760 as paying £10 a year in wages was valued at £6 in vails.[3] Still more remunerative in terms of vails was the footman's place for which the same advertiser sought a candidate. The wages offered were £8 *per annum*, the value of the vails exactly the same.[4] It was no uncommon thing, according to Grosley's observations, for a servant's vails thus to double his wages.[5] The consensus of opinion was that they sometimes even trebled or quadrupled them. It was with this abundant revenue from vails in mind that Dr. Shebbeare concluded 'the place of a domestic' to be 'a more considerable thing, than many small trades. . . .'[6]

To the employer class vails-giving was a much less agreeable institution than it was to servants. Many condemned it for the criticism it occasioned amongst visitors from other nations. 'It is well known', expostulated one sensitive writer, 'that we are extremely ridiculed and censured by foreigners on this account,

---

[1] *Diary and Letters of . . . Thomas Hutchinson*, II. 218.
[2] *Daily Advertiser*, 1762, No. 9682, Jan. 16, 3b.
[3] *Ibid.*, 1760, No. 9288, Oct. 14, 3a. [4] *Ibid.*
[5] Grosley, *Londres*, I. 132.
[6] Angeloni, *Letters on the English Nation*, II. 39. Cf. Hanway, *Eight Letters*, p. 39.

who compare every gentleman's house they visit to an inn, where they are obliged to pay their reckoning before they go away.'[1] Imbued with equal concern, another demanded:

> With what contempt must foreigners consider us, when they see the numerous and splendid train of servants attending on the Great, and reflect that not a fourth, perhaps not a tenth part of these fellows' income is supplied by the man whose livery they wear; the rest is raised by extorted contributions from his friends and guests?[2]

And Josiah Tucker complained that many foreigners would not visit England because they thought these exactions so outrageous.[3] Vails-giving was also condemned for its disruptive influence on social intercourse. The impositions it placed on guests were such that 'persons of small fortune could scarcely visit each other'; nor could they enter a great man's house 'but at an expence much greater than they could dine at a tavern with comfort and elegance'.[4] Baron de Pöllnitz in 1738 remarked on it disapprovingly as an impediment to visiting: '. . . if a Duke gives me a Dinner four Times a Week, his Footmen would pocket as much of my Money, as would serve my Expences at the Tavern for a Week.'[5] And later in the century Archenholz remembered how 'a visitor was obliged to distribute a great deal of money among the servants, when he dined with a man of quality: so that it was much cheaper to go to a tavern, than to accept such an invitation'.[6] But the effective barrier it presented to a man of moderate means appears most strikingly in an anecdote told by Saussure:

> My Lord Southwell stopped me one day in the park, and reproached me most amicably with my having let some time pass before going to his house to take soup with him. 'In truth, my lord,' I answered, 'I am not rich enough to take soup with you often.' His lordship understood my meaning and smiled.[7]

---

[1] *London Chronicle*, 1760, VII. 386b.

[2] *Ibid.*, 1760, VII. 260a. Cf. *Town and Country Magazine*, 1776, VIII. 201; Hanway, *Eight Letters*, pp. 43, 47.

[3] Josiah Tucker, *A Brief Essay on the Advantages and Disadvantages which Respectively Attend France and Great Britain with Regard to Trade*, 1753, 3rd ed., p. 47.

[4] *London Chronicle*, 1790, LXVII. 342c. Cf. *Public Advertiser*, 1768, No. 10534, Aug. 3, 4d.

[5] *Memoirs of . . . Baron de Pöllnitz*, II. 464–5.

[6] Archenholz, *Picture of England*, p. 207.

[7] Saussure, *Foreign View of England*, p. 194.

It was not only to people of modest circumstances, however, that vails-giving was a source of discomfort; the same tendency to decline invitations for fear of the costs existed in the very highest ranks. Queen Caroline said in the presence of Lord Hervey that because of the high vails demanded 'she had found it a pretty large expense . . . to visit her friends even in town'.[1]

Insults and ill-treatment were the certain rewards of those who failed to give generously. Their orders were likely to be ignored, their requests at table misunderstood. The serious plight of the guest whose meagre disbursements had earned him the enmity of his friends' servants is humorously set forth in a paper in the *World*:

> I am a marked man. If I ask for beer, I am presented with a piece of bread. If I am bold enough to call for wine, after a delay which would take away its relish were it good, I receive a mixture of the whole sideboard in a greasy glass. If I hold up my plate, nobody sees me; so that I am forced to eat mutton with fish sauce, and pickles with my apple-pye.[2]

Sometimes domestics repaid niggardliness in a more violent fashion. A guest whose gifts did not meet their expectations might find that his horse had been injured or might himself be subjected to some minor species of physical abuse. '. . . it is no uncommon language among servants,' declared a writer in 1767, 'when visitants pay not according to their wishes, Hang him scrubby rascal; but I'll take care to throw a plate of soup or boat of gravy upon his clothes, next time he comes. . . .'[3] Rather than run the risk of being treated in this way many preferred to remain at home.

But neither the criticism vails-giving evoked from continental visitors nor the check it imposed on social life was the prime cause for its condemnation. It incurred most disapproval for the bad effect it had upon servants. According to Hanway, by providing them with abundant funds over which the heads of families had no power, it 'wounded the *authority of masters*, created an impatience of *control*, and [sowed] the seeds of contempt of superiors'.[4] The independence that servants derived from vails

---

[1] John, Lord Hervey, *Some Materials towards Memoirs of the Reign of George II*, ed. Romney Sedgwick, 1931, II. 501.

[2] *World*, II. 50. Cf. Hanway, *Eight Letters*, p. 29.

[3] *London Chronicle*, 1767, XXI. 239a. Cf. [James Ridley,] *The Schemer*, 1763, p. 143.

[4] Hanway, *Reflections, Essays and Meditations*, I. 49.

likewise inspired Dr. Shebbeare to write: '... the domestic scarce conceives himself the menial servant of him who supplies him with his daily bread and apparel, and in general has very little good-will towards him.'[1] And a third critic of vails-giving expressed precisely the same opinion as to the principal evil arising from the practice:

> This custom has totally destroyed the reciprocal relation between master and servant, instituted by authority no less than divine. On whom does a servant where vails are taken depend, on his master? No, on the guests; as these increase the servant is willing to keep or leave his place. Can a master expect fidelity, love or gratitude, from a servant who is always grumbling when the house is not filled with vails-giving company; and lives with him with such uncertainty, that his staying or going from quarter to quarter depends merely on the number and disposition of the visitants?[2]

This sentiment against vails, militant enough before 1750 to produce sporadic efforts to uproot the custom, increased sharply in violence about the middle of the century. Vails-giving became a favourite subject of complaint for public spirited contributors to the press, and there was even talk of Parliament's suppressing it by legislation.[3] Men of prominence such as Lord Chesterfield, whose activities later led Archenholz to credit him with the destruction of the practice, and Jonas Hanway, the merchant-philanthropist, sought to awaken masters to its inconveniences and ill effects. Above all, Townley's *High Life Below Stairs*, by exposing 'to the opulent a part of their domestic economy that they had not before examined', brought out in bold relief the most undesirable aspects of vails-giving.[4] Defenders of the custom were not entirely lacking, some stressing its antiquity and distinctly English character,[5] others arguing that its abolition would be a stroke of the grossest meanness and that the proposed raising of wages would inadequately compensate servants for their loss.[6] But despite these protests, the feeling against vails-giving continued to mount.

So strong did it become that in 1757 the more resolute among

---

[1] Angeloni, *Letters on the English Nation*, II. 41.
[2] *London Chronicle*, 1767, XXI. 239ab.
[3] *Ibid.*, 1760, VII. 260a, 347a; 1762, XI. 164c.
[4] Pugh, *Life of Jonas Hanway*, p. 181.
[5] *London Chronicle*, 1760, VII. 202a, 260b; 1762, XI. 380a.
[6] *Ibid.*, 1760, VII. 347ab.

employers entered into an agreement to forbid their servants to accept vails, and during the following year the number of homes in which the practice was prohibited slowly increased. But these efforts at extirpation accomplished little. Vails-giving gradually reappeared.[1] Eventually, however, feeling against the practice crystallized into an organized movement to abolish it.

The movement to abolish vails had its origin in Scotland. Remedial measures were under general discussion there at least as early as 1757, when the Edinburgh Society for the Encouragement of Arts, Science, Manufactures, and Agriculture proposed as the topic for an essay: 'What is the proper method to abolish the practice of giving vails.'[2] But the initial steps were not taken until almost three years later. At the end of 1759 the freeholders and commissioners of the land tax for the county of Aberdeen resolved to do all in their power to discourage the practice and engaged neither to give vails nor to permit their domestics to receive them.[3] Within a month the Company of Scots Hunters at Edinburgh had followed their example.[4]

An event that occurred shortly after the adoption of these resolutions did much to accelerate the growth of the movement. The night Townley's *High Life Below Stairs* was to be given at Edinburgh, the managers of the playhouse received a menacing letter from a group of servants who had organized to prevent its performance. When the audience insisted that the piece be presented as scheduled, the servants in the gallery created so much noise and confusion that they finally had to be ejected.[5] These audacious acts deepened the widespread belief that much of the unsatisfactory conduct of servants was due to the custom of giving vails, and masters in and around Edinburgh hastened to effect its abolition. In the Capital such bodies as the Faculty of Advocates, the Select Society, the Clerks of the Signet, and the Scottish Masons declared against it; in the country a similar stand was taken by meetings of the freeholders.[6]

It was not long before the movement spread southward. The

---

[1] Grey, *Apology for the Servants*, p. 6.
[2] *Scots Magazine*, 1757, XIX. 164.
[3] *Ibid.*, 1759, XXI. 661; *Gentleman's Magazine*, 1760, XXX. 44; *London Chronicle*, 1760, VII. 62a.
[4] *Scots Magazine*, 1760, XXII. 42.
[5] *Ibid.*, 1760, XXII. 12–13, 42.   [6] *Ibid.*, 1760, XXII. 42, 43, 98.

Opera Club in London was perhaps the first to take up the cause.[1] But the freeholders of Cumberland, who united against vails in the summer of 1760, were also among the earliest adherents. The movement progressed much less rapidly in England, however, than in Scotland. A larger population made unanimity more difficult to achieve; prejudice caused many to oppose a reform that the Scots had been the first to introduce. Symptomatic of the slow rate of advance is the fact that, although individuals in all parts of the country promptly imitated their northern neighbours, by the middle of 1763 only in Cumberland, Westmorland, Northumberland, Lancashire, Yorkshire, and Devonshire had collective action been taken.

During the next few years, however, a good deal of ground was gained. One county after another fell into line, and a meeting of the nobility and gentry at Almack's in 1764 'unanimously determined neither to give nor allow any vails to servants'.[2] Even the wealthier London merchants joined in rooting out the custom. In 1767 Hanway could therefore say with some degree of accuracy that vails-giving had been 'nearly abolished'.[3]

Nevertheless, there long remained a considerable number of houses in which it continued to be practised. As late as 1778, Hutchinson, who described it as having been 'laid down almost everywhere', found that it was kept up at Lord Hardwicke's;[4] and some upper-class families continued to maintain it well into the nineteenth century.[5] Among the higher clergy and the judiciary it was especially tenacious.[6] In certain sections of the middle class it also lingered for a considerable time. Declaring in 1771 that vails-giving was 'not suffered in any genteel families', a writer made it clear that the custom was still quite prevalent among small merchants and tradesmen. He supposed, however, that 'fashion, and a reputation for politeness' would eventually 'bring over those vulgar families' that continued to preserve it.[7] His expectations were largely realized in time; but in 1785 the Rev. Trusler could

---

[1] Hanway, *Eight Letters*, p. 62.
[2] *London Chronicle*, 1764, XV. 479b.
[3] Hanway, *Letters on . . . the Rising Generation*, II. 159.
[4] *Diary and Letters of . . . Thomas Hutchinson*, II. 218.
[5] Smith, *Nollekens and His Times*, I. 348.
[6] *London Chronicle*, 1790, LXVII. 342c.
[7] *Oxford Magazine*, 1771, VI. 84.

still write: 'Though vails are abolished among the first class of people, they are not so among the second.'[1]

The inertia of employers was much to blame for the dilatory advance of the reform. But the fierce resistance of the servant class was even more responsible. From the first it reacted with open hostility. The Scottish resolutions of 1760 'raised a general mutiny among servants'; and 'many of them left their services all at once, and got into ships in order to come to London in quest of new places and vails. . . .'[2] Those who remained behind expressed their resentment by treating their masters' guests with studied discourtesy. A gentleman from Renfrew described their attitude in 1761:

> I can assure you, from my own experience, and from what I hear every day told happening to others, who as often visit the Nobility and Gentlemen of the counties around, that by the servants not now receiving vails, most people, who have not always their own servants attending them on such visits, are very badly used. . . . In short, they [servants] have fallen on every step that can be thought on, to show the Gentlemen their error in abolishing their vails. . . .[3]

When the reform was introduced in England, it met with similar opposition. Servants grumbled, grew insolent and, in not a few instances, quit their masters to serve others who would permit them to accept vails. It required fortitude to challenge this fractious spirit; and there were not many masters like Major John Cartwright's father, who unhesitatingly made the first move to ban vails in Norfolk, even though 'it was expected that the attempt would be attended with very unpleasant consequences'.[4] In most households the reform was initiated cautiously; grave misgivings were entertained as to how it would go down. It was with a sense of relief that Mrs. Harris wrote to her son, the first Earl of Malmesbury: 'Mr. Harris has settled with his men servants the *grand affair* of vails, . . . it went off better than I expected.'[5] But even when vails-giving had been successfully abolished, all cause for apprehension did not disappear. Commenting on a sumptuous

---

[1] [John Trusler,] *Modern Times*, 1785, 2nd ed., III. 46.
[2] *London Chronicle*, 1762, XI. 164c.
[3] *Lloyd's Evening Post*, 1761, VIII. 55ab.
[4] Frances D. Cartwright, *The Life and Correspondence of Major Cartwright*, 1826, I. 3.
[5] *Letters of the First Earl of Malmesbury*, I. 113.

Michaelmas dinner at his patron's, the Rev. Stotherd Abdy says in his journal: 'I am afraid indeed as to the inferior order of Domesticks, so much goose eating served only to put them in mind of the *want* of money, and to revive some of their *good-natured reflexions* upon the *Loss of Vails*.'[1]

The mood of the servants in London was particularly ugly. In 1761, when action was first taken against vails, an admiral's valet, out of pique, cut to pieces the hat of a guest; and upon examination 'A bottle of aqua fortis was found in his room, which he intended to sprinkle on the cloaths of gentlemen and ladies that visited his master'.[2] About the same time Sir Francis Dashwood, one of the leading opponents of vails-giving, was threatened with death by an enraged domestic:

> Sir Frans Dashwood I have taken this hoper tunet to a Quent You That if Yo do go hon as You do You sartenly lose Your Life and that black that Lord Northampton and some more that I have not mentioned for when you go to dine You go hout hand neare leaves won farthing nor wont let Your Sarvants tak One farthen for if You dont leave of You sarten shall have a dose of Leden Piils and tha hare vere hard to digest for if Sarvants has but nine Pounds tha cannot Ceep a Wife and Femele. For You must bild Work Houses and Cep Them but You will not live to see them bilt for I wod have Yout be all wase prepared for Deth for You do se thare is nothing but robin upon the hi Way and that is o caisened by no thing Else but by Starven the Poore Sarvants and so you must concider a bout this a fare for Dam You You shall suffer and hall such Blacks and more such Blacks as Youer selfe and so I am Youer and be damd.[3]

Three years later, when the movement against vails had acquired wide support in the Metropolis, hot-heads among the servants resorted to violence in an effort to intimidate those masters who had instituted the reform. In a letter dated May 10, 1764 Mrs. Harris told her son how there had been 'Great riots at Ranelagh among those *beings*, the footmen'. She wrote: 'It began Friday when three were taken into custody; but on asking pardon, they were discharged. Last night it was more violent, and there was fighting with drawn swords, for some hours; they broke one chariot

---

[1] Alice A. Houblon, *The Houblon Family*, 1907, II. 144-5.
[2] *London Chronicle*, 1761, IX. 230c.
[3] *Ibid.*, 1761, X. 483ab; *London Magazine*, 1761, XXX. 610. See also *London Chronicle*, 1761, IX. 230bc.

all to pieces; six are now in custody.'[1] And on May 12 she wrote of 'another riot, much more considerable than the former ones'.[2] Horace Walpole hints cryptically that the bad humour of the servant class at this time could easily have led to bloodshed and 'civil commotions'.[3]

But formidable as resistance to the movement was, it could do little more than retard the spread of the reform. Those who sought to outlaw vails never ceased to gain adherents. In consequence, when Archenholz visited England about 1780 he found vails-giving almost entirely abandoned;[4] some five years later Richard Cumberland, diplomat and playwright, listed its abolition as one of the improvements of the times;[5] and in 1788 Hannah More, descanting on the evils of card money, pointed to the disappearance of vails as evidence of what could be effected by the example of the élite.[6]

V

Although vails were eliminated as a source of income during the last quarter of the century, there was another tax on visiting that continued to flourish in that period. The playing cards, and sometimes the candles, used when the master of the house entertained were supplied by the footman, the butler, or the groom of the chambers and were paid for by the guests. The usual procedure was for the host to inform the company how much he had agreed to allow the servant or servants who were to provide the cards. This amount—always well in advance of the actual cost—was then placed under the candlesticks on the card tables as new packs were needed.

It is only necessary to recall that card-playing was the favourite diversion of the age in order to realize that this practice yielded considerable returns. Most upper- and middle-class houses prob-

---

[1] *Letters of the First Earl of Malmesbury*, I. 108. Cf. *Gentleman's Magazine*, 1764, XXXIV. 247; *Annual Register*, 1764, VII. 74–5.
[2] *Letters of the First Earl of Malmesbury*, I. 109.
[3] Horace Walpole, *Memoirs of the Reign of King George the Third*, ed. Sir Denis Le Marchant, 1845, II. 2–3.
[4] Archenholz, *Picture of England*, p. 207.
[5] Richard Cumberland, *The Observer*, 1788, IV. 10.
[6] Hannah More, 'Thoughts on the Importance of the Manners of the Great', *The Works of Hannah More*, 1830, XI. 22.

ably bore a strong resemblance to the one of which Hutchinson wrote: 'At Lord Barrington's they play a shilling a game or corner, and pay for cards. He says everybody that plays is a loser at the year's end. His butler is the only person who gains. . . .'[1]

As a source of great profit to servants card money came under heavy fire at the same time as vails. It was denounced as a nuisance and as an inexcusable violation of ordinary hospitality, and employers were severely blamed for allowing it to exist. In 1760 'A Country Gentleman', after proposing that it be dropped, laid its continuance to 'no other motive, but a pitiful avarice in the masters'. He went on to suggest sarcastically that if it were retained, the cook might just as well be permitted to provide the butcher's meat, the gamekeeper the venison, the butler the liquors, the coachman the oats, and the groom the hay. At the departure of the guests, he suggested, the reckoning could then be called for; and the master could 'collect the several quotas according to the established rate'.[2] Another irate enemy of card money even went so far as to insinuate that some employers shared the proceeds with their domestics.[3]

As in the case of vails, however, the opposition to card money arose principally from the belief that by unduly enriching servants it tended to lessen their dependence on their masters. '. . . it serves,' said a writer eager to see its suppression,

> only to supply fuel for the unruly passions of a set of pampered fellows, whose matchless impudence and debauched idle behaviour, have been long a well-grounded complaint; the depriving them of it would therefore be doing good; it would be giving a check to their vices and insolence; and also would make them more obedient to their masters and mistresses, which they greatly want. . . .[4]

A serious attempt to do away with it was made in 1760, when several upper-class employers agreed that all card money collected during the year be donated for the relief of English soldiers disabled in Germany. The manner in which this agreement was carried out at a young lady's debut was described at the time by one of the guests. She reported

> that after the usual ceremonies she sat down to cards, when looking to the candlesticks she saw a card hung to each with these words (no

---

[1] *Diary and Letters of . . . Thomas Hutchinson*, I. 250.
[2] *London Chronicle*, 1760, VII. 260b.
[3] *Ibid.*, 1762, XI. 380b.   [4] *Ibid.*, 1760, VII. 100b.

card money, but you may speak to the drummer) and on looking about she perceived the figure of a drummer in wood standing on a box with a hole in the top to receive money, and the figure held a paper in its hand containing, a supposed dialogue between Dick and John, two of the lady's servants; wherein they mutually agreed, that their wages being full sufficient to defray all their reasonable demands, to dispose of the card money as a token of their regard to the Minden heroes. . . .[1]

The appearance later on of advertisements in which prospective candidates were informed that they need expect no card money strongly suggests that the movement was not confined to a small circle or a single year.[2]

But whatever the strength and duration of the movement, card money survived. When Hutchinson visited England in 1774, he noted in his diary: '. . . the custom is kept up for each person to pay 18d for cards when they play with two packs, and a shilling when with one.'[3] And Hannah More found it still necessary to arraign card money more than a decade later.[4]

VI

Admittance fees formed another tariff that, along with card money, visitors were made to bear throughout the period. They were exacted under varying circumstances, but their existence was almost universal.

A toll on callers was levied by the porter in large houses, by the footman or maid who attended the door in small ones; and it was almost impossible to gain entree without paying out the requisite amount. Saussure makes this plain in his account of England: 'If you wish to pay your respects to a nobleman and to visit him, you must give his porter money from time to time, else his master will never be at home to you.'[5] And Letitia Pilkington comments with acerbity on the callousness and avarice of the average porter: 'If you have the smallest suit to make to his master, the fellow

---

[1] *London Chronicle*, 1760, VII. 159a.
[2] See, for example, *Daily Advertiser*, 1763, No. 10278, Dec. 13, 3c; 1768, No. 11597, Feb. 29, 2c; 1769, No. 11962, Apr. 29, 2c.
[3] *Diary and Letters of . . . Thomas Hutchinson*, I. 250.
[4] More, 'Thoughts on the Importance of the Manners of the Great', *Works*, XI. 20–1.
[5] Saussure, *Foreign View of England*, p. 194.

will be as dull of apprehension as the Mock Doctor, till you tip him the symptoms. . . .'[1] The case was not overstated, then, by a writer who in 1762 declared that people of rank and fortune had, in a sense, become the property of their servants, who either concealed them or exposed them to view at arbitary rates.[2]

Fees similar to those imposed upon callers were collected from tourists. Gentlemen's seats with their picture galleries and gardens were centres of interest both for the ordinary traveller and the man of taste. Road maps seldom failed to indicate their location, and even so serious-minded a guide as Defoe mentions those most worthy of inspection. The interiors were usually exhibited as well as the grounds, and certain servants were assigned the task of showing tourists about. Those who performed this duty were rewarded with gratuities by the visitors they attended. In some of the great show places all or part of the take was turned over to the master to be used in defraying household expenses, especially those occasioned by the crowds of tourists. This practice was followed, for example, at Cannons.[3] But in most houses the servants who took the visitors through pocketed the proceeds.

There is good reason to believe that the proceeds were often substantial. The fees were high. John Byng, a gentleman who on frequent jaunts about the country seldom passed up an opportunity to examine an imposing pile or an unusual garden, was loud in his complaints of the costs of such visits. After viewing the seat of the dukes of Marlborough, he set down in his diary: '. . . The expence of seeing Blenheim is very great; the servants of the poor D—— of M being very attentive in gleaning money from rich travellers.' Of his visit to the grounds at Chatsworth he wrote: 'Seeing this little of garden, cost us much money; because we were shewn about by a wou'd be gentleman, and felt ourselves to be really so.'[4] When a house held sufficient interest to attract a great many like Byng, those who showed it reaped handsome returns. At Strawberry Hill, for instance, the housekeeper collected so

[1] *Memoirs of Mrs. Letitia Pilkington, 1712–1750*, ed. Iris Barry, New York, 1928, p. 378.
[2] *London Chronicle*, 1762, XI. 164b. Cf. *Gentleman's Magazine*, 1734, IV. 131.
[3] Baker, *James Brydges First Duke of Chandos*, pp. 181–2.
[4] *Torrington Diaries*, I. 53; II. 37. Cf. Arthur Young, *A Six Weeks' Tour through the Southern Counties*, 1769, p. 128; Austin, *Letters from London*, p. 260.

much money from the droves of people who came to see the house that Walpole jested that he ought to marry her and so recoup himself for the sums he had laid out on the place.¹ At Cannons, another mecca for tourists, the Groom of the Chambers, who had the privilege of showing the inside, took in an average of £38 a year between 1732 and 1736; and this was some time after the heyday of public interest in the house.² Dr. Shebbeare, then, was guilty of exaggeration rather than invention when, discussing the fees collected from tourists at country houses, he contended that 'by this means a domestic in many families has as good an employment as many at court; and as much money has been paid for the seeing of many houses, as they have cost building'.³

VII

Just as visitors contributed to the income of servants by giving vails, card money, and admittance fees, shopkeepers contributed by paying commissions and by handing out Christmas gifts. These benefactions were designed to secure the patronage of those servants who did the purchasing for their employers. The business that such servants brought in was considerable, and they held the whip over shopkeepers by favouring those who gave them fees and avoiding those who did not. 'There is not one Tradesman to be named,' wrote a pamphleteer, 'but is dependent on these Wretches to procure and continue them a Nobleman's custom. . . .'⁴

The commissions that shopkeepers were thus compelled to grant were known as poundage. The term is self-explanatory. A percentage of the monthly or yearly bill was allowed the purchaser for every pound's worth of merchandise he ordered.

The practice of taking poundage lent itself to grave abuses. In return for a good rate of poundage servants often connived at their employers being overcharged.⁵ To increase their poundage they often bought much more lavishly than necessity demanded.⁶

---

[1] *Letters of Horace Walpole*, XIII. 39.
[2] Baker, *James Brydges First Duke of Chandos*, p. 182.
[3] Angeloni, *Letters on the English Nation*, I. 93.
[4] *Treatise on the Use and Abuse of the Second . . . Table*, p. 33.
[5] [John Scott,] *Observations on the Present State of the Poor*, 1773, p. 121*n*; Gisborne, *An Enquiry into the Duties of Men*, II. 498–9*n*.
[6] Gisborne, *An Enquiry into the Duties of Men*, II. 499*n*.

These abuses swelled the yield of what in any case must have been an important source of income. Its consequence is attested by Hanway's mouthpiece, Thomas Trueman, who, referring to employers, observes: 'By *them* we *gain* no more than the *regular wages* we receive; and this is reckoned as a thing of course; whereas our *profits* arise from a *right understanding* with their *Tradesmen*. . . .'[1]

Whether or not a servant was granted poundage, he usually received a Christmas gift from each of the shopkeepers with whom he dealt. The practice of giving these Christmas boxes was of ancient origin, and servants tended to regard them as something they might expect by right. Their attitude is exemplified by an incident that occurred in 1771. In that year the London grocers entered into an agreement not to give Christmas boxes, whereupon 'the female servants, from the Lady's maid down to the Cook', retaliated by resolving 'to drink no more tea'.[2]

Christmas boxes occasioned the same sort of outcry that was raised against vails and card money. They were spoken of as bribes intended to undermine the honesty of servants.[3] The money, it was said, generally went 'to the idle and disorderly' and was therefore 'productive of much mischief'.[4] One newspaper correspondent even claimed that if the giving of Christmas boxes were to be abandoned, 'it would have no small effect towards bringing about a general reformation of manners among the lower sort of people. . . .'[5] Evidently the sums given out as Christmas boxes were generous. For at the root of the clamour lay the conviction that a full purse made a servant too independent.

VIII

Besides the income from wages and from the various sources that supplemented them, service provided the possibility of other rewards. Paternal feeling nourished a generosity in employers that was often expressed in the form of legacies and gifts. These benefactions varied greatly in size. The determinants of this variation

[1] Hanway, *Sentiments and Advice of Thomas Trueman*, p. 34.
[2] *London Chronicle*, 1771, xxx. 632b.
[3] *An Enquiry into the Melancholy Circumstances of Great Britain*, n.d., p. 30.
[4] *General Advertiser*, 1779, No. 843, Dec. 16, 3c.
[5] *London Packet*, 1774, No. 807, Dec. 21–3, 3cd.

THE REWARDS OF SERVICE

included the rank of the servant, the length of his service, the degree of satisfaction he gave, the attachment he inspired, and, of course, the circumstances of his master. Although the causes were not as readily identifiable, the benefactions of employers also varied in form.

A legacy was frequently left as a lump sum. Richard Orlebar willed £5 to each of his servants in 1729.[1] In 1741 Sir Francis Page left £10 to each servant who had lived with him a year.[2] And Jonas Hanway, who died in 1786, left two servants £10 each.[3] These amounts, although respectable enough by the standards of the time, by no means represent the maximum liberality of outright bequests. In some instances hundreds and even thousands of pounds were left as legacies. When Sir Richard Lyttleton died in 1770, he bequeathed one of his servants £500.[4] The bequests left by Lord Berkeley in 1773 included £600 to his gentleman-in-waiting, £500 to his valet, £500 to his housekeeper, and £200 to each of his two stewards.[5] General Pultney left £1,000 a piece to his steward and valet in 1767.[6] And Sarah, Duchess of Marlborough, who died in 1744, left £15,000 to her lady's maid.[7]

A servant was often left an annuity rather than a bequest in this form. Dr. William Gibbons left £20 a year to one of his domestics in 1728.[8] Alderman Beckford, whose death occurred in 1770, was reported to have left £25 a year to one servant and £10 a year to each of two others.[9] And Admiral Forbes was said to have left his housekeeper and two other members of his household annuities of £30 each in 1796.[10] Such bequests were designed to insure subsistence (for a single person) and they did no more. Some annuities, however, were large enough to provide a life of comfort; and still others permitted even a degree of luxury. When in 1784 Dr. Johnson inquired what the proper amount to leave a favourite

---

[1] Orlebar, *Orlebar Chronicles*, I. 279.
[2] Brooks, *Steeple Ashton and Middle Ashton*, p. 231.
[3] Pugh, *Life of Jonas Hanway*, p. 257.
[4] *The Grenville Papers*, ed. William J. Smith, 1852–3, IV. 528.
[5] *London Magazine*, 1773, XLII. 255.
[6] Peake, *Memoirs of the Colman Family*, p. 208.
[7] Colville, *Duchess Sarah*, p. 373.
[8] Gerald P. Mander, *The Wolverhampton Antiquary*, Wolverhampton, 1903, I. 110.
[9] *Middlesex Journal*, 1770, No. 205, July 21–4, 2b.
[10] *London Chronicle*, 1796, LXXIX. 272c.

PECUNIARY PROFITS

servant was, he was told that in the case of a nobleman £50 a year was considered an adequate reward for many years of service.[1] Throughout the period, however, there were noblemen and commoners alike whose liberality dwarfed that figure. The Duchess of Marlborough, for instance, left her housekeeper, butler, and head housemaid each £200 a year.[2] Lt.-Gen. John Huske left his valet an annuity of £200 in 1760.[3] And the Duke of Queensberry, who died in 1810, left his head groom, his confectioner, and one of his footmen each £200 a year, while he left his valet £300 a year.[4]

Employers did not always wait until they died to bestow annuities on deserving servants. When John Baker disbanded his establishment preparatory to taking lodgings, he dismissed his housekeeper, granting her at the same time a life pension of £21 a year.[5] Similarly, the Duke of Kingston allowed his master of the horse £60 a year when that official retired after years of service.[6]

Sometimes instead of supplying the funds for an annuity himself, an employer through the exertion of influence got his servant a government sinecure. When this was the case, the servant, having hired a deputy who would discharge the duties of the post for a fraction of the salary, either retired or entered some occupation other than service. An illuminating account of the whole practice appeared in a London newspaper in 1780. 'Investigator,' who contributed the piece, asserts that 'The Lords of the Treasury, through their influence, get their servants appointed to places, and as soon as they are initiated, procure them leave of absence, for a whole year, at the expiration of that for another, &c.'. As an example he cites Lord North's valet, who, he claims, has a post in the Customs that will bring him £100 a year for life; and this, he says, is but one case out of many. He goes on to concede that old and faithful servants are 'intitled to such places', since they ought to be put 'out of the reach of want'. But he insists that they ought to 'do the duties of office, if capable, and not saddle the nation with a substitute'.[7] 'Investigator' singles out the Lords of the Treasury for criticism, but they were by no means the only offenders. Nor was the Customs the sole quarter where sinecures

[1] Hawkins, *Life of Samuel Johnson*, p. 582.
[2] Colville, *Duchess Sarah*, p. 373.   [3] *London Chronicle*, 1760, ix. 77.
[4] Jesse, *George Selwyn*, 1. 208–9.   [5] *Diary of John Baker*, p. 36.
[6] Whitehead, *Original Anecdotes*, p. 130.
[7] *London Courant*, 1780, May 3, 2c.

THE REWARDS OF SERVICE

were obtained. The place of stamper in the Stamp Office, for instance, was regularly used to provide for servants, until the younger Pitt put a stop to the practice.[1] Joseph Addison, for example, secured a place as stamper for one of his servants.[2] Byng took care of a favourite groom in the same way.[3]

[1] N[athaniel] W. Wraxall, *Historical Memoirs of His Own Time*, 1836, IV. 463, 464.
[2] *The Letters of Joseph Addison*, ed. Walter Graham, Oxford, 1941, p. 299.
[3] *Torrington Diaries*, II. 305n.

Chapter Seven

THE REWARDS OF SERVICE: SOCIAL ADVANCEMENT

IF service could mean a comfortable and protected existence, and an opportunity to acquire a competence, it also functioned as a path for social ascent. Many who enlisted in its ranks were thereby enabled to improve their social status, some rising a few degrees in the social scale, others radically altering their condition.

I

In order to trace the process of ascension it is necessary to define the standing of service as an occupation. The limitations of the available material and the presence of certain ambiguities in the hierarchy of occupations itself make it impossible to do this with precision, but it can be done in a general way.

Enough contemporary comment has survived to indicate that, on the whole, service was considered a somewhat demeaning occupation. A certain stigma attached to much of the servant class. The readiness with which both men and women became domestics, however, testifies to the stigma's mildness. So, too, does the general tone of the group. There appears to have been none of the gloomy discontent, none of the acute sense of degradation or personal indignity so common among servants in more recent times.[1] Austin, who visited England in the opening years of the nineteenth

---

[1] For the attitude of the twentieth-century domestic toward service see Violet M. Firth, *The Psychology of the Servant Problem*, [1925,] pp. 18–19, 21, 31–2; *The Report of the Committee Appointed to Enquire into the Present Condition as to the Supply of Female Domestic Servants*, pp. 15–16; Elaine Burton, *Domestic Work*, [1944,] p. 4.

century, observed of the London footmen: '. . . these people wear the appearance of the most perfect contentment. They are pleased with their party coloured clothes, and never seem more happy than when they expose themselves to the public.'[1] And Silliman, who came a few years later, commented with surprise on the complacency of servants in general. 'In England', he wrote, 'the servant is contented with his condition.'[2] Had these American travellers come fifty or a hundred years earlier, they undoubtedly would have carried away the same impression. But, however mild it may have been, a stigma did exist.

It derived, in part, from the nature of the servant's social role. The real or imagined importance of an occupation for the subsistence and survival of the society in which it exists is one of the factors responsible for its standing.[3] In eighteenth-century England servants were looked upon as valueless to the community, as people who contributed little or nothing to the common welfare. This view was given expression time and again in the incidental remarks of writers concerned with divers subjects. In 1767 Nathaniel Forster called attention to 'the numbers of servants . . . of both sexes entertained in gentlemen's families; who consume without mercy the produce of the state, with very little return of advantageous labour. . . .'[4] Terming the whole class 'an unnecessary set of people in their present capacity', a 'Yorkshire Tradesman' pointed out in 1772 that they 'might be made very useful in other stations in life'.[5] And in 1784 another writer referred to them 'as drones in the hive, consuming the produce of others' labour and industry without contributing anything thereto. . . .'[6] As the most conspicuously idle of domestics, livery servants were sometimes singled out for comment. In 1743, for example, a contributor to

---

[1] Austin, *Letters from London*, p. 274.
[2] Silliman, *Journal of Travels*, I. 87.
[3] Kingsley Davis and Wilbert E. Moore, 'Some Principles of Stratification', *American Sociological Review*, 1945, x. 243–4; Pitirim A. Sorokin, *Social Mobility*, New York and London, 1927, p. 100.
[4] [Nathaniel Forster,] *An Enquiry into the Causes of the Present High Price of Provisions*, 1767, p. 45.
[5] *London Chronicle*, 1772, XXXI. 421c.
[6] *Heads of a Plan*, p. 47. Cf. *London Chronicle*, 1766, XX. 560b; *An Address to the Gentry of the County of Durham*, Newcastle, 1779, pp. 19–20; [John Gray,] *A Plan for Finally Settling the Government of Ireland*, 1785, p. 20; *Manufactures Improper Subjects of Taxation*, p. 12.

the *Champion* voiced regret at finding so many husky young men living the unproductive life of a footman:

> When I see four or five able Fellows swinging behind a gilt Chariot, and reflect, that they have no other Business to do than what, perhaps, might be better undone; that they are . . . of so little Use to Society, that in the Course of their whole Lives not one of them adds a *Shilling* to the publick *Stock*, I am grieved to see *Englishmen* in such a Situation.[1]

This being the general attitude, servants naturally enjoyed anything but a high repute.

Another source of the stigma they bore was the generally accepted theory of the relationship of master and servant. The servant, as has been shown, was viewed as a person who had temporarily relinquished his freedom; his position was conceived to be but a step or two removed from serfdom. In consequence, there attached to him at least a modicum of the ignominy that invariably attaches to the unfree. Thus the author of the piece in the *Champion* quoted above maintained that servants were 'so far Slaves, as to make a part of the Equipage of their Masters. . . .'[2] And a newspaper correspondent in 1757 roundly declared: 'I consider an Englishman in Livery, as a kind of Monster. He is a Person born free, with the obvious Badge of Servility, and I should think myself in better Company with the Farmer's Servant who buys his own Clothes. . . .'[3] An interesting rejoinder to these remarks, signed 'R. D.' and almost certainly by Robert Dodsley,[4] appeared in the same newspaper later in the year. The writer argues that 'the Necessity of the subordinate Ranks, Conditions, and Offices of Men, sufficiently obviates the Dishonour and Disgrace of Servitude'. Yet he reluctantly admits that 'a Livery Suit may indeed fitly be called a Badge of Servility'.[5]

A great many servants, however, entirely escaped the stigma. Those who served the nobility and the gentry were free of all taint. This is made quite clear by Hanway when he writes: '. . . I

---

[1] Quoted in *Gentleman's Magazine*, 1743, XIII. 433. Cf. *Lloyd's Evening Post*, 1780, XLVI. 307c; [John Feltham,] *A Picture of London for 1803*, 1803, pp. 273–4.
[2] Quoted in *Gentleman's Magazine*, 1743, XIII. 433.
[3] *London Chronicle*, 1757, II. 468c.
[4] Ralph Straus, *Robert Dodsley*, 1910, p. 388.
[5] *London Chronicle*, 1757, II. 612c.

do not think that the Domestic in a *private livery*, is equal in office to a *husbandman* or a *mechanic*. On the other hand, the servant who is near the person of a Nobleman, or a Gentleman, . . . derives an importance from it which renders him respectable. . . .'¹

The respectability of such servants was mirrored in their bearing towards those engaged in other occupations. They had neither the humility nor the diffidence normally characteristic of a despised group; rather, their manner was uniformly haughty, and their actions were often insolent in the extreme. '. . . we find them', says an anonymous author, 'so puffed up with Pride and Insolence, that it is no uncommon thing to see a good Tradesman, nay, sometimes People of Superior Rank, cringing to a saucy Lacky. . . .'² A satirical essay entitled *Below Stairs*, which was published in 1792, effectively reproduces their lofty attitude. Speaking of a grocer, a lady's maid says in Slipslop manner: 'Such low people are beneath our attention; though some of them have the *frontery* to put themselves upon a footing with a nobleman's attendant, or a gentleman's servant.' And she continues by remarking:

> We sometimes condescend indeed to talk with them in familiar terms, as if they were our equals, and this has encouraged them to be arrogant. That enormous mass of a woman, our butcher's wife in St. James's market, accosts me with as much freedom, and as little *emberassment* as if she had belonged to a family of rank as well as myself. But I always discountenance such people and convince them that I know how to support the *spear* of life to which my stars have elevated me.³

To be sure, much of this hauteur originated in the servant's close identification with the social status of his employer, a fact with which contemporary observers were fully cognizant. A writer discoursing in 1767 on 'The insolence . . . so much complained of among noblemen's servants' asserted: '. . . a consciousness of the dignity of the noble personage they serve . . . naturally make[s] them arrogant and proud.'⁴ And in 1782 the perceptive Vicesimus Knox saw their conduct in the same light: 'They assume a share

---

¹ Hanway, *Eight Letters*, p. 59. Cf. *London Chronicle*, 1765, XVII. 459a.
² *An Enquiry into the Melancholy Circumstances of Great Britain*, p. 21. Cf. [John Corry,] *A Satirical Review of London at the Commencement of the Nineteenth Century*, 1801, p. 79.
³ *Carlton House Magazine*, 1792, I. 163.
⁴ *Court Miscellany*, 1767, III. 413.

SOCIAL ADVANCEMENT

of the grandeur from the rank of their masters, and think themselves intitled to domineer over their equals, and to ridicule their superiors.'[1] But equally important as a cause of their arrogance was the prestige that the social status of their employers conferred upon them in the eyes of the general public. They were proud because they were respected.

The quantum of respect naturally varied with the nominal rank of the domestic. The duke's valet was held in greater esteem than his footman. Among the servants employed by the middle classes the same sort of variations prevailed.

In the hierarchy of occupations, then, service stood neither wholly above nor wholly below such employments as keeping a shop or working as an artisan. There was considerable overlapping. While, as Hanway observed, the social status of the lower domestics who served the nobility and gentry was superior to that of the mechanic and the servant or labourer in husbandry, the social status of the lower domestics in middle-class families was not. Again, while the social status of the upper servants employed by the nobility and gentry was superior to that of the small tradesman, the social status of those employed by the middle classes probably was not.

II

From the foregoing analysis it is apparent that in itself entrance into service might or might not bring an improvement in social status, depending chiefly on the provenance of the servant, his nominal rank, and the social status of his employer. The clergyman's widow or the merchant's daughter whom circumstances forced to serve as housekeeper in a middle-class family suffered a distinct loss of prestige. On the other hand, the girl from the parish poorhouse who became a maid in a tradesman's home and the farmer's son who became footman to a duke undoubtedly improved their condition.

The domestic's initial place did not necessarily fix his social status for the duration of his career in service. He could rise by receiving promotion in the family in which he served or by exchanging his employer for one more elevated in the social scale.

Promotion was frequently given in order to fill a vacant post; it

[1] *London Chronicle*, 1782, LII. 287a.

was often the easiest method of securing a servant with the experience that was necessary for so many household offices. A domestic might learn outside of service how to discharge the mechanical part of his duties, but practice was often the only way he could perfect himself in the elaborate system of forms that had to be observed when those duties were carried out. Ineptitude would imply that his master could not afford to engage a well-trained servant; that is, it would argue an inability to pay for the consumption of time and effort required for the preparation of such a servitor. More often than not, then, the awkward servant was wholly unacceptable. A letter written by Mrs. Montagu in 1745 perfectly illustrates the impatience with which his deficiencies were likely to be regarded. 'The servant I part with', she explains, 'is very honest, but I cannot bring him to deliver his sincerity in such delicate terms as are necessary in a message. He told a lady of quality who inquired after my health, that I was *pure stout*, and if I am in good spirits he tells people I am *brave*. . . .'[1] To avoid such maladroitness the common practice was to choose some servant who was already a member of the staff, train him for the post to be filled and then, after a brief novitiate, advance him permanently to that position.

Such preferment was also customarily given as a reward for satisfactory and extended service. The servant who acquitted himself well over a period of years was likely to be advanced to a higher post. Had it been otherwise, during the controversy over vails Hanway could hardly have named 'greater *promotion*' as one of the compensatory benefits domestics would probably receive if those gratuities were abolished.[2]

A single promotion might raise a servant several degrees in the scale of rank. In giving an account of Elizabeth Chudleigh's domestic machinations after her marriage to the Duke of Kingston, Thomas Whitehead, who was at one time His Grace's valet, presents a number of examples. He tells how Thomas Philips, the butler, was made steward of one of the Duke's estates; how Williams, a footman, was raised to the position of butler; how one Dicks, who had been a gardener, was made a bailiff.[3]

Transitions such as that of Williams, from the lower ranks of the

---

[1] *Elizabeth Montagu*, I. 225.
[2] Hanway, *Sentiments and Advice of Thomas Trueman*, p. 30.
[3] Whitehead, *Original Anecdotes*, pp. 79, 159, 171.

hierarchy to the upper, were not unusual. A mock petition purporting to have been drawn up by a group of waiting-women who sought the right to be styled 'ladies', just as valets were called 'gentlemen', plaintively observed: "The most pitiful, paltry, insignificant fellows in being, can get a Livery on their backs; and by a subordinate obedience, some insinuation, and great compliance, do very often get themselves promoted to the second table out of livery...."[1] An essay in a series entitled the *Whimsical Philosopher* confirms this observation. Describing how the nobility and gentry chose their servants in medieval times, it asserts approvingly: 'No fawning or pimping footman could then expect to become an upper servant in a great family....'[2] The implied contrast with the eighteenth century is, of course, unmistakable. Further confirmation is supplied by the highly critical remarks of a newspaper correspondent who signed himself 'Clytus'. He assails the practice of 'setting some minion to the government of the house, brought from the most servile drudgery, and without the least education, more than barely writing his name'. How is it possible, he asks,

> to suppose such a person, assisted by a female ... who never studied anything beyond the use of the mop and duster (set aside airs and impertinence) should be able to dispose a family of thirty, forty or fifty servants, in that good order which should rendound honour and give a grace to dignity.

The badness of upper servants, he contends, is due largely to the fact that they are frequently persons who have been promoted from the lower staff; and he comments with surprise 'that these promotions are rewards of a disposition which all gentlemen seem to hold in the utmost contempt'.[3]

The promotion that elevated a servant to the upper staff sometimes came after he had risen by slow stages through the ranks of the lower household; sometimes, too, it proved but the prelude to further advancement. In fact, it was by no means uncommon for a servant who remained in the same family for a considerable time to rise gradually from a lowly office to one of the most exalted in the hierarchy. The case of Nancy Bere is typical. Taken from the local poorhouse by the Hackmans of Lymington to be a weeder in

---

[1] *London Chronicle*, 1765, XVII. 434b. Cf. *ibid.*, 1760, VII. 196b.
[2] *London Magazine*, 1750, XIX. 557.
[3] *London Chronicle*, 1765, XVII. 459ab.

their garden, Nancy Bere was later employed by them as a kitchen maid. She evidently discharged her duties in that capacity satisfactorily; for in time Mrs. Hackman preferred her to the post of lady's maid, having first 'had her carefully instructed in all the elementary branches of education'.[1] Very similar was the ascent of a boy employed in the establishment of the younger Pitt. Beginning his rise as a helper in the stables, he was next made under-groom, then 'taken to town to wait on the upper servants', 'afterwards made a footman', and eventually promoted to the post of valet.[2] A news item published in 1757 mentions yet another case of the same order: the rise of a stable boy 'in a certain Nobleman's Service' to the office of butler.[3]

Even the position of land steward, as John Mordant makes clear, was frequently attained by servants who rose in this manner. Discussing some of the errors into which the owners of estates commonly fall, Mordant cautions against 'that of advancing *menial servants to the office of steward, that are not duly qualified*. . . .' He then proceeds to give what purports to be an actual instance of such advancement:

> There was a postillion advanced to the office of steward in the following manner. While in this low situation he behaved well, learned his A. B. C. of the *butler*, who also taught him to write his name, and in a little time could do so tolerably well, nay, in time he wrote a print hand so well as to be able to ticket the casks in the cellar: after some time he was made coachman, could cut the figure of 8 in smacking his whip and by a certain motion, or rather spring of it, would take a straw out of a dirt wall three times together, and not miss; nay, even when upon the coach box, and full speed, could by the elasticity of a certain whip of his own projecting, take up a fowl, or almost anything within its reach. In this situation he continued some years, drove with a great deal of care, improved himself in *letters*, could write a bill of his outgoings, and make a sum total, give a discharge upon receipt of it, speak good horse language, and had some notion of speaking well to the *pointers*, would curse the postillion with an *air*, and gave the wheel-horses the pretty names of *Gooseberry* and *Hard-arse*; when he gave them the whip upon the rump, would fetch the guttural sound of hoay, hoay, up the rough artery, as if his lungs was a curtal bag: he set his hat well, swore

---

[1] Warner, *Literary Recollections*, I. 48–9.
[2] R[obert] Chambers, *The Book of Days*, 1864, I. 155–6.
[3] *London Chronicle*, 1757, I. 298a.

upon a proper accent. In short, he performed everything with propriety, and an uncommon gracefulness, would turn off a horn of October, and give a genteel hem after it; and at watering, &c. would whistle a horse till he drank or pissed to some tune. . . . In fine, he behaved so well, that he merited so much good will of his *lady*, that one day, John, says she, I have often thought of advancing thee, and as often mentioned it to your ——. Here is Mr. —— the steward of the —— estate, is almost superannuated and no *son* to succeed him, what think you of that——? replies John, with his wonted modesty, M—m, I have thought of such a thing; but then thought it too great a favour to ask, but M—m, it is what I could do perhaps as well as another, and if I should be so fortunate as to succeed, your *ladyship* may depend upon my utmost endeavours in that capacity also. John succeeds (Mr. ——) marries the housekeeper, and as soon as possible takes three or four hundreds a year of the *best* land in the lordship into his own hands, buys horses for his —— and most of the nobility and gentry in that part of the country; his wife brings him an only daughter, who is brought up at a French school, dances very fine, and plays as fine as any young *lady* on the spinet, &c. makes a grand appearance at the horse-race and assizes, as genteel as Miss —— And John and Madam on a winter evening by the parlour fire often talk (*if it could be brought about*) to marry Miss with *Master* —— the *counsellor*.[1]

Manifestly this is satire, yet it is no less convincing as evidence than if it were an actual case history; for Mordant would scarcely have written it if employers had not been in the habit of preferring to the post of steward servants who, starting from the lower ranks, had risen through the *cursus honorum*.

A passage in the diary of the Rev. William Jones, written in 1800 but outlining events that had taken place some time earlier, describes the upward progress of such a servant:

A few years ago this great mushroom-man [Rogers] began his career in Lord Monson's stables. I had heard it frequently declared, but could hardly believe it, on account of his affected consequence, till Mrs Shuldham, a most aimiable lady, a relative of the Monson family, assured me it was truth. By degrees he worked himself into the house, &, in the absence of the *great* family, he had charge of the *great* house, which I suppose inspired him with *great* ideas. . . . Rogers had continued in the house so long & tasted so many sweets arising from the house, that he almost seemed to dream that the whole was his own. . . .

[1] Mordant, *Complete Steward*, I. 208–10.

THE REWARDS OF SERVICE

> On the death of Mr Parkinson, the Steward, a very honest, worthy man . . . Rogers started up into a great, a very great man; for he now received the rents.[1]

The picture certainly differs little in essentials from that presented by Mordant.

A servant might be helped, similarly, by the paternalism of his employer to transfer his services to an employer of higher social status. As a rule the aid a servant received in making a change of that sort was confined to the usual written or verbal character: he secured the place through his own efforts. Thomas Whitehead's account of how he became valet to the Duke of Kingston illustrates the point. While in the service of Sir Henry Oxenden, a country gentleman, he decided to look for a more advantageous position. '. . . accordingly,' he writes,

> I gave him warning, telling him I thought I might at my age, do better for myself in London; and hoped he would not be my hindrance. . . . Soon afterwards I was informed that the Duke of Kingston wanted a travelling valet. This news pleased me much: I thought, if I could get into a Duke's service, I should be provided for, for life. I mentioned it to my worthy master, who gave me a letter of recommendation to his Grace, which I lost no time in taking to the Duke.[2]

By leaving the household of a country gentleman for that of a duke Whitehead improved his social status. He appears to have been chiefly concerned with the material benefits the change would bring, but he must also have been aware that it would increase his prestige.

Two servants employed at different times by the Rev. Woodforde altered their social status in much the same way. In 1784 his maid Lizzy, having been recommended by him, left his service to join the household of the local squire.[3] Again, in 1793 his footboy, whom he described as 'being too big for his present place and deserving of a better', was taken on by the squire's brother.[4] In both instances the servant gained prestige by passing from the employ of a lesser man to that of a greater. But the footboy's social

---

[1] *The Diary of the Revd. William Jones, 1777–1821*, ed. O[ctavius] F. Christie, 1929, pp. 115–16.
[2] Whitehead, *Original Anecdotes*, pp. 126–7.
[3] *Diary of a Country Parson*, II. 142.　　　　　　　　[4] *Ibid.*, IV. 1, 3.

SOCIAL ADVANCEMENT

status may also have been improved in another way. From Woodforde's remark about his having outgrown his place, it seems likely that his new position may have been of a higher nominal rank than his old one: in changing places he may have received promotion.

Such promotions were probably not uncommon. It is reasonable to suppose that the servant who sought to better himself by changing places tried to capitalize to the full the training and experience he had acquired in his last position. Mandeville affirms the existence of such a tendency. 'Ask for a Footman that for some time has been in Gentlemens Families,' he says, 'and you'll get a dozen that are all Butlers.'[1]

But whether or not it entailed a rise in the hierarchy of rank, the transit of a servant from one employer to another higher in the social scale might be followed later on by several similar removes. A succession of changes might be a series of upward steps.

A change of places did not always bring social advancement. Just as a domestic might pass from the service of a middle-class employer to that of a gentleman or from the service of a gentleman to that of a nobleman, so he might move in the opposite direction, sinking in the social scale. Sally Gunton, for instance, after a term of service with the Townshends, one of the most eminent families of the Norfolk squirearchy, went to live with the Rev. Woodforde.[2] And in the course of his career as a servant John Macdonald made at least two such changes. After serving Maj. Deibbiege, a gentleman, he entered the employ of Charles Ferguson, a wine merchant; and after living with Sir John Stuart of Allan Bank, he became footman to another wine merchant, James O'Neil.[3]

During a career of service changes of this kind might alternate with changes of the opposite order, the domestic's social status rising or falling with each new place. Macdonald, for example, moved back and forth between middle- and upper-class employers.[4]

Such a course stood in sharp contrast to the sort in which every change of place was a step in social advancement. Just how common either type was remains a matter of conjecture; both were possible lines that a servant's career might follow.

---

[1] Mandeville, *Fable of the Bees*, p. 345.
[2] *Diary of a Country Parson*, IV. 153.
[3] *Memoirs of an Eighteenth-Century Footman*, pp. 70–1, 238.
[4] *Ibid.*, introd., p. xvii and *passim*.

III

A career of service might lead to social advancement in other ways than through promotion and change of place. It might enable a servant to secure some employment or set up in some business that ranked above service in the hierarchy of occupations, or entitle him to a greater degree of respect than he had received before he entered service; it might even bring him financial independence.

The occupations that domestics entered on quitting service varied greatly. Sally Bussy, who had served Dr. Francis, father of Sir Philip Francis, became the landlady of a genteel lodginghouse.[1] Thomas Knowles, who had lived in the capacity of coachman to a Miss Clayton of Liverpool, set up as a brushmaker, selling both wholesale and retail.[2] Mrs. Delany's footman Richard went into the grocery business.[3] Hossack, the Earl of Egmont's valet, took up the practice of medicine and later wrote 'a book on the mechanism of human bodies'; Henekin, another of his servants, left his employ 'to study physic'.[4] Adam Charles, the Duke of Chandos' valet, became a surgeon.[5] Joseph Bramah, the father of the perfector of the water closet, having been coachman in the Earl of Strafford's family, spent the later years of his life as a tenant on one of His Lordship's estates.[6] Lord Palmerston's coachman also eventually became a tenant of a farm that belonged to his former master.[7] And Mr. Newport, who had been butler to the Duke of Northumberland, became gaoler of New Prison, Clerkenwell.[8]

One occupation stands out as having been especially favoured. A great many domestics became keepers of public houses. They did so, according to Sir John Fielding, because they lacked the training and experience requisite for success in other lines.[9] A more

---

[1] *The Francis Letters*, ed. Beata Francis and Eliza Keary, 1901, I. 172–3.
[2] Richard Brooke, *Liverpool during the Last Quarter of the Eighteenth Century*, Liverpool, 1853, p. 177.
[3] *Autobiography and Correspondence of . . . Mrs. Delany*, Second Series, I. 239.
[4] *H. M. C. Egmont*, II. 215, III. 22.
[5] *James Brydges First Duke of Chandos*, p. 174.
[6] *Wilkinson, Worthies, Families and Celebrities of Barnsley*, p. 226.
[7] Tipping, *English Homes*, Period VI. I. 244.
[8] *Lloyd's Evening Post*, 1779, XLV. 419b.
[9] Fielding, *Origin and Effects of a Plan of Police*, p. xi; *London Chronicle*, 1757, II. 221a. Cf. Hanway, *Eight Letters*, p. 60.

SOCIAL ADVANCEMENT

compelling explanation for their preference is that the skills and training required for service were also ideal equipment for tavern keeping. But whatever the reason, there is no doubt that they were to be found operating hostelries of all kinds. Writing in 1777, a newspaper correspondent observes how 'The menial servant tired of his Master's *company*, and mid-night revels, becomes the landlord of a snug public house,' and how 'The *Lady's-Maid*, sick with hasty jaunts and toilet fancies, listens to *Phillip's* soothing tale, then tastes hymenial joys, and takes up her *constant residence* in the bar of a coffee-house....'[1] A review of Patrick Colquhoun's *Observations and Facts Relative to Public-houses* written in 1797 likewise calls attention to the frequency with which servants set up as publicans and innkeepers:

> When we consider who are the sort of persons who occupy public houses of every sort, from the best inn on the Bath road to the lowest small-beer pothouse, or hedge ale-house, they are servants of all descriptions; the butler and the housekeeper, the footman and the lady's maid, the coachman and the cook, the gardener and the dairy-maid, the groom, or stable-boy, with the nursery-maid, or kitchen-maid, the carter and the plough-boy with maid-servants of their own rank, whether they have acquired an independent competency by cheating their masters and mistresses, or by long and faithful service, all direct their settlements for life to a public house.[2]

These general statements are substantiated by a good deal of other evidence. The King's Head Tavern at Islington was kept in the 1730's by Mrs. Robotham, a former servant of Elizabeth Purefoy.[3] The George Inn at Warminster was taken in 1774 by Simon Hayward, who had been butler to Edward Southwell.[4] The Red Lion Inn at Bagshot was taken in 1780 by Peter Harvey, who had formerly been cook to the Duke of Bolton.[5] The White Swan Inn at Alnwick was occupied in 1782 by a man named Wilson, who at one time had lived as footman in the Hervey family.[6] The Essex Head Tavern in London, the meeting place of the club of that

---

[1] *Morning Post*, 1777, No. 442, June 4, 4a. Cf. Daniel Defoe, *The Complete English Tradesman*, 1745, 5th ed., II. 315.
[2] *Gentleman's Magazine*, 1797, LXVII. 223.   [3] *Purefoy Letters*, II. 240.
[4] *London Chronicle*, 1774, XXXVI. 39a.
[5] *London Courant*, 1780, May 20, 4c.
[6] 'Journals of the Hon. William Hervey, in North America and Europe, from 1755 to 1814', *Suffolk Green Books*, XIV. 335.

THE REWARDS OF SERVICE

name organized by Dr. Johnson in 1783, was run by Samuel Greaves, a former servant of the Thrales.[1] And the Fountain Inn at Biggleswade was opened in 1790 by J. Scarborough, who had served as butler to the Duke of Chandos.[2]

A career of service often made possible the accumulation of the modest capital necessary to set up in such a business. This is evident from the remarks of an anonymous author who lamented the destiny of retired servants. '. . . they marry,' he wrote, 'and pine away their small Gains in some petty Shops, or Publick Houses. . . .'[3] The same inference may be drawn from the observations of 'Footmanius', who in 1762 addressed himself on the subject of vails to the editor of a London newspaper: '. . . if a servant chances to save a little money in his place why it enables him to get into some business, and keep his family from going to the Parish. . . .'[4]

Service also often provided the domestic with a beneficent patron through whose efforts he gained suitable employment or was launched in a suitable trade. The patron might either be one of his employers or else some person he had met through one of his employers; the patron's efforts might take the form of either financial assistance or the exercise of influence.

A proposal that Thomas Whitehead, while in the service of the Duke of Kingston, received from a former master well illustrates how the kind employer might finance a servant. After Whitehead had been valet to the Duke for a number of years, Sir Henry Oxenden, with whom he had previously lived, sent for him and offered to put him in possession of the Crown Inn at Rochester.[5]

One of Whitehead's fellow servants received financial aid from a similar source. Mr. Frozard, who had entered the Duke's employ as a youth and had eventually been advanced to the post of butler, on quitting service took Hall's Stables at Hyde Park Corner. His savings made up part of the necessary funds; but he was also

---

[1] *Letters of Samuel Johnson LL.D.*, ed. G[eorge] B. Hill, Oxford, 1902, II. 390*n*.
[2] *Torrington Diaries*, II. 276*n*. For further examples see *ibid.*, I. 352; *Autobiography and Correspondence of . . . Mrs. Delany*, First Series, III. 423; Stirling, *Annals of a Yorkshire House*, II. 311; *Diary of John Baker*, p. 412; *Wynne Diaries*, II. 199; *Memoirs of . . . Mrs. Catherine Cappe*, p. 55.
[3] *An Enquiry into the Melancholy Circumstances of Great Britain*, p. 21.
[4] *London Chronicle*, 1762, XI. 380b.
[5] Whitehead, *Original Anecdotes*, pp. 128–9.

SOCIAL ADVANCEMENT

assisted by Col. Litchfield, a former employer, who had recommended him as a boy to the Duke.[1]

Robert Dodsley's retirement from service was also made possible by a generous gift, although in this case the donor had never been his master. The son of a country schoolmaster, Dodsley was early apprenticed to a stockinger; but disliking the work, he ran away and became a domestic. He may have gone up to London to look for a place, or he may have been taken up by some employer who had engaged him in the country. In any case, soon after his arrival there, he entered the household of Charles Dartiquenave, the epicure. It is possible that he next served Sir Richard Howe, who, he said, encouraged him to write verse. The turning point in his career occurred when, about 1728, he became footman to Jane Lowther, daughter of the first Viscount Lonsdale. In her house he came in contact with a host of literary celebrities, some of whom probably took notice of him. Moreover, she is said to have placed her library at his disposal. As a result, his muse thrived. In 1729 he published *Servitude*, after Defoe had revised it and supplied a preface and postscript. A second edition bearing the title *The Footman's Friendly Advice to His Brethren of the Livery* was brought out the next year; and this was followed in 1732 by *A Muse in Livery, or the Footman's Miscellany*, a collection of verse. The eighteenth century's interest in untutored genius rather than the intrinsic merit of these works gave Dodsley something of the vogue enjoyed by Stephen Duck, the thresher-poet, and Anne Yearsley, the poetical milkwoman. Like several other literary domestics, including Mary or Molly Leapor, whose poems first appeared in 1748,[2] and Elizabeth Hands, whose verses were initially published in the newspapers of Birmingham and Coventry and then reprinted in a collected edition about 1787,[3] Dodsley was hailed as clear proof that poetic spirit might be found in the scullery and the pantry as well as in the library and the study. Successful as a poet, Dodsley next became a playwright, turning out a piece in prose entitled *The Toy-shop*. Through the influence of Pope, whose acquaintance he had probably made at his mistress', if not earlier at Dartiquenave's, *The Toy-shop* was produced in 1735. Soon after it had been put on,

---

[1] Whitehead, *Original Anecdotes*, p. 187.
[2] *Gentleman's Magazine*, 1784, LIV. 806–7.
[3] W. K. Riland Bedford, *Three Hundred Years of a Family Living*, Birmingham, 1889, pp. 112–13.

Dodsley left service to become a bookseller and publisher. The proceeds of the play, along with his savings, helped to establish him in his new occupation. But a donation of a hundred pounds from his patron, Pope, was perhaps decisive in enabling him to make the change.[1]

The exertion of influence, the other way a patron might render assistance, is exemplified by the manner in which many domestics entered government service. Undoubtedly there were some who, having laid up sufficient funds, purchased comfortable berths. This is evidenced by an advertisement that appeared in 1796:

> A Sober Steady Elderly Man, who has passed the principal part of his time in servitude, with reputation and profit to himself, wishes to pass the remainder of his days in some easy situation, in any of the Public Offices, where much attendance or the exertion of literary talents may not be deemed necessary. A handsome gratuity will be given to any Person who can procure the advertiser such a situation.[2]

But the majority of those who entered government service did so through the good offices of their masters. It was a common thing for a master to use his connexions to obtain a post for a deserving servant. In 1750 a writer grumbled that

> if any gentleman of a small estate applies to a lord or member of parliament, to get some little place in the government's service for a younger son, he may perhaps succeed, after his lordship or his honour, has provided for all his favourite servants, even down to his postilion; for the footman or valet of a lord, or member, now stands a better chance of being thus provided for, than the best qualified poor gentleman in the kingdom.[3]

A somewhat more subtle attack was made by the *Whimsical Philosopher*. The essayist, posing as one of the commissioners of a government board, confesses to having 'enjoyed a salary or 1000£ a year, besides the advantage of providing for a favourite groom or footman, or the husband of my wife's favourite maid. . . .'[4] And in the farce *High Life Below Stairs* Townley satirizes the practice by making Kitty lecture Lovel out of *The Servant's Guide to Wealth, by* Timothy Shoulderknot, *formerly Servant to several Noblemen,*

---

[1] Straus, *Robert Dodsley*, pp. 1–37.
[2] *Morning Chronicle*, 1796, No. 8273, Apr. 15, 4a.
[3] *London Magazine*, 1750, XIX. 558.   [4] *Ibid.*, 1750, XIX. 129.

and now an Officer in the Customs.[1] Actual examples can be cited. In 1701 Henry Guy wrote to Robert Harley about 'one Shepherd' who, at the request of his master, had been given a post in the Customs.[2] Writing in his diary in 1739, the Earl of Egmont says of a Mr. Castars, who was 'son to a French under cook in King William's kitchen', that 'Mr. Horace Walpole the elder took him into his family, and afterwards got him made Consul at Alicant'.[3] In 1741 Egmont noted in his diary that 'one Mr. Thearie, alias Terry, a Frenchman by extraction', who had been house steward to Sir Gustavus Hume and also to Lord Chetwynd, was recommended to him for the post of Recorder of Frederica (Georgia).[4] John Macdonald mentions in his *Travels* a Mr. Vernon 'who had been butler to Lord Murray and by him placed in a good office in the Excise. . . .'[5] And a news item in 1777 related, doubtless with some exaggeration, how a certain domestic, through the interest of Henry Fox and his son Charles, had been 'advanced to places and appointments under government, to the amount of near one thousand per annum. . . .'[6]

It was not only in the civil and consular services that domestics acquired places in this manner; they were also sometimes appointed to posts in the army. Sir John Ligonier, for instance, bestowed a commission on his valet.[7] That such appointments were not uncommon was intimated by a writer who declared: '. . . when a Member of —— happens to be —— a thorough thick and thin Man, he can recommend a Son, a Nephew, a Brother, a Friend, and sometimes a Footman to a P——st in the A——y. . . .'[8]

Like these different branches of government service, the Royal Household, too, was utilized by those with influence to provide for servants. In 1736 the Duke of Chandos commended his valet to the Duke of Grafton, the Lord Chamberlain, for a place in the King's Band of Music.[9] Similarly, after Lord Chesterfield had been made Lord Steward in 1730, Swift appealed to him on behalf of 'an honest man' who had 'been long a servant to my Lord Sussex'.[10]

---

[1] Townley, *High Life Below Stairs*, p. 29.
[2] *H. M. C. Portland*, IV. 13.   [3] *H. M. C. Egmont Diary*, III. 24.
[4] *Ibid.*, III. 219.   [5] *Memoirs of an Eighteenth-Century Footman*, p. 11.
[6] *Morning Post*, 1777, No. 1353, Feb. 20, 2c.
[7] *Memoirs of Mrs. Letitia Pilkington*, p. 214.
[8] *Common Sense*, 1738, I. 157.
[9] Baker, *James Brydges First Duke of Chandos*, p. 131.
[10] *Letters of . . . Chesterfield*, II. 158n.

Chesterfield replied that he had already committed himself to several of his own retainers for whatever places were in his gift: 'Some old Servants, that have served me long and faithfully, have obtained promises of the first four or five vacancies. . . .'[1] As Groom of the Stole, the Earl of Rochford practised the same sort of paternalism, appointing his house steward to be one of the King's Pages of the Bedchamber.[2] And in a like manner the second Viscount Townshend, when Captain of the Yeomen of the Guards, gave several posts at his disposal to domestics 'who had serv'd him faithfully'.[3]

The influence of patrons was exerted to place servants in other quarters besides government service and the Royal Household. The Duke of Richmond in 1740 urged a governor of the newly founded London Hospital to have a former laundry maid appointed a nurse there.[4] And Francis Charlton secured a place in the service of the East India Company for a footman who at one time had lived with his father.[5]

It would be erroneous to suppose that the domestics whom service in these different ways enabled to pass on to other occupations, invariably improved their social status by doing so. In some cases change meant sinking rather than rising in the social scale; in others it probably effected no alteration in the servant's social status. The difficulty of perceiving from so great a distance the subtler nuances of social evaluation makes it impossible to demonstrate this with certainty. Yet it may well be questioned whether Sally Bussy, for instance, raised her social status when she left the Francis family to become landlady of a lodginghouse and whether Peter Harvey, to take another example, raised his when he abandoned the post of cook in a ducal household to undertake the operation of an inn.

There can be no doubt, on the other hand, that in many cases the change from service to another occupation did bring an improvement in social status. Hossack certainly gained prestige when, after being valet to the Earl of Egmont, he became a member of the

---

[1] *Letters of . . . Chesterfield*, 157.
[2] *London Chronicle*, 1760, VII. 66b.
[3] R[obert] W. Ketton-Cremer, *Country Neighbourhood*, 1951, p. 154.
[4] Mary L. Matcham, *A Forgotten John Russell*, 1905, p. 130.
[5] *Memoirs of William Hickey, 1749–1809*, ed. Alfred Spencer, 1913–25, I. 22.

medical profession. So, too, did Castars, Old Horace Walpole's servant, when he forsook his household duties to accept a consular post. Yet another example of a definite rise is Thomas Knowles, who, having been coachman to a middle-class employer, became a brushmaker, with his own shop and warehouse. The change in this instance erased the stigma that attached to all domestics save those who served the nobility and gentry; henceforth—in the language of the day—he 'lived free of dependence'. Precisely the same transformation occurred in the case of Peacock, a footman who, having served Sir John Forbes, the merchant, became a clerk in his business house.[1]

To these individual examples may be added, categorically, those servants who were fortunate enough to secure posts as officers in the army. Whatever their previous social status, the character of military service raised them above it and gave them a special dignity. Thus Letitia Pilkington speaks of the commission bestowed on Sir John Ligonier's valet as making him a gentleman.[2]

But the social status of the domestic who left service was not necessarily given permanent definition by his new occupation. He might subsequently improve it by any one of several means.

In Dodsley's case personal connexions coupled with commercial success raised him far above the ordinary publisher. He apparently felt obliged to comport himself with humility. Walpole speaks condescendingly of him as a 'decent, humble, inoffensive' creature, 'little apt to forget or disguise his having been a footman!'[3] Nevertheless, he lived on terms of some intimacy with the Great and the near-great, a token of the degree of respectability he enjoyed.[4]

Lancelot Brown's achievement resembled Dodsley's in essentials. Having begun as gardener on a small estate in Northumberland, he later moved south, first serving Sir Richard Grenville and then Lord Cobham. His improvements at Lord Cobham's seat, Stowe, and elsewhere gained him such a wide celebrity that when he renounced service in 1749, he had no difficulty in establishing himself as an independent landscapist. His success was phenomenal. Within a short time he was being consulted on all sides, and

[1] *Verney Letters*, II. 256.
[2] *Memoirs of Mrs. Letitia Pilkington*, p. 214.
[3] *Letters of Horace Walpole*, IV. 135–6.
[4] Straus, *Robert Dodsley*, p. 309.

each year brought him more business and greater wealth. By 1756 he had reached the peak of his profession; and royal recognition came in 1764, when a group of his noble patrons succeeded in having him made Surveyor of His Majesty's Gardens at Hampton Court.[1] As the most eminent landscapist of the day, Brown was generally respected. Many of the élite treated him almost as an equal, and some even stooped to court him. The heights he attained were graphically described by Lord Chatham: 'He writes Lancelot Brown, Esquire, *en titre d'office* . . . shares the private hours of the King, dines familiarly with his neighbour of Sion the [Duke of Northumberland] and sits down at the tables of all the House of Lords.'[2]

Elizabeth Raffald rose in a rather different fashion. After filling the position of housekeeper in a succession of families for fifteen years, Mrs. Raffald left service in 1763, when she married the gardener of the establishment in which she was employed. Settling with her husband in Manchester, she opened a confectionery shop, acted as a caterer and at the same time ran a normal school where young women were taught both elegant accomplishments and the domestic arts. Her husband, meanwhile, set up as a seedsman and florist. About 1769, however, Mrs. Raffald abandoned her various enterprises, Mr. Raffald gave up his seed and flower business, and together they took the Bull's Head Inn, occupying it profitably for many years. This change of occupations probably did not greatly alter their social status, either for better or for worse. But the outside activities in which Mrs. Raffald engaged definitely affected hers. While plying the trade of publican, she helped maintain *Harrop's Manchester Mercury* and founded *Prescott's Manchester Journal*; she also compiled a commercial directory of the city. Her most profitable venture, however, was her *Experienced English Housekeeper*, a work for which she received £1,400. When added to the income from the Bull's Head, the proceeds of these excursions into publishing and writing placed Mrs. Raffald in very comfortable circumstances, as is apparent from her ability to afford a nurserymaid for each of her three daughters when they were young. Moreover, because of the way in which it was achieved, her prosperity lifted her above the usual social status of an innkeeper's

---

[1] For details of Brown's career see Dorothy Stroud, *Capability Brown*, 1950, *passim*.
[2] Quoted in *ibid.*, p. 43.

wife: she was highly regarded by the most respectable people of Manchester.¹

Like Dodsley and Brown, the ex-servant might rise by distinguishing himself in his regular occupation; like Elizabeth Raffald, he might do so by undertaking some well chosen by-work. But these were not the only avenues that were open to him.

Another means whereby the ex-servant might rise was to exchange his occupation for a more honorific one. Tom Broughton's career illustrates this perfectly. Broughton, having been employed in the Whately family, quit service and opened a punch house. But his years as a publican were only an interlude, the punch house was only a stepping stone; ultimately he rose to be a successful broker.²

Sometimes the financial success of the ex-servant permitted him to withdraw altogether from the struggle for gain and to pursue a life of respectable leisure. Anthony Fletcher, a livery servant of Bishop Cumberland, 'by a series of good conduct and good fortune, established himself in an affluent and creditable situation at Bath. . . .' He lived out his later years in the Crescent, one of the most fashionable sections of town, 'well known and universally respected'.³ The process of ascent can be more clearly traced in the rise of a servant named Lowe. A livery servant at the outset of his career, Lowe later became proprietor of a tavern, which appears to have flourished. According to one account, it enabled him to amass 'a small fortune'; according to another, it was merely the means whereby "he scraped up some money" which he later managed to increase greatly by the simple expedient of lending it at usurious rates. After he had acquired a tidy sum he retired and 'commenced gentleman'.⁴

Service itself sometimes made possible such retirement. Domestics who were generously pensioned, who received substantial legacies, or who were given lucrative sinecures at the public expense no longer found it necessary to work; those who contrived to save a sizable portion of the profits of service gained a like exemption.

---

[1] John Harland, 'Collecteana Relating to Manchester and Its Neighbourhood', II. *Chetham Society Publications*, 1867, New Series, LXXII. 144-73.

[2] *Grenville Papers*, IV. 420.

[3] *Memoirs of Richard Cumberland*, 1807, I. 133.

[4] *Lloyd's Evening Post*, 1779, XLIV. 365b; *Annual Register*, 1779, XXII. 207.

THE REWARDS OF SERVICE

But the sweets of retirement consisted of more than mere leisure; they included security and at least modest comfort. The circumstances of most retired servants probably approximated those Henry Angelo depicts when, alluding to the munificence of the Duke and Duchess of Queensberry, he remarks that it was 'perpetuated for many years, in certain old families, all of whom were living in respectable style in the neighbourhood of Grosvenor-square, about thirty years ago, having derived their means in their graces' service.'[1]

In some instances it was not to the comfortable refuge of middle-class existence, but to the luxurious life of the gentleman that the servant retired. Thomas Whitehead relates how Mr. Poynter, who had been master of the horse to the Duke of Kingston, purchased an estate in the country with the money he had saved in service. 'It was worth two hundred per annum,' says Whitehead, 'contained seven miles of manor for sporting, and plenty of game. . . .'[2]

One type of servant was heavily represented amongst those who established themselves in this fashion. The nature of his duties, the breadth of his authority, and the height of his salary combined to provide the land steward with opportunities to build up a private fortune; and frequently he invested part of that fortune in land. Edward Laurence speaks of 'Stewards, who, after they have made *haste* to be rich, . . . have purchas'd out the Freeholders, thereby making an Estate for themselves, even within their own Lord's Manors. . . .'[3] Lord Monson's steward, Rogers, whose ascent from the stables is described above, may not have followed precisely this course; but he is an example of the retired steward who purchased landed property. The acreage in his hands appears to have been considerable; on one occasion he described himself 'as a very great *landholder*'.[4]

Rogers' position in the local community is worth examining. According to the Rev. William Jones, he dominated the parish, engrossing two or three parish offices and making his power 'an engine of terror to all around him'. Although he seems to have been generally disliked as an upstart and tyrant, his wealth and influence commanded respect. He was sometimes referred to as 'Lord

---

[1] *Reminiscences of Henry Angelo*, 1828–30, I. 21.
[2] Whitehead, *Original Anecdotes*, p. 132.
[3] Laurence, *Duty of a Steward*, p. 36.
[4] *Diary of the Revd. William Jones*, pp. 116–25, 140.

SOCIAL ADVANCEMENT

Rogers', half in derision, half in awe. Evidently his social status was sufficiently high to permit him to associate with members of the local squirearchy, at last outside their homes. He was to be found, says the Rev. Jones, 'spunging with every gentleman' who did not have 'resolution enough to repulse, & kick out of his party, such an impudent, niggardly intruder'.[1]

To live comfortably without working, it need scarcely be said, conferred a high degree of prestige upon those former servants who were able to do so; to acquire a country estate, as Rogers did, was to gain a place in the social scale more or less equivalent to that of the middle-class parvenu who, retiring from business, bought land and in myriad ways sought to identify himself with the gentry. It could hardly have been more than a tiny fraction of the servant class, however, that attained these heights.

[1] *Diary of the Revd. William Jones*, pp. 116–18, 125, 140.

Chapter Eight

THE SERVANT CLASS AS A CULTURAL NEXUS

VIEWED in the context of eighteenth-century English society, the domestic servant class has a special significance. It was an important agent in the process of cultural change.

I

The cultural tone of eighteenth-century England was set by an élite composed of the highest nobility, the wealthiest gentry and their satellites. Variously styled the Ton, the Great, the Polite, the Beau Monde, the World of Fashion, and, simply, the World, this small group constituted the fount of norms and values. No level of the social structure escaped the impact of its scheme of life, its modes of behaviour.

Some knowledge of the élite was acquired by all classes through face to face contacts. Social life might bring the small squire and the duke together in the drawing-room; politics might gain the prosperous merchant an invitation to the dinner table of the earl. The merchant of modest means, the tradesman, and the artisan also had opportunities of observing the élite at close range. In London there were abundant points of contact. Although many coffee houses were frequented by members of a single class or occupational group, the patronage of others was heterogeneous. Typical of these was the Bedford. The Bedford, writes an anonymous author,

> may be looked upon as the centre of gravitation between the court and the city; the noxious effluvia of St. Bride's is here corrected by the genuine eau-de-luce from Pall Mall, and the predominance of ambergris at St. James's is qualified by the wholesome tar of

THE SERVANT CLASS AS A CULTURAL NEXUS

Thames Street. Nor does the conversation receive a less happy effect from this junction; the price of stock and the lie of the day from the Alley are softened by the *bon mot* of Lady Dolabella which set every soul at the Duchess Triffle's rout in a titter, or the duel that was fought this morning between Captain Terrible and Lord Puncto, when both of them were mortally wounded in the coat.[1]

A similar convergence of classes occurred at the theatre. 'In our Playhouses at London . . .,' explains a pamphleteer ostensibly bent on dissuading country gentlemen from coming up to the Metropolis,

> we have three . . . different and distinct Classes; the first is called the *Boxes*, where there is one peculiar to the King and Royal Family, and the rest for the Persons of Quality, and for the Ladies and Gentlemen of the highest Rank, unless some Fools that have more Wit than Money, or perhaps more Impudence than both, crowd in among them. The second is call'd the *Pit*, where sit the *Judges*, *Wits* and *Censurers*, . . . in common with these sit the *Squires*, *Sharpers*, *Beaus*, *Bullies* and *Whores*, and here and there an extravagant *Male* and *Female Cit*. The third is distinguished by the Title of the *Middle Gallery*, where the Citizens Wives and Daughters, together with the *Abigails*, Serving-men, Journey-men and Apprentices commonly take their Places. . . .[2]

In the public parks, too, the company was mixed. Describing the Mall in St. James's Park, Baron de Pöllnitz, the German traveller, calls it 'one of the most diversified Scenes imaginable' and complains of 'the Mobility being suffer'd to walk [there] as well as Persons of Distinction. . . .'[3] The different classes also mingled promiscuously at the principal pleasure resorts. No doubt thinking of Ranelagh and Vauxhall, Henry Fielding speaks of 'those great Scenes of Rendez-vous, where the Nobleman and his Taylor, the Lady of Quality and her Tirewoman, meet together and form one common Assembly. . . .'[4] And this was not all; there were many other places where an intermingling of classes occurred. At boxing matches 'Noblemen of the first rank' were often to be seen 'laying bets with butchers and cobblers'.[5] In the country there was a

---

[1] *Memoirs of the Bedford Coffee House*, 1763, pp. 2–3.
[2] 'The Tricks of the Town Laid Open', 1747, reprinted in Ralph Straus, *Tricks of the Town*, New York and London, 1928, pp. 37–8.
[3] *Memoirs of . . . Baron de Pöllnitz*, II. 436; IV. 239.
[4] Fielding, *Enquiry into the Causes of the Late Increase of Robbers*, p. 15.
[5] William Guthrie, *A New Geographical, Historical and Commercial Grammar*, 1782, 7th ed., p. 192.

greater separation of classes in terms of physical distance;[1] members of the subordinate classes, from the yeoman downwards, had fewer opportunities of rubbing elbows with the élite. Yet just as in London, there did exist certain points of contact, such as churches, inns, and racecourses. There were even dances at which the lower and middle classes mixed with their betters. In 1738 Lady Thanet 'set an assembly on foot' and in order 'to make up a number' included 'all the parsons, apprentices, tradesmen, apothecaries, and farmers, milliners, mantua-makers, haberdashers of small wares, and chambermaids' in the vicinity.[2]

Probably the most effective points of contact outside London were the watering places; no crowds could be more varied than those that flocked there. In each place, around a nucleus of the élite, there swarmed a motley crew in which all classes above the mechanic level were represented. Smollett depicts this melange in his classic description of the most popular of the resorts. 'Every upstart of fortune,' he writes, 'harnessed in the trappings of the mode, presents himself at Bath. . . .' He mentions as prominent types 'Clerks and factors from the East Indies', 'planters, negro-drivers and hucksters from our American plantations', 'agents, commissioners and contractors' who had made fortunes out of the nation's wars, and 'usurers, brokers and jobbers of every kind'. And he goes on to analyse their intentions:

> Knowing no other criterion of greatness, but the ostentation of wealth, they discharge their affluence without taste or conduct, through every channel of the most absurd extravagance; and all of them hurry to Bath, because here, without any further qualification, they can mingle with the princes and nobles of the land. Even the wives and daughters of low tradesmen . . . are infected by the same rage of displaying their importance, and the slightest indisposition serves them with a pretext to insist upon being conveyed to Bath, where they may hobble country-dances and cotillions among lordlings, 'squires, counsellors and clergy. . . .[3]

Defoe's impression of Tunbridge Wells must have corresponded pretty closely to Smollett's impression of Bath, for he writes:

> Here you have all the Liberty of Conversation in the World, and any thing that looks like a Gentleman, has an address agreeable,

---

[1] Gilboy, *Wages in Eighteenth Century England*, p. 70.
[2] *Elizabeth Montagu*, I. 29.
[3] Smollett, 'Humphry Clinker', *Works*, VII. 41–2.

and behaves with decency and good Manners, may single out whom he pleases that does not appear engag'd, and may talk, rally, be merry, and say any decent thing to them. . . .[1]

At such spas as Harrogate and Cheltenham (after the patronage of George III had popularized it) and, once surf-bathing had come into vogue, at such seaside resorts as Scarborough, Margate, and Brighthelmstone there was the same mixed company.

Besides these primary contacts there were also secondary contacts through which knowledge of the élite was gained. The eighteenth century possessed nothing comparable to the cinema, which so effectively portrays for mass consumption the culture pattern of the present-day élite; nor was there a slick-paper press that provided glimpses into the lives of the exalted few.[2] From the early years of the period, however, the newspaper carried the details of the pageant of 'high life' to an increasing proportion of the literate public. 'People of rank,' maintained a writer in 1789, '. . . do nothing unobserved, for indeed our newspapers are more than half filled with their private transactions. . . .'[3] Moreover, beginning with the *Tatler* and the *Spectator*, the periodical essay supplemented newspaper notices and accounts by making the dissection of 'high life' one of its favourite themes. What the periodical essay did in words the print did in line and colour: from Hogarth to Gilray and Rowlandson caricaturists, whose paintings and drawings were published in print form, delighted in satirizing the foibles of the élite. Finally, individuals who had acquired a knowledge of the élite gave it currency by word and act. The hearsay story—the retailing of what His Grace said or what Her Ladyship did—perfectly exemplifies this medium of diffusion.

In one way or another, then, the subordinate classes gained a certain familiarity with the manners of the élite; and, for the most part, they sought to imitate it as closely as possible. This was natural. In virtually all societies that possess social solidarity the highest social strata tend to be taken as models by the strata

[1] Defoe, *Tour*, I. 126–7. Cf. Thomas B. Burr, *The History of Tunbridge-Wells*, 1766, pp. 120–1.
[2] For a discussion of the part these media play in spreading a knowledge of the twentieth-century élite see Henry C. Durant, *The Problem of Leisure*, [1938,] pp. 18, 21, 37.
[3] *Lady's Magazine*, 1789, xx. 291.

THE SERVANT CLASS AS A CULTURAL NEXUS

beneath.¹ Imitation may not be carried very far; in fact, where there are specific tabus against it or where there are wide fissures in the social structure, it may scarcely occur at all. Nevertheless, the tendency normally exists; and in eighteenth-century England it existed under optimum conditions.

The prevalence of such imitation is amply attested by the comments of contemporary observers. One writer declared: 'The present rage of imitating the manners of high-life hath spread itself so far among the gentlefolks of lower-life, that in a few years we shall probably have no common people at all.'² The impressions of another moved him to exclaim: 'The most ignorant naturally *look up* for example: the common people will be what their superiors are. . . .'³ Referring to the élite, still another asserted: '*Their* example is the fountain from whence the vulgar draw their habits, actions, and characters.'⁴ and a fourth writer, taking fashions in clothing as an illustration, maintained that

> The vanity of the great and opulent will ever be affecting new modes, in order to increase that notice to which it thinks itself exclusively entitled. The lower ranks will imitate them as soon as they have discovered the innovation. . . . The pattern is set by a superior; and authority will at any time countenance absurdity. A hat, a coat, a shoe, deemed fit to be worn only by a great grand-sire, is no sooner put on by a dictator of fashions, than it becomes graceful in the extreme, and is generally adopted from the first lord of the Treasury to the apprentice in Houndsditch.⁵

But if, as the prime exemplar of the subordinate classes, the élite was assiduously imitated, it was not, for the most part, imitated directly, except by the stratum just below it. Each of the other classes aped the one next above, so that a chain of emulation ran from the apex to the base of the social pyramid. This was noticed in 1734 by a writer in the *Universal Spectator*: 'The *Alderman's* lady aims at the *Taste* of her *Grace*; Mr. *Deputy's* Wife

---

[1] Gabriel Tarde, *The Laws of Imitation*, New York, 1903, pp. 198–9, 217; Thorstein Veblen, *The Theory of the Leisure Class*, New York, 1935, pp. 84, 104 and *passim*; Neal E. Miller and John Dollard, *Social Learning and Imitation*, New Haven, 1941, p. 190.
[2] *British Magazine*, 1763, IV. 417.
[3] Hanway, *Virtue in Humble Life*, 1774, I. introd., p. xx.
[4] More, 'Thoughts on the Importance of the Manners of the Great', *Works*, XI. 57. Cf. *ibid.*, XI. 3, 58.
[5] *Works of Vicesimus Knox*, I. 374.

THE SERVANT CLASS AS A CULTURAL NEXUS

imitates the *Alderman's*; the *Common-Council Man's* the *Deputy's* and so on down to the *Constable* and the *Headborough's*. . . .'[1] Arguing in 1751 that the manners of the élite were 'as infectious by Example, as the Plague itself by Contact', Henry Fielding also described the phenomenon:

> Thus while the Nobleman will emulate the Grandeur of a Prince; and the Gentleman will aspire to the proper State of the Nobleman; the Tradesman steps from behind his Counter into the vacant Place of the Gentleman, Nor doth the Confusion end here: It reaches the very Dregs of the People. . . .[2]

And in 1773 'Arcadius' observed: '. . . each of the different ranks of men are perpetually pressing upon that above them. . . .' As he saw it, the gentry imitated the nobility, the tradesmen and farmers the gentry. '. . . and even the lower class,' he maintained, 'both in town and country are so much infected with this preposterous ambition, that all ranks and degrees of men seem to be on the point of being confounded. . . .'[3]

The reasons for the existence of this chain of emulation are not far to seek. Eighteenth-century England was a relatively dynamic society: many members of each class sought to advance to the social status of the class above. As a consequence, although the ultimate model was the élite, the immediate model was very naturally the class that the socially ambitious person wished to enter. Imitation of such a model, moreover, was likely to prove much more successful than direct imitation of the élite; for, as a rule, the culture patterns of contiguous classes possess a high degree of affinity, the differences tend to be slight, and so displacement can readily occur.[4] Then again, in many instances direct imitation of the élite would have subjected the climber to ridicule, whereas imitation of the class above did not. Lack of wealth also tended to confine his attempts at imitation to the next class above. But most important by far in giving him this focus was the nature of his contacts. Of the classes above his own that immediately above

---

[1] Reprinted in *Gentleman's Magazine*, 1734, IV. 124.
[2] Fielding, *Enquiry into the Causes of the Late Increase of Robbers*, p. 6.
[3] *London Chronicle*, 1773, XXXIV. 213a. Cf. *Gentleman's Magazine*, 1800, LXX. 1043.
[4] Pitirim A. Sorokin, *Social and Cultural Dynamics*, New York, 1937–41, IV. 265–6.

was the one with which he had the greatest intercourse and familiarity; it was therefore the one he was best able to copy.

The preoccupation of each stratum with that above it did not preclude the imitation of other models. To a certain extent each copied the strata that stood between it and the élite; to a certain extent each copied the élite directly. It was an extensive system of capillaries through which cultural elements passed from the élite to the classes below.

One of the most effective sections of the system was the servant class. It linked the élite and the lower levels. Moreover, it linked various lower levels distant from each other in the social structure.

II

Consciously and unconsciously the servant tended to identify with his master. He assumed something of his master's social status; he took his master as a model to be imitated in detail.

As a member of the household, he had an unparalleled opportunity to acquire the knowledge essential to successful imitation. He could observe his master at close range; he could observe him for protracted periods. In large households his opportunity varied somewhat with his nominal rank; upper servants, particularly personal attendants, enjoyed a greater freedom of access than lower servants. Even the most lowly menial, however, was not entirely excluded from the presence of his employer.

But it was not merely his master who was exposed to the servant's scrutiny. His master's friends and associates, people of a class superior to his own, passed in review before his eyes; indeed, their whole scheme of life lay open to his inspection.

The possibilities of the domestic's point of vantage were not lost on contemporaries. In one of his essays Vicesimus Knox makes a servant say: 'I usually stand behind my master's chair at dinner and attend very closely to all the conversations; so that I often pick up a great deal of improvement. . . .'[1] And the author of the satirical *Directions to Lords and Ladies*, who posed as a livery servant, asked: '. . . who have greater Opportunities of Observing Men and Manners, than the Gentlemen of our Corps?' And he continued in

---

[1] *Works of Vicesimus Knox*, I. 346.

explanation: 'At Table we in Silence hear all Conversations, and remark and refine upon them for our own Use and Conduct. . . .'[1]

An authentic servant's appreciation of the scrutiny his position permitted is expressed in *The Footman*, one of the poems Dodsley wrote before discarding his livery suit to become a bookseller. Referring to dinner time at his mistress' house, he versified:

> This is the only pleasant Hour
> Which I have in Twenty-four;
> For whilst I unregarded stand,
> With ready Salver in my Hand,
> And seem to understand no more
> Than just what's call'd for, out to pour,
> I hear, and mark the courtly Phrases,
> And all the Elegance that passes;
> Disputes maintain'd without Digression,
> With ready Wit, and fine Expression;
> The Laws of true Politeness stated,
> And what Good-breeding is, debated. . . .[2]

To a certain extent the probing eyes and attentive ears of the servant even imposed on his master an onerous constraint. It seemed to the Scotsman Alexander Carlyle that the average English employer was so aware of being observed and had such deference for the opinion of his servant that he regulated his conduct with him constantly in mind.[3] That there was a good deal of truth in Carlyle's impression is suggested by the highly disapproving attitude taken by Horace Walpole whenever some indiscretion was committed before servants. It is with evident shock, for instance, that he writes Conway in 1756 of how Charles Townshend had been rude to Lady Dalkeith in front of the members of the household staff. Again, in a letter written in 1763 his tone is extremely censorious when he tells how Lady Halifax, despite the presence of a similar audience, had remarked on the lowly origins of an illustrious cleric. Another incident of this kind called forth his disapprobation in 1765. 'I dined to-day with a dozen *savants*,' he wrote to Montagu from Paris, 'and though all the servants were waiting, the conversation was more unrestrained, even on the Old

---

[1] *Directions to Lords and Ladies*, introd., p. 4. Cf. *Guardian*, 1756, II. 324; *London Chronicle*, 1765, XVIII. 300b.
[2] [Robert Dodsley,] *A Muse in Livery*, 1732, pp. 27–8.
[3] *Autobiography of . . . Alexander Carlyle*, p. 442.

Testament, than I would suffer at my own table in England, if a single footman was present.'[1]

It was a desire to ease the constraint Walpole so clearly accepted as normal that brought dumb-waiters into vogue in the early decades of the century. The Earl of Bristol purchased one in 1727.[2] In 1732 a piece in the *Weekly Register* remarked that footmen had been 'supplanted by a certain stupid utensil call'd a *Dumb Waiter*. . . .'[3] And writing in 1756, Soame Jenyns corroborates this account. Servants, he says, 'By their impertinence . . . have reduced us to dumb-waiters, that is, to wait upon ourselves. . . .'[4] The dumb-waiter was a tier table, which, prior to the dinner hour, was stocked with food, drink, and eating utensils by the servants, who then withdrew, leaving the guests to serve themselves.[5] Mary Hamilton discloses the sense of emancipation that the use of this contrivance produced. On one occasion in 1784 she wrote: 'My cousin Charles Cathcart din'd with us at Lady Stormont's; we had dumb waiters so our conversation was not under any restraint by ye Servants being in ye room.' The following year, after another visit to the Stormonts', she reported: 'At dinner we had y*e* comfortable *dumb waiters*, so our conversation was not obliged to be disagreeably *guarded* by y*e* attendance of Servants.'[6] Boswell likewise testifies to the effectiveness of the dumb-waiter in dissolving restraint. While carrying on a flirtation with the wife of his friend Col. Stuart in 1775, he wrote to Wilkes: 'We dined in all the elegance of two courses, and a dessert, with dumb-waiters, except when the second course and the dessert were served. We talked with unreserved freedom, as we had nothing to fear.'[7] But even in those houses where dumb-waiters were regularly used, the relief they afforded lasted only as long as the dinner hour; at other times servants were still free to observe their masters and their masters' friends.

Their observations enabled them to adopt the culture patterns of the classes they served. Both material and non-material cultural elements were taken over on an extensive scale.

[1] *Letters of Horace Walpole*, III. 387; V. 416; VI. 301.
[2] *Diary of John Hervey*, p. 153.
[3] Quoted in Straus, *Robert Dodsley*, p. 20.
[4] *World*, IV. 15.
[5] For a full discussion of the dumb-waiter see Margaret Jourdain, 'Dumb-waiters and What Nots', *Country Life*, 1945, XCVII. 286.
[6] Anson, *Mary Hamilton*, pp. 225, 268.
[7] *Letters of James Boswell*, I. 225-6.

THE SERVANT CLASS AS A CULTURAL NEXUS

In the matter of dress, for instance, the servant imitated his master in every detail. Defoe complained of this early in the century. On every side he saw 'the Maid striving to out-do the Mistress'.[1] No sooner does the country girl arrive in the Capital and get into service, he wrote, than

> Her Neat's Leather Shoes are . . . transformed into Stuff or Sattin ones, with high Heels: her Yarn Stockings are turned into fine Silk or Cotton ones; and her high wooden Patterns are kicked away for leathern Clogs; she must have a Trollopee and long Ruffles too, as well as her Mistress; and her poor scanty Linsey-Woolsey Petticoat, is changed into a good Silk one. . . .[2]

Eliza Haywood's comments on the subject pretty well substantiate Defoe's account. In an attack on what she terms 'Apeing the Fashion' she takes maidservants to task for having 'the ambition of imitating [their] Betters in point of Dress . . . .'—'Ribbands, Ruffles, Necklaces, Fans, Hoop-Petticoats, and all those Superfluities in Dress,' she goes on to say, are the things for which they spend their money. And addressing them directly, she declares: 'This Folly is indeed so epidemic among you, that few of you but lay out all you get in these imagin'd Ornaments of your Person. . . .'[3] Some very similar remarks appeared in a London newspaper towards the end of the century:

> Servants complain that their wages are too small, and they cannot dress decently without an advance: the word *decently* means apeing all the fashions of those they live with: muslins, caps, and mobs to go under the chin, are all exploded; silks, and muslins, and tasty slippers, supplant the stuff and cotton gowns, and strong soaled shoes, formerly used.[4]

The efforts of servants to dress like their employers appear to have been highly successful. For, according to Defoe, it was 'a hard Matter to know the Mistress from the Maid by their Dress. . . .'[5]

---

[1] Defoe, *Everybody's Business*, p. 13.
[2] *Ibid.*, p. 5. Cf. *A Trip from St. James's*, p. 60; [Susannah] Centlivre, 'The Artifice', *The Works of the Celebrated Mrs. Centlivre*, 1761, III. 322.
[3] Haywood, *A Present for a Servant-Maid*, p. 24. Cf. Broughton, *Serious Advice*, p. 21.
[4] *London Chronicle*, 1791, LXIX. 165b. Cf. Hanway, *Domestic Happiness*, p. 100.
[5] Defoe, *Everybody's Business*, p. 4. Cf. Defoe, *Law of Subordination*,

THE SERVANT CLASS AS A CULTURAL NEXUS

And Defoe's opinion was echoed later on by foreign travellers who were struck by the fine appearance of English maidservants. Saussure, whose impressions were gathered in the reigns of the first two Georges, did not go quite so far. '... servant-maids wear silks on Sundays and holidays,' he says, 'when they are almost as well dressed as their mistresses.'[1] But Grosley, whose visit was made in 1765, remarks: '... si on ne connoît pas la maîtresse, il est bien difficile de la distinguer de sa suivante.'[2] And although he confines his comments to servants of a single rank, Archenholz, writing about 1780, makes the same observation: 'As to a *Lady's Maid*, the eye of the most skilful *connoisseur* can scarcely distinguish her from the mistress. The appearance of a waiting-woman is that of an opulent and fashionable person....'[3]

Menservants no less than women copied the dress of their employers; they too sought as far as possible to be in the mode. Hence John Fuller, discussing the faults of domestics in 1799, includes both sexes when he condemns those 'who ape their superiors in dress'.[4] It was, of course, impossible for livery servants even to approximate their masters' appearance while on duty. But they did what they could in choosing their shoes, stockings, and linen, and in dressing their heads. Some whose liveries did not differ radically from ordinary clothes even went so far as to remove the tell-tale shoulder knot in order to 'look more like a Gentleman'.[5] Most, however, waited until they were off duty or out of place before attempting to shine sartorially. At such times they donned the 'rich vests' and 'laced ruffles' that earned John Macdonald the sobriquet of 'the Scotch Frenchman'.[6]

The endeavours of menservants to match the appearance of their employers were evidently quite as successful as those of maids. '... the valet de chambre,' declared Soame Jenyns, 'cannot be distinguished from his master, but by being better drest....'[7] And another writer expressed the same opinion, though in more general terms: 'The Servant is so blended with the Gentleman, that 'tis

p. 284; *World*, IV. 12; *Batchelor's Monitor*, p. 64; *London Magazine*, 1754, XXIII. 410; *European Magazine*, 1784, V. 245.
[1] Saussure, *Foreign View of England*, p. 204.
[2] Grosley, *Londres*, I. 132.   [3] Archenholz, *Picture of England*, p. 208.
[4] John Fuller, *History of Berwick upon Tweed*, 1799, p. 444.
[5] *London Chronicle*, 1757, II. 263c.
[6] *Memoirs of an Eighteenth-Century Footman*, pp. 236–7.
[7] *World*, IV. 12. Cf. *Annual Register*, 1761, IV. 201.

hard to know one from the other.'¹ These assertions are supported by the account Kielmansegge, the German traveller, gives of a dinner he attended at the Duke of Newcastle's: 'At least ten to twelve servants out of livery waited on us, of whom the majority wore long wigs, which would naturally make it difficult for a stranger to distinguish between guests and servants.'²

Two facts go a long way to explain the success of servants in imitating the dress of their employers. For one thing, they frequently received and wore their employers' cast-off clothing. Secondly, in many instances they were given every possible encouragement by their employers to dress in the height of fashion.³

At the same time they were also encouraged, or rather obliged, to adopt their employers' standards of cleanliness. The stress placed upon cleanliness is clearly revealed in Heasel's handbook for servants. While warning that they ought never 'aim at dress above their circumstances', Heasel enjoins them to make it their study to be neat and clean.⁴ Similarly, a handbook intended primarily for women who kept house asserts that to be personally cleanly is an obligation 'incumbent on servants in general', that in a cook cleanliness is 'as indispensably necessary as a knowledge of cookery' and that a 'want of cleanliness is no where so unpardonable' as in a dairy maid.⁵ Lord Chesterfield, then, was not out of step with his class in allowing his 'footmen forty shillings a year extraordinary, that they [might] be spruce and clean',⁶ nor was the third Earl of Egremont in making his postilions change the white jackets of their liveries every other day.⁷

But not only did employers prescribe standards of cleanliness for their domestics; they also inspired conformity by their example. For in this, as in so much else, servants took their masters as models. Sir Charles Hotham attests their bent when he warns his young daughter that unless she is cleanly herself her servants will never be so.⁸

The cleanliness that servants learned from precept and example

[1] *London Chronicle*, 1765, XVII. 300a.
[2] Kielmansegge, *Diary of a Journey to England*, p. 53.   [3] See Chap. IV.
[4] Heasel, *Servants Book of Knowledge*, p. 87. Cf. *ibid.*, p. 68.
[5] *Every Woman Her Own House-Keeper*, I. 195, 320, 358. Cf. Hanway, *Virtue in Humble Life*, 1774, I. 399; Barker, *Complete Servant Maid*, p. 6.
[6] *Letters of . . . Chesterfield*, IV. 1769.
[7] *Letters of Horace Walpole*, VIII. 347.
[8] A[nna] M. W. Stirling, *The Hothams*, 1918, II. 120.

was noted by contemporary observers. Defoe, who, as a rule, was highly critical of domestics, remarks in the introduction he wrote for Dodsley's *Servitude*: 'As to Neatness, I need not say much about it; we [servants] seem fond enough of appearing clean and handsome....'[1] And both Le Blanc and Grosley were in solid agreement with him; indeed, Le Blanc thought cleanliness the only good quality English servants possessed: 'La seule vertu qu'on trouve assez communément dans les Domentiques Anglois, est celles qui sont particulières à cette Nation, je veux dire le propreté.'[2]

Along with dress and standards of cleanliness, servants tended to assume their employers' way of speech. Smollet brings this out in his portrait of Winifred Jenkins, lady's maid to Tabitha Bramble: '... she seems to have adopted Mrs. Tabby's manner with her cast cloaths. She dresses and endeavours to look like her mistress.... She enters into her schemes of oeconomy, learns her phrases, repeats her remarks, imitates her style in scolding the inferior servants....'[3] A passage in one of Steele's essays is similarly revealing in this connexion: 'The very footman will be a fine gentleman in his master's way.... He practises the same oaths, the same ribaldry, the same way of joking.'[4]

The efforts of servants to imitate the speech of their employers were often highly successful. Archenholz found the conversation of maidservants 'such as if they kept the best company',[5] and doubtless there were many menservants who spoke equally well. But the endeavours of some in this direction fell considerably short of the mark. These failures are pilloried in the literature of the period: plays and novels alike contain pretentious servants who mouth malapropisms and other species of verbal error.

Literary sources also provide evidence that domestics imitated the gestures as well as the speech of their employers. In his poem *Servitude* Dodsley advises his fellow footmen to avoid the

> affected Ways
> And uppish Gestures practis'd now a days....[6]

---

[1] Dodsley, *Servitude*, p. 12.
[2] Le Blanc, *Lettres d'un François*, I. 147. Cf. Grosley, *Londres*, I. 132.
[3] Smollett, 'Humphry Clinker', *Works*, VII. 264.
[4] *Guardian*, II. 324. Cf. Darrell, *The Gentleman Instructed*, Pt. III. 511.
[5] Archenholz, *Picture of England*, p. 207.
[6] Dodsley, *Servitude*, p. 12.

Again, in one of Arthur Murphy's plays the footman upbraids the lady's maid with: '... second-hand airs! You take them at your ladies toilet with their cast gowns....'¹ And in a minor novel of the mid-century sometimes attributed to Sarah Fielding the heroine is depicted as encountering a gentleman's valet who, in imitation of his master, 'practised every affected air in a manner perfectly consistent with his tawdry trimmings, and threw himself into ... many odd contortions of body....'²

The bow of the manservant and the curtsy of the maid were often perfect copies. Sometimes, however, servants distorted almost beyond recognition the gestures they adopted. In such cases they resembled the fictitious valet described above, of whom the novelist says in conclusion: '... he betrayed himself, by overdoing the original.'³

But whatever the success of domestics in their attempts to imitate the speech and gestures of their employers, it is certain that their employers gave them strong inducements to try. '... pride,' says Soame Jenyns, 'has put it into our heads, that it is most honourable to be waited on by gentlemen and ladies....'⁴ And not only were domestics expected to be 'gentlemen and ladies' in point of dress, but also in accent and phrasing, and in bow and carriage.

No such encouragement spurred them on to imitate the social life of their employers; the force of example alone was responsible for their efforts in that direction. The effect of their employers' pursuit of pleasure was noticed by a writer in 1788: '... where Servants see their superiors living in ease, plenty, luxury, and festivity, it raises desires to which they might otherwise have been strangers.'⁵ Somewhat more pointed but having the same purport were the observations made by a writer in 1796. 'From you,' he said, directing his remarks to the employer class,

> they have imbibed certain notions of pleasure, gayety, amusements, which they had not before. They begin to experience wants of which

---

[1] *The Works of Arthur Murphy*, 1786, III. 10. Cf. Corry, *Satirical View of London*, p. 80.
[2] *The History of Betty Barnes*, 1753, II. 20.
[3] *Ibid.*
[4] *World*, IV. 11–12.
[5] *County Magazine*, 1788, II. 44. Cf. *An Enquiry into the Melancholy Circumstances of Great Britain*, p. 34; *Universal Magazine*, 1768, XLIII. 350.

they were not before conscious, they begin to stand in need of amusements, of idle time, of visiting seasons, and of days of pleasure. . . .¹

Not only the scope of the recreational activity of servants, but many of its forms as well were inspired by the example of the employer class. Their card parties and assemblies, their play-going, their visits to pleasure resorts, such as Vauxhall and Ranelagh, were all more or less conscious attempts to follow in their masters' footsteps. This was fully realized at the time, as a piece that appeared in a London newspaper in 1725 clearly demonstrates. Recounting how the magistrates had broken up a masquerade in Covent Garden, the writer reports that the participants had been 'either Chamber-maids, Cook-Maids, Foot-Men, or Apprentices' who had intended 'there to be very silly and very affected in Imitation of their Betters'; and he then goes on to moralize about the impetus that gave rise to such affairs: 'Thus we may see how Vice descends, and Servants seem to think that they have a Right to the Vices and Follies of their Masters and Mistresses, as well as to their old Cloathes. . . .'²

Along with the various forms of entertainment that they adopted, servants took over much of the related social ritual. The extent to which this variety of imitation was carried was described by a writer in 1757:

> The present Age are grown so unfortunately polite . . . that common Servants (I mean the Female part of them) send Cards to one another to make up a Party at Whist, or pass an Evening. . . .
> At a Meeting all Housewifery is laid aside and at once the Kitchen or Servants' hall is forgot; for you hear Nothing; but—'Why don't you help the Ladies?'—'The Ladies seemed disposed for this or that;' while on the other Hand, the Title of Gentleman is given promiscuously to every Scoundrel Lick-plate of a [Man-] Servant. . . .³

A letter addressed to the editor of a London newspaper enlarged on the same theme in 1780. The writer relates how the servant of a friend of his had received a card reading: 'Mr. Senegambia Mungo's compliments to Mr. John Skip, and should be proud of his company this evening at ——, Esqr's, in Cheapside,' and how the servant had explained that Mr. Senegambia

---

¹ *Universal Magazine*, 1796, XCVIII. 238.
² *Weekly Journal*, 1725, No. 337, Apr. 10, 2093-4.
³ *London Chronicle*, 1757, II. 263c.

was a black servant of Mr. ——, in Cheapside; that though an ignorant African, who could neither write nor read, he had all the pride of an East-Indian nabob; that he had before lived in a Nobleman's service, where the Steward had been accustomed to have his routs as well as his Master, and therefore thought he now had an equal right to have his. . . .

The writer continues by quoting the servant's description of the manner in which he had been received at the party:

> I was introduced . . . by the Cook, who apologized for her greasy condition, by saying that, she was obliged to cook the supper; and that as her Master kept very few servants, she was forced to act the part of the Mistress of the Ceremonies herself, it being very improper for 'Squire Senegambia to appear in that character. On entering the room, 'Squire Senegambia, who sate at the head of the table, rose, and saluted me, in broken English, with, 'Squire Skip, I am happy to be honoured with your company this evening. . . .[1]

Obviously, the whole account owes something to Townley's farce. But although the writer admits having invented the names, he presents it as a recital of fact and with the serious purpose of showing the punctilio observed by domestics in carrying on their social life.

Moralists insisted that in patterning their social life on that of their employers, servants adopted vices as well as amusements. In fact, much of the moral corruption said to exist amongst them was commonly blamed on the example set by their employers. The nobility and gentry were considered most culpable, hence the most vigorous indictments were aimed in their direction. Richard Graves baldly declared that the morals of 'servants in the more elevated ranks of life' suffered greatly 'from the examples of their masters'. And lashing out with shrill insistence at the upper classes, he asserted:

> Until some reformation . . . takes place in the manners and modes of life amongst the higher circles, in vain will the promoters of Sunday Schools, Schools of Industry, and other charitable institutions labour to reform the morals of the lower classes of people, which are infallibly corrupted, in the first fashionable family that takes them into service.[2]

[1] *Lloyd's Evening Post*, 1780, XLVII. 180c.
[2] Richard Graves, *The Reveries of Solitude*, 1793, p. 38; *Universal Magazine*, 1794, XCIV. 185. Cf. *Guardian*, II. 27; *Gentleman's Magazine*, 1746, XVI. 254; Jonas Hanway, *Midnight the Signal*, 1779, I. 115–16.

Thomas Day, the reformer, delivered himself on the subject in a similar vein. In a dialogue between a farmer and a justice of the peace, who is supposed to represent the upper classes, he makes the former say:

> So great is the contagion of your example that it extends to all about you. The laborious and simple youth that we are continually sending you out of the country, are, by a few months residence in your houses, transformed into the most worthless and contemptible characters: idle, luxurious, delicate, and abandoned, as their betters. Many an honest and laborious parent is left to weep in tears of blood, the hour when a misguided ambition first made him consent to send his child even into the service of a gentleman.[1]

Exactly what were the vices to which these strictures allude? Principally gambling and sexual licence. It was generally felt that the mania for play that infected the upper classes was invariably contracted by their servants. Thus Colquhoun expresses a widely held opinion when he states that *'menial Servants* in general, all over the Metropolis; but particularly... the pampered male and female domestics in the houses of men of fashion and fortune,' are encouraged in gaming by 'the example of their superiors'.[2] As for sexual irregularity, Ignatius Sancho, the Negro footboy who became a literary figure of some note, succinctly sets forth the common view in one of his Shandyesque letters: 'The example [of upper-class masters] spreads downwards from them to their domestics;—the laced valet and the livery beau either debauch the maids, or keep their girls. . . .'[3]

No doubt there is a certain amount of exaggeration in all this criticism. The effect of example is probably overstated. Yet there is no question that the moral standards of employers exerted a very real influence on the conduct of their servants.

It is equally certain that the reading habits of employers were taken over in the same way. Swift tells Stella that he noticed his

---

[1] Thomas Day, *A Dialogue between a Justice of the Peace and a Farmer*, 1786, 3rd ed., pp. 49–50.
[2] Colquhoun, *Police of the Metropolis*, pp. 150–1. Cf. Townley, *Apology for Servants*, pp. 11–12; Murphy, 'The Way to Keep Him', *Works*, III. 6; *London Chronicle*, 1787, LXI. 590b.
[3] *Letters of the Late Ignatius Sancho, an African*, ed. Joseph Jekyll, 1803, 5th ed., pp. 267–8. Cf. *Treatise on the Use and Abuse of the Second ... Table*, p. 14; *London Chronicle*, 1760, VII. 420c.

footman had borrowed one of his volumes of Congreve.[1] And Hanway cites 'as proof how servants imitate their master or mistress' the fact that he had often 'seen on the kitchen dresser, volumes of fictitious tales. . . .'[2] Dodsley, then, was not unique in being led to good literature by his employer. Such imitation was greatly facilitated by the access to books and other reading matter that servants enjoyed in many homes. Even where they were not permitted the use of the library or where no library was available, the newspapers and periodicals taken by their masters were usually within their reach. A writer commented on this in 1769: '. . . in this age of political speculation, few families are without newspapers carelessly scattered up and down the house, for the perusal of maids and foot-boys. . . .'[3]

According to one discerning observer, in music, too, the taste of domestics was derived from their masters. He confidently asserted: 'The Love of Musick is now descended from the Operahouse in the *Hay-market* to the little Publick Houses about this Metropolis, and common Servants may be now met with, who pretend as much Judgment of an Opera Tune as my Lady Duchess. . . .'[4]

Another sphere in which servants followed the lead of their employers was politics. Those masters who took an active part in political life used the members of their households for purposes of electioneering and for the staging of demonstrations.[5] Moreover, masters in general usually gave explicit instructions on election day to such servants as possessed the franchise. It was considered worthy of newspaper comment when in 1774 'A great lady' was rumoured to have told her servants 'to vote agreeably to their private choice'.[6] It seems probable, however, that in most cases it was unnecessary to bring pressure to bear. Very likely the majority of servants adopted their employers' politics of their own volition. That they did so is strongly suggested by an institution maintained

---

[1] Swift, *Journal to Stella*, p. 325.
[2] Hanway, *Virtue in Humble Life*, 1774, I. 407.
[3] *Oxford Magazine*, 1769, III. 84.
[4] *An Enquiry into the Melancholy Circumstances of Great Britain*, p. 34.
[5] For examples of the use of servants in political life see Hearne, *Collections*, I. 180; John Latimer, *Annals of Bristol*, 1893, p. 107; Wilkinson, *Worthies, Families and Celebrities of Barnsley*, p. 412; *Letters of Horace Walpole*, I. 208; *Letters and Journals of Lady Mary Coke*, IV. 425.
[6] *London Packet*, 1774, No. 779, Oct. 17–19, 4b.

by the livery servants of members of Parliament. From the reign of Charles II those servants met regularly as a mock legislature. In imitation of their employers they elected a presiding officer and debated the issues of the day, each of them taking his own master's political position. Swift alludes to one of their elections when, writing to Stella in 1710, he announces that Col. John Hill's servant 'designs to stand speaker for the Footmen', and then goes on to say: 'I am engaged to use my interest for him and have spoken to Patrick to get him some votes.'[1] Another of their elections was fully described in a news item that appeared in 1715:

> Last Week, the Foot-men belonging to the Members of the House of Commons, according to the Custom of their Masters . . . proceeded to the Choice of a Speaker; where those that espouse the cause of the Whigs chose Mr. Strickland's Man, and the Tory-Livery Gentry, the Servant of Sir Thomas Morgan. Hence a Battle ensu'd between the two contending Parties, wherein several broken Heads discover'd the Resolution of each to abide by its respective Choice, tho' the Combatants were at that Time forc'd to leave the Victory undeceided upon the breaking up of the House. But on Monday last, they return'd to their former Tryal of Skill; and the Tories, after an Obstinate Resistance from the Whigs, . . . had the better of their Adversaries, and carri'd their Mock-Speaker three Times round Westminster-Hall. After which, he that was chosen to fill their Chair, as well as his Predecessor, according to ancient Usage, spent their Crowns a-Piece in Drinks at a Dinner, which an adjacent Ale-house entertain'd them with Gratis.[2]

The scope of the imitation carried on by domestics, then, was very extensive. Indeed, to contemporaries it seemed that they virtually transformed themselves into replicas of their employers.

Perhaps imitation was carried farthest by the servants of the élite. Their identification with those they served was so complete that they even assumed their names and titles.[3] Steele portrays this practice in a humorous vignette of the servants who made up the mock House of Lords:

> Falling in the other Day at a Victualling-House near the House of Peers, I heard the Maid come down and tell the Landlady at the

---

[1] Swift, *Journal to Stella*, pp. 76–7.
[2] *Weekly Packet*, 1715, No. 143, Mar. 26–Apr. 2, 3a.
[3] *Connoisseur*, III. 238; *The Footman: an Opera*, 1732, pp. vii, 7; Townley, *High Life Below Stairs*, passim.

Bar, That my Lord Bishop swore that he would throw her out at Window, if she did not bring up more Mild Beer, and that my Lord Duke would have a double Mug of Purle. My surprise was increased, in hearing loud and rustick Voices speak and answer to each other upon the Public Affairs, by the Names of the most Illustrious of our Nobility; till of a sudden one came running in, and cry'd the House was rising. Down came all the Company together, and away! The Alehouse was immediately filled with Clamour, and scoring one Mug to the Marquis of such a Place, Oil and Vinegar to such an Earl, three Quarts to my new Lord for wetting his Title, and so forth.[1]

Steele also alludes to this mummery in his play *The Conscious Lovers* (1722). Referring to the corps of London livery servants, Tom says: 'Nay, sir, our order is carried up to the highest dignities and distinctions; step but into the Painted Chamber, and by our titles you'd take us all for men of quality.'[2]

It should not be overlooked that much of the imitation carried on by servants was viewed with stern disapproval by employers. In some quarters the slightest mimetic venture was frowned on as unbecoming; in others, while the prestige value of servants who dressed and acted like ladies and gentlemen was fully appreciated, it was felt that imitation ought to stop there. But all deterrents were unavailing in the face of the independent spirit of the servant class—the same spirit that expressed itself in insubordination and in the vigorous pursuit of self-interest. Had it been otherwise, domestics would have been far less effective than they were as cultural intermediaries between their employers and the members of other classes.

III

Just as servants modelled themselves on their employers, they were in turn taken as models by those beneath them in the social scale. The imitators varied according to the social status of the individual servant: those who looked to the shopkeeper's maid were not of the same class as those who looked to the land steward of the duke. But none of the social levels from the lower middle class down failed to find exemplars among servants.

Extensive intercourse between these levels and the servants provided the contact necessary for imitation. The execution of their

[1] *Spectator*, II. 34.   [2] *Steele's Plays*, p. 281.

routine duties, for instance, brought servants into touch with the members of diverse classes and occupations. So, too, did their social life: the visits paid to friends and relatives, the visits received at home, the parties and assemblies at which there were guests from outside the servant class. Moreover, their constant movement from one household to another had the same effect; for during periods of unemployment they naturally mingled with the people amongst whom they lived.

The range of contact provided by this intercourse would have been less broad but for the independent spirit of the servant class. For if servants had conformed to the pattern of conduct prescribed by the accepted theory of the relationship of master and servant, they would have led a relatively isolated existence. They would have had little or no social life; there would have been few intervals of unemployment.

But since domestics were far from being isolated, they diffused the cultural elements they took over from their masters. Their efficiency in this respect was pointed out by Vicesimus Knox, a writer concerned with 'the Effects of the bad Example of the Great among their menial Servants, Domesticks and Dependents'. After stating that largely because of the example set for them by their employers there were 'few orders in the community more profligate than servants and domestic dependents in rich and noble families', he averred: 'Where-ever they go, they diffuse among the lower orders, a spirit of impudence, discontent, extravagance, and debauchery. . . .'[1] Colquhoun, writing in 1795, made essentially the same points:

> The examples of the great and opulent, operate most powerfully among the tribe of *menial servants* they employ; and these carry with them into the lower ranks that spirit of gambling and dissipation which they have practised in the course of their servitude; thus producing consequences of the most alarming nature to the general interest of the Community.[2]

And another writer, who viewed the role of domestics as cultural intermediaries from an economic rather than a moral standpoint,

---

[1] *London Chronicle*, 1782, LII. 287a. Knox appears to have altered the wording later on; cf. *Works of Vicesimus Knox*, I. 344–5.
[2] Colquhoun, *Police of the Metropolis*, p. 143. Cf. Seaton, *Conduct of Servants*, p. 214; *World*, IV. 15–16.

contended in 1785 that 'by their example they spread the contagion of luxury and idleness among the lower ranks of people'.[1] All three of these observers confined their remarks to the influence exerted by the servants of the nobility, gentry, and upper middle class; but there is no reason to suppose that those who served the less well-to-do members of the middle classes were not effective in the same way.

The cultural elements relayed by domestics descended along two different courses. There were lines of transmission that ran directly from servants to their imitators. There were also lines that ran down through the servant class before reaching imitators outside it. Such a line is amusingly illustrated by a sketch written in 1761. It relates how my lord, having been entrusted with a court secret, confided it to his lady, who whispered it to her woman, who told it to the valet, who passed it on to a servant of lesser rank, from whom it descended by similar stages, until it finally reached the footmen of the family, who gave it general currency.[2] But this sort of line did not necessarily run through the servants of a single household. It might, for instance, run from the land steward of a duke to the valet of a gentleman, then to the butler of a merchant and finally to some such outsider as a milkwoman, chandler, or ironmonger.

Whatever the sequence, servants with the higher occupational and social statuses were imitated by those below them. 'The generality of common servants,' asserts a handbook for domestics, 'ape the servants of the quality in every particular. . . .'[3] A fuller description might have added that both among 'common servants' and among 'the servants of the quality' the chain of imitation ran in this same direction: the shopkeeper's housemaid copied the merchant's housemaid; the valet of the gentleman copied the valet of the duke.

The cultural elements thus relayed were of all sorts: articles of clothing, gestures, moral values, ideas. A new attitude towards church or state was as likely to be passed on as a new way of cocking a hat. James Lackington, the bookseller, writing in 1804, makes the point that Gentlemen's servants, having been taught infidelity in London, and while waiting at table, have spread the contagion

[1] *Manufactures Improper Subjects of Taxation*, p. 12.
[2] *London Chronicle*, 1761, IX. 369c–70a.
[3] *Servants Pocket-Book*, p. 9.

throughout the region of their acquaintance.[1] During the whole of the preceding century servants had been similarly effective in disseminating their employers' views.

In some cases this process of diffusion can be clearly traced. Snuff and tea are excellent examples.

Snuff was first introduced into England in the late sixteenth century.[2] It was promptly taken up by the élite. But it was not until the eighteenth century, when the importation of larger quantities and coarser varieties lowered the price, that other classes followed their example. The spread of snuff-taking was a gradual process, but by the middle of the century the practice had become universal. Thomas Alcock, writing in 1752, observes that snuff-taking

> for some Time was practised chiefly by the better Sort; but as Inferiors are always apt to imitate the Ways of their Superiors, tis now become general among the lowest Class; and you shall scarce meet with a common Handicrafts-Man . . . but what is more or less addicted to this Habit.[3]

It was to a large extent through servants that the habit descended. As early as 1709, Mrs. Manley mentioned footmen and chambermaids as using snuff;[4] in 1725 Defoe spoke of maidservants as habitual users;[5] and in 1752 Alcock wrote: 'The Custom is become so prevalent and notorious, especially amongst the Females, that in Advertisements for Servant-Maids, we see it particularly mentioned very often, that no Snuff-takers will be accepted'.[6] Having thus taken over the use of snuff from their employers, servants passed it on in turn.

Tea descended in precisely the same way. At the end of the seventeenth century tea was still a luxury confined to the élite; in the early years of the eighteenth century it began to make its way among the subordinate classes. As in the case of snuff, increased importation and the introduction of inferior grades, especially Chinese green tea, made its diffusion possible by reducing the price; and by mid-century it had reached the lower classes. Han-

---

[1] *The Confessions of J[ames] Lackington*, 1804, p. 78.
[2] Mattoon M. Curtis, *Snuff and Snuff Boxes*, New York, 1935, p. 46.
[3] Thomas Alcock, *Observations on the Defects of the Poor Laws*, 1752, p. 46.
[4] *Female Tatler*, 1709, No. 10, July 27–9, 2a.
[5] Defoe, *The Maid-Servant's Modest Defence*, p. 8.
[6] Alcock, *Defects of the Poor Laws*, p. 46.

way, descanting on the evils of tea-drinking in 1756, commented on their addiction to it with stern disapproval:

> It is the curse of this nation, that the *labourer* and *mechanic* will *ape* the *lord*. . . . To what a *height* of folly must a nation be arrived at, when the *common people* are not satisfied with *wholesome* food at *home*, but must go to the remotest regions to please a *vicious palate!* There is a certain lane near *Richmond*, where beggars are often seen, in summer season, drinking their *tea*. You may see labourers who are *mending the roads* drinking their *tea*; it is even drank in *cindercarts*; and what is not less absurd, sold out in cups to *Haymakers*.[1]

The part played by servants in the diffusion of the tea habit is obvious. Having seen their employers drink tea and having drunk it themselves, they transmitted the practice to those who stood beneath them in the social scale. Hanway was alive to their responsibility for its downward spread. Considering how tea-drinking could be eliminated, he says:

> The suppression of this dangerous custom depends entirely on the example of ladies of rank in this country. Tea will certainly be acknowledged a bad thing, as soon as [they] leave off drinking it. No *lady's* woman, or gentlewoman's chambermaid, will drink a liquor which her mistress no longer uses.[2]

Alcock also realized the part played by servants in this. 'It is now [1752] usual with many Female Servants,' he wrote,

> to insist on Tea in their Agreement, and to refuse serving where this is not allowed. And when from Servants they go to be poor Men's Wives, we may naturally suppose they carry the same expensive Appetites and Habits with them, which being propagated by Example to the Offspring, the Evil becomes still more epidemical.[3]

Another aspect of the role of servants as cultural intermediaries is touched on here: their continued effectiveness after they quit service. Much of what they adopted in imitation of their employers they retained after they entered other occupations; much of what

---

[1] Jonas Hanway, *An Essay on Tea*, 1757, p. 272. Cf. *Considerations on the Dearness of Corn and Provisions*, p. 9; Alcock, *Defects of the Poor Laws*, p. 47.
[2] Hanway, *Essay on Tea*, p. 275.
[3] Alcock, *Defects of the Poor Laws*, p. 48.

they learned while in service they carried over into later life. This is well brought out in an imaginary dialogue between a haberdasher of small wares and his wife written for a London newspaper in 1777. The wife, a former servant, declares: 'I'm resolved that Jack's next Livery shall be the same as our Butler had when I lived at Sarvice at Squire Brewer's, and have double Rows of Lace, and two *Eblets*.' And the long-suffering husband replies with ironical humour: '. . . what a Fool I was to marry into a Squire's Family. . . .'[1] The German traveller Wendeborn noted ex-servants like the haberdasher's wife on every side and expressed the belief that the habits and tastes they had acquired through their former way of life eventually brought many of them to impoverishment and ruin:

> Servants in general live nearly as well as their masters and mistresses; and when servant-men or maids marry, they frequently begin the married state with a life of more expense, or rather profusion than their circumstances will admit, and continue the same until children and want force them to apply to their parish.[2]

Clara Reeve, who having herself lived as a domestic, knew service, intimately as an occupation, in one of her novels gives an account of two former servants such as Wendeborn describes: '. . . the habit of imitating the manners of their superiors, in the way of life they had seen, made them go to the extent of their fortune, and sometimes exceed it.'[3] But whether extravagance drove them to the parish or prudence brought them prosperity, ex-servants were imitated by their neighbours and acquaintances, who thus received cultural elements that employers had passed on in former years.

IV

Servants not only carried cultural elements from class to class; they also promoted the flow from city to country. In fact, they were among the principal supports of the cultural dominion that London exercised over the rural regions.

London was the Capital; it was the great urban centre and home of the élite for a considerable portion of the year. In consequence, it was there that the vast majority of cultural innovations had their

---

[1] *St. James's Chronicle*, 1777, No. 2522, May 8–10, 2a.
[2] Wendeborn, *View of England*, I. 115–16.
[3] Reeve, *Two Mentors*, p. 32.

THE SERVANT CLASS AS A CULTURAL NEXUS

origin and began their downward course. Only later did they penetrate the countryside and make their way by stages into the more remote counties.

At the beginning of the period they moved very slowly, since the difficulties of travel severely limited contact between the country and the Metropolis. The result was naturally vast differences in such particulars as dress, speech, and modes of behaviour. As the century advanced, these differences became less pronounced and all but disappeared. For the demands of an ever-growing internal commerce brought about an improvement in the condition of the roads; with improved roads came better vehicles and more and faster coach service; and these changes, in turn, fostered intercourse between London and the country, which, as it increased, accelerated the flow of cultural elements. Sir John Hawkins, writing in 1787, calls attention to the fact 'that a new fashion pervades the whole of this our island almost as instantaneously as a spark of fire illuminates a mass of gunpowder'.[1]

Those whose movement thus gradually weakened the distinctions in culture between country and Capital belonged to many different classes. As the conditions of travel and the means of transportation improved, noblemen and gentlemen, yeomen and farmers, labourers and servants in husbandry all visited London in greater numbers and with greater frequency; and for the same reasons London merchants, tradesmen, and artisans more often made excursions into the country.

When noblemen and gentlemen came up to London, whether for a brief stay or for 'the Season', they brought along their servants; when they left, they carried them back. Similarly, the London merchant took his household with him when he visited rural parts. Very often, too, servants journeyed to London on their own and later drifted back into the country again.

It was this mobility that made the servant class an important link between London and the rural regions. For in London servants encountered many cultural innovations at their source, and these they subsequently carried down into the country.

Some servants, of course, never visited London; and many visited it but infrequently. In the early decades of the century these country servants retained some degree of rusticity, despite their imitation of their employers and other social superiors. Later, under

[1] Hawkins, *Life of Samuel Johnson*, p. 262.

the influence of servants who had experienced the life of the Metropolis, the number of those whose thinking and behaviour bore the distinctive stamp of the country declined. Commenting in 1790 on their gradual disappearance, Tate Wilkinson, the actor, remarks that 'in some bye villages some traces are still to be seen; but in every country gentleman's family the servants at present are as forward fine gentlemen's gentlemen as the metropolis can boast of. . . .'[1]

Servants who had lived in London affected the general population of the countryside even more profoundly than they did their own rustic brethren. Pointing out in 1773 that 'The conveniency of trade', 'the necessary calling together of the Legislature' and 'the attachment to courts and other amusements' draw noblemen and gentlemen to London, John Arbuthnot observes:

> These necessarily carry with them a suite of attendants, which I cannot but think mischievous to a state; for the loitering life of a gentleman's servant not only debauches his own mind, but by his attendance on the great, and his intercourse with the inferior class, makes him the vehicle of conveyance of those manners which ruin the industrious tradesman, though necessary accomplishments in the rich. If they unfortunately see a bad example, they retail it out with all its mischievous consequences; and in this manner does their appearance and example operate when they return with their masters to the country.[2]

Wendeborn, writing in 1790, also credits them with having a considerable effect upon the inhabitants of the country. The ways of country people, he says, were formerly characterized by a greater simplicity; and he accounts for the change by explaining that when the roads were bad and travel was difficult, 'the great and the rich' did not 'so frequently and expeditiously, as they now do, go into the most distant parts of the kingdom with their servants and attendants, who carry the follies and vices of the capital, so successfully among the people who live remote from it'.[3]

The diffusion that these observers describe is still further elucid-

---

[1] Tate Wilkinson, *Memoirs of His Own Life*, York, 1790, IV. 105.
[2] Arbuthnot, *Inquiry into the . . . Present Price of Provisions*, pp. 48-9.
[3] Wendeborn, *View of England*, I. 359-60. Cf. Thomas Short, *A Comparative History of the Increase and Decrease of Mankind in England*, 1767, p. 24; Huntingford, *Laws of Masters and Servants*, pp. 99-100; *Gentleman's Magazine*, 1791, LXI. 986-7.

ated by Vicesimus Knox. In one of his essays Knox exposes the actual mechanics of the process. The servant, he writes, having spent 'the Season' in London, goes down into the country.

> He is finely dressed, and naturally excites the admiration of the village, and his own family. What he says, comes from him with the authority of an oracle. He considers himself, indeed, as greatly enlightened, and undertakes to communicate the illumination. In the first place, he ridicules the rusticity of his friends and neighbours, and laughs at their awkward dress and behaviour. Their patient submission to labour, he calls plodding and slavery; their sobriety and temperance, covetousness and meanness. . . .
>
> He commonly confirms his opinions by alleging the example of my Lord. 'My Lord (says he) I would have you know, is a great man, a very great man. . . .'
>
> The lads and lasses of the village listen to his lesson with open mouths, and hearts which pant to imitate their kind instructor.[1]

V

The role of the servant class in the process of cultural change thus becomes clear. It was vitally involved in many of the mutations that transformed the England of Queen Anne into the England of George IV.

During the eighteenth century the standard of living of the lower classes progressively improved. Many overseas imports whose consumption had previously been confined to the élite filtered down to the lowest social level. The descent of snuff and tea has been traced; sugar is another example. Certain native products, too, such as butter and white bread, for the first time became articles of popular consumption, at least in some regions.

In the same way standards of dress and personal cleanliness percolated down to the lower classes. During the second half of the century foreigners repeatedly commented on how well English labourers dressed; doctors attested their cleanliness.

Modes of behaviour likewise descended. The studied decorum and conscious refinement of the élite by degrees worked their way through the middle classes to the base of the social structure. Each decade witnessed a certain amount of improvement. At the close

---

[1] *London Chronicle*, 1782, LII. 287ab; *Works of Vicesimus Knox*, I. 345–6.

of the century, in consequence, it was possible to look back and marvel at how the lower classes had been transformed.

Ideas and moral values followed a similar downward course. The growing benevolence of the élite, to take an outstanding example, gradually spread to the lower classes, producing amongst them a greater regard for human life and limb, and tenderness towards animals. The new attitude developed very slowly, but by the close of the period the lower classes had lost much of the callousness and brutality depicted earlier by Hogarth.

By promoting the circulation of cultural elements the servant class was instrumental in furthering all these changes and many others like them. It also accelerated the rate at which such changes took place, for cultural elements descended much more rapidly through servants than when they passed less directly from one level to another.

BIBLIOGRAPHY

Listed below are the most important works on servants and service in eighteenth-century England. The editions are those cited in the footnotes. As in the footnotes, unless otherwise stated, the place of publication is London.

I. CONTEMPORARY WORKS

Anon. *Every Woman Her Own House-Keeper*, 1796, 4th ed., 2 vols.
Anon. *Laws Concerning Masters and Servants*, 1768, 2nd ed.
Anon. *A Present for Servants*, 1768, 8th ed.
Anon. *A Proposal for the Amendment and Encouragement of Servants*, 1752.
Anon. *The Servant's Friend*, n.d.
Anon. *The Servants Pocket-Book*, 1761.
Anon. *A Treatise on the Use and Abuse of the Second, Commonly Called, the Steward's Table*, n.d.
Barker, Anne, *The Complete Servant Maid*, n.d.
Broughton, Thomas, *Serious Advice and Warning to Servants*, 1763, 4th ed.
[Cook, Ann,] *Ann Cook and Friend*, ed. Regula Burnet, 1940.
[Defoe, Daniel,] *Everybody's Business is Nobody's Business*, 1767.
Defoe, Daniel, *The Great Law of Subordination Consider'd*, 1724.
[Defoe, Daniel,] *The Maid-Servant's Modest Defence*, 1725.
Dodsley, Robert, 'The Footman', *A Muse in Livery*, 1732.
[Dodsley, Robert,] *Servitude*, 1728.
Glass, Hannah, *The Servants Directory*, 1761.
[Hanway, Jonas,] *Eight Letters to His Grace —— Duke of ——, on the Custom of Vails-Giving*, 1760.
Hanway, Jonas, *The Sentiments and Advice of Thomas Trueman*, 1760.
Haywood, Eliza, *A Present for a Servant-Maid*, Dublin, 1743.
Heasel, Anthony, *The Servants Book of Knowledge*, 1773.
Huntingford, James, *The Laws of Masters and Servants Considered*, 1790.
[Johnson, Mary,] *Madam Johnson's Present*, 1769, 5th ed.
Laurence, Edward, *The Duty of a Steward to His Lord*, 1727.
Macdonald, John, *Memoirs of an Eighteenth-Century Footman*, ed. John Beresford [1927].
Mordant, John, *The Complete Steward*, 1761, 2 vols.
Seaton, Thomas, *The Conduct of Servants in Great Families*, 1720.
Swift, Jonathan, *Directions to Servants in General*, 1745.

BIBLIOGRAPHY

Tancred, Christopher, *A Scheme for an Act of Parliament for the Better Regulating Servants, and Ascertaining Their Wages*, 1724.
[Townley, James,] *An Apology for Servants*, 1760.
[Townley, James,] *High Life Below Stairs*, 1775.

II. RECENT WORKS

George, M. Dorothy, 'The Early History of Registry Offices', *Economic Journal* (Supplement), 1929, IV.

Hecht, J. Jean, 'Continental and Colonial Servants in Eighteenth-Century England', *Smith College Studies in History*, XL.

Hughes, Edward, 'The Eighteenth Century Estate Agent', *Essays in Honour of James Eadie Todd* [1949].

Marshall, Dorothy, 'The Domestic Servants of the Eighteenth Century', *Economica*, 1929, IX.

Simpson, Violet, 'Servants and Service in [the] Eighteenth Century', *Cornhill Magazine*, 1903, XIV.

INDEX

Abdy, Rev. Stotherd, 167
Aberdeen, 164
'A Country Friend', 119
'A Country Gentleman', 169
Adam, Robert, 104
Addison, Joseph, 176
Admittance fees, 170-2
Advice to a Sister, 73
Agent-in-Chief, the, 40
Alcock, Thomas, 222, 223
Alicant, 193
Almack's, 165
Althorp, 106
Angelo, Henry, 198
Anne, Queen, 227
Appeal to the Public, 23
Arbuthnot, John, 226
'Arcadius', 205
Archenholz, Johann W., describes magnetism of London, 13; on legal actions brought by servants, 79; on servants' quarters, 105; on crowding caused by servants, 107; on appearance of maidservants, 119, 210; on the size of vails, 161; credits Chesterfield with abolition of vails, 163; finds vails-giving abandoned, 168; on conversation of maidservants, 212
Arkwright, Sir Richard, 1
Arundel, 5
Ashby, Rev. George, 56, 57
Asylum for Orphan Girls, 21
Axwell Park, 103

Bagnigge Wells, 135
Bailiff, the, 44-5

Baker, John, on Duke of Norfolk's retinue, 5; size of his household, 8; on suit brought by servant, 80; turnover of his servants, 82; care of his servants, 98; teaches maid, 99-100; agrees about livery, 118-19; describes visit of servants' guests, 129; his servants visit Sadler's Wells, 135; board wages paid by, 155; pension given housekeeper by, 175
Baker, the, 44
Barrels, 49
Barrington, Lord, 169
Bath, 197, 202
Baynards, the, 3
Beckford, William, the elder, 1, 174
Bedford Coffee House, 200-1
Bedford, 4th Duke of, 5, 97, 136, 150, 151
Bedford, 5th Duke of, 125
Bedford House, 97, 104, 106, 107, 108, 117
Bedfordshire, 126, 128
Bedingfeld, Sir Robert, 100
Below Stairs, 180
Benefactions, 173-6, 197
Bere, Nancy, 183-4
Berkeley, Lord, 174
Berry, Mary, 7
Betts, Rev. George, 7
Betty's, 44
Bidewell, Billy, 129
Birmingham, 191
Blenheim, 104, 126, 171
Board wages, 132, 153-6, 157
Bodham, Mrs., 128
Bogle, Mr., 134

INDEX

Bolton, Duke of, 189
Bond Street, 135
Boscawen, Frances, 7, 82
Boswell, James, 62, 208
Bow Street, 133
Bramah, Joseph, 188
Bramble, Matt., 2, 14, 49, 135
Bramble, Tabitha, 212
Bray, Thomas, 24
Brighthelmstone, 203
Bristol, Earl of, 5, 113, 116, 158, 208
Bristol, Lady, 116
British Society for Rewarding Servants, 94
Brocket Hall, 104
Brocklesby, Dr. Richard, 95
Broughton, Thomas, servant, 197
Broughton, Thomas, writer, 72, 87
Brown, Lancelot, 195–6, 197
Browne, Hawkins, 95
Bull's Head Inn, Manchester, 196
Burley-on-the-Hill, 50, 58
Burnet, Gilbert, 4–5
Burney, Fanny, 52, 126
Burrell, Timothy, 116
Bussy, Sally, 188, 194
Butler, the, 46–8, 104
'B.X.', 89
Byng, Admiral, 60
Byng, John, 171, 176

Cannons, 97, 107, 112, 113, 115, 118, 171
Cappe, Mrs. Harrison, 3, 125
Card money, 168–70
Carlisle House, 135
Carlyle, Dr. Alexander, 49, 207
Caroline, Queen, 119, 162
Carter, Mrs. Elizabeth, 11, 71
Cartwright, Maj. John, 166
Castars, Mr., 193, 195
Cast-clothes, 115–16, 211
Cathcart, Charles, 208
Cave, Lady, 97
Cawley, 128
Chambermaid, the, 65–6
Champion, 179

Chandos, Duke of, 97, 112, 118, 150, 188, 190, 193
Characters of servants, 32, 83–5, 92–5
Charity schools, 21, 22
Charles II, 218
Charles, Adam, 188
Charlton, Francis, 194
Chastisement of servants, 78–80
Chatham, Lord, 196
Chatsworth, 171
Cheapside, 214, 215
Cheltenham, 126, 203
Chenlis, William, 99
Chesterfield, Lord, 60, 71, 163, 193, 194, 211
Chetwynd, Lord, 193
Chickwell, Sir John, 3
Christmas boxes, 172, 173
Chudleigh, Elizabeth, 182
Claremont, 5
Clark, William, 127
Clarke, Ned, 98
Clavering, Sir Thomas, 103
Clayton, Miss, 188
Clerkenwell, 188
Clerk of the kitchen, the, 42–3, 104
Clerk of the stables, the, 42
Clerks of the Signet, 164
Cleveland, Duke of, 125
Clubs of servants, 85–7, 132
'Clytus', 183
Coachman, the, 51
Cobham, Lord, 195
Coke, Edward, 100
Coke, Lady Mary, 96, 97, 100
Cole, Rev. William, 11, 79, 99, 117, 128, 130, 131
Coleraine, Lord, 99
Colquhoun, Patrick, on servant unemployment, 25; on number of servants, 34; proposes legal penalties for bad servants, 88–9; his tract on public houses, 189; on the gambling of servants, 216, 220; on servants as agents of diffusion, 220

INDEX

Combinations of servants, 85–7
Companion, the, 62–3
Confectioner, the, 43, 44
Congreve, William, 217
Conscious Lovers, 219
Conway, Henry, 207
Cook, the, 65
Copley, Mr., 129
'Cornelius', 20
Cornelys, Teresa, 135
Country servants, 10–12, 80, 225–7
Coutts, James, 116
Covent Garden, 133
Covent Garden Journal, 83
Coventry, 191
Cowslade, John, 99
Craftsman, 2
Crauford, John, of Errol, 96
Crescent, the, 197
Crown Inn, Rochester, 190
Cumberland, 27, 153, 165
Cumberland, Bishop, 197
Cumberland, Richard, 168
Curwen, Samuel, 28–9
Custance, John, 6, 129

Dacre, Lord, 17
Dairy maid, 68
Dalkeith, Lady, 207
Darrell, William, 75
Dartiquenave, Charles, 191
Dartmouth, Lord, 131
Dartry, Lady, 99
Dashwood, Sir Francis, 167
Davers, Sir Robert, 103
Dawson, John, 97
Day, Thomas, 216
Defoe, Daniel, on country girls, 15; on tradesmen, 16; on Yorkshire grooms, 57; on the inconstancy of servants, 81; on combinations of servants, 85–6; proposes remedies for bad servants, 88, 90, 91; proposes maids wear liveries, 119; on maidservants' clothing, 122, 209–10; notes great houses, 171; assists Dodsley, 191; on Tunbridge Wells, 202–3; on cleanliness of servants, 212; on maids taking snuff, 222
Deibbiege, Maj., 187
Delany, Mary, 82, 188
Delany, Rev. Patrick, 72, 76
Derby, Lord, 105, 120
Derbyshire, 16
Descriptions, 4
Devonshire, 27, 153, 165
Directions for Servants, 87
Directions to Lords and Ladies, 206
Dodsley, Robert, on obedience, 73, 74; on status of servants, 179; career of, 191–2, 197; status of, 195; on scrutiny of masters by servants, 207; admonishes footmen against affectation, 212; led to letters by employer, 191, 217
Donelli, Dr., 97
Dorset, Duke of, 60
Doubleday, Dr., 97
Dow, Col., 156
Drake family, 107
Drury Lane Theatre, 137, 138
Duck, Stephen, 191
Duff, Mr., 134
Dumb-Waiters, 208
Duncan, Sir William, 97
Du Quesne, Rev., 7

East India Co., 194
Edinburgh Society for the Encouragement of Arts, 164
Education of servants, 99–100
Edwards, Jane, 126
Egmont, Earl of, 193, 194
Egremont, Earl of, 211
Elliot, Sir Gilbert, 125
Elliott, Sir John, 97
Ely, Bishop of, 4
Enclosures, 15–16
Essex Head Tavern, London, 189–90
Experienced English Housekeeper, 196
Exton, 126

INDEX

Faculty of Advocates, 164
Farington, Joseph, 86
Faulkner, Alderman, 87
Female Orphan Asylum, 22
Female Tatler, 2
Ferguson, Charles, 187
Ferguson, Sir Adam, 95
Fermanagh, Lady, 18, 99
Fielden, Joshua, 1
Fielding, Henry, 66, 83, 139, 201, 205
Fielding, Sarah, 213
Fielding, Sir John, on occupations of women, 20; employs girl from Orphan Asylum, 22; notes shortage of maids of all work, 24; on size of servant class, 33; on effects of dishonest testimonials, 83; on advantages of a state register office, 93; register office of, 94; requests information on illegal assemblies, 133; on servants taking public houses, 188
Fitzroy, Lt.-Gen., 6
Fleet, Mr., 129
Fleetwood, Charles, 137
Fletcher, Anthony, 197
Foley, Lord, 126
Footboy, 59, 60
Footman, 207
'Footmanius', 190
Footman, the, 8, 13, 14, 51–5, 86
Forbes, Admiral, 174
Forbes, Sir John, 195
Forster, Nathaniel, 178
Foundling Hospital, 21
Fountain Inn, Biggleswade, 190
Fox, Charles, 193
Fox, Henry, 193
Frances family, 194
Francis, Dr., 188
Francis, Sir Philip, 188
Frederica, Georgia, 193
Free, James, 85
French servants, 44, 46, 62, 87
Frozard, Mr., 190
Fuller, John, 210

Gage, Lord, 5
Galloway, Earl of, 125
Gamekeeper, the, 58, 59, 104
Gardener, the, 48–50
Garrick, David, 138
Gentleman, 132
Gentleman-in-waiting, the, 42
Gentleman's Magazine, 12
George III, 196, 203
George IV, 227
George Inn, Warminster, 189
Gibbons, Dr. William, 174
Gilpin, Rev. William, 7
Gilray, James, 203
Gisborne, Thomas, 69–70
Glass, Hannah, 68
Gloucestershire, 85, 126
Gonzalez, Don Manoel, 86
Grace, William, 11, 130
Grafton, 2nd Duke of, 193
Grafton, 3rd Duke of, 6
Grant, Mr., 134
Graves, Richard, 215
Gray, Thomas, 116
Great Queen Street, 133
Great Saxham House, 104
Greaves, Samuel, 190
Greenwich Hospital, 98
Grenville, George, 127
Grenville, Sir Richard, 195
Grey, Lady, 160
Groom of the chambers, the, 50–1
Groom, the, 51, 57
Grosley, Pierre, 156, 160, 210, 212
Grosvenor Square, 105, 198
Gulwell, 31
Gunning, Sir Robert, 99
Gunton, Sally, 187
Guy, Henry, 193

Hackfall, 106
Hackman family, 183
Halifax, Lady, 207
Hall's Stables, 190
Ham, Elizabeth, 130
Hamilton, Mary, 99, 208
Hampshire, 126
Hampton Court, 196

INDEX

Hands, Elizabeth, 191
Hanway, Jonas, on migrants to London, 12; on enclosures, 16; on servants' concern with profit, 23; advertises for cook, 24; on servant unemployment, 25; warns of register offices, 31; advertises for servants, 33; on master-servant relationship, 72, 76; commends humility, 73–4; on vails, 89, 159, 165, 182; on meat consumed by servants, 111; on liveries, 121; on servants' play-going, 136; on servants' recreation, 139–40; on poundage, 173; on status of servants, 179–80, 181; on promotion of servants, 182; on imitation of employers, 217; on servants' tea-drinking, 222–3
Hardwicke, Lord, 5, 160, 165
Harewood House, 104
Harewood, Lord, 104
Harley, Robert, 193
Harris, Mr., 166
Harris, Mrs., 126, 166, 167
Harrison, William, 4
Harrogate, 203
Harrop's Manchester Mercury, 196
Hart, Thomas, 17
Harvey, Peter, 189, 194
Hawkins, Sir John, 225
Hayward, Simon, 189
Haywood, Eliza, praises timidity, 73; on inconstancy of servants, 81; her *Present for a Servant-Maid*, 87; on hauteur of employers, 96; on servants' expecting delicacies, 112; on the security of service, 123; warns against pleasure resorts, 135; on time off, 140; on imitation of employers, 209
Hearne, Thomas, 60, 99
Heasel, Anthony, on valet, 45; on butler, 47; on groom, 57; on cook, 65; on maidservants, 67; on laundry-maid, 68; on loyalty of servants, 75; on housekeeper, 128; on attractions of public houses, 132; on cleanliness, 211
Henderson, Mathew, 107
Hertford, Earl of, 18
Hertford, Lady, 82
Hervey family, 189
Hervey, Lord, 162
High Life Below Stairs, 37, 85, 87, 129, 138, 163, 164, 192
Hill, Col. John, 218
Hill, Dr., 98
History of the Poor, 91–2
Hogarth, William, 203, 228
Holden, Tom, 128
Holkham, 9
Holroyd, Maria, 127
Hotham, Sir Charles, 211
Household, size of, 2–8; dining arrangements in, 36; controlled by house steward, 40, 41; footman the mainstay of, 51; authority of housekeeper in, 63–4; authority of upper servants in, 69–70
Housekeeper, the, 63–5, 104
Housemaid, the, 67
House Steward, the, 41
'How d'ye's', 52
Howe, Sir Richard, 191
'Humanus', 18
Hume, Sir Gustavus, 193
Humphry Clinker, 2
Huntingford, James, 12, 24, 32, 84, 94, 95
Huske, Lt.-Gen. John, 175
Hutton, Catherine, 16
Hutton, William, 56
Hyde Justice, 134
Hyde Park, 134
Hyde Park Corner, 190

Imitation, 203–30; of the élite, 200, 203–4; chain of, 204–6; 219–24; reasons for, 205–6; mechanics of, 206–30; by country people, 224–7
Indian servants, 19
Insubordination, 78–9, 80, 88–90

INDEX

'Investigator', 175
Irish servants, 19

Jackson family, 82
Jacob, Giles, 6, 41, 58, 69
Jeanes, Rev., 7
Jenkins, Winifred, 212
Jenyns, Soame, 121, 122, 129, 136, 153, 208, 210
Jernegan, Sir William, 131
Johnson, Dr. Samuel, 127, 174–5, 190
Johnson, Mary, 33
Jones, Rev. William, 185, 198, 199
Joseph Andrews, 66

Kedleston, 103
Kendal, deputy steward of, 3
Kielmansegge, Frederick, 211
King, Gregory, 34
King, Richard, 30
King's Head Tavern, Islington, 189
Kingston, Duke of, 110, 113, 115, 157, 175, 182, 186
Knowles, Thomas, 188, 195
Knox, Vicesimus, 14, 180, 206, 220, 227

Lascelles family, 104
Lackington, James, 221
Lady's Magazine, 63
Lady's maid, the, 60–2, 63
La Motte, Mr., 46
Lancashire, 153, 165
Land steward, the, 38–41, 158, 184–6, 198–9
Lane, Captain, 55
Lardner, Rev. Richard, 78
La Rochefoucauld, Duc de, 5, 66, 114
Laundry-maid, the, 68
Laurence, Edward, 39, 59, 152, 198
Leapor, Molly, 191
Le Blanc, Jean, 80, 126, 159, 212
Legacies to servants, 173–5
Legh, Peter, 6, 17, 82
Lewis, Mrs., 54

Lichtenberg, Georg, 133
Ligonier, Sir John, 193, 195
Lincoln, 153
Linfield, Dr., 98
Litchfield, Col., 191
Liveries, 53–4, 117, 118–19, 120–1, 139, 179, 180, 211
Liverpool, 188
Locock, Mrs, 128
London, 13, 14, 15, 16, 22, 29, 31, 32, 33, 34, 82, 93, 129, 130, 175, 190, 201; abundance of places in, 10–11; ill-repute of servants in, 11; number of migrants to, 12; attractions of, 12–14; importance of livery servants in, 3; size of establishments in, 7–8; charity schools in, 21; prestige of living in, 23; place to better self, 23; darkness of streets in, 52–3; testimonials in, 84; physicians in, 97; servants' quarters in, 130, 131, 139; migration of Scottish servants to, 166; vails riots in, 167; grocers' boycott in, 173; pleasure resorts in, 135, 201, 214; class contacts in, 200–2; centre of cultural diffusion, 224–7; contacts between country and, 225
London General Office, 29
London Hospital, 194
Lonsdale, Viscount, 191
Lowther, Jane, 191
Luxborough, Lady, 49, 82, 97
Lying Lover, 85
Lyttleton, Sir Richard, 174

Macdonald, John, his attitude toward unemployment, 24–5; studies with *friseur*, 45–6; his numerous employers, 82, 187; tells of master's pride, 96; is rewarded with clothes, 115–16; boasts of livery, 20; is rejected because of dress, 122–3; tells of hunting, 125–6; has guests, 129; seeks company, 132; describes

INDEX

servants' ball, 133; fluctuations of his social status, 187; mentions Mr. Vernon, 193; is called 'Scotch Frenchman', 210
Maclean, James, 53
Magdalen Hospital, 21
Maid of all work, the, 67–8
Maître d'hôtel, the, 41
Malmesbury, Earl of, 166
Man-cook, the, 43–4
Mandeville, Bernard, 81, 86, 187
Manley, Mrs., 222
Marchant, Thomas, 17, 41
March, Lord, 55, 56
Marlborough, Duchess of, 6, 116, 171, 174, 175
Martin, Mr., 98
Marylebone Gardens, 135
Massie, Joseph, 25
Master of the horse, the, 41–2
May, Ned, 100
Medical care of servants, 97–8
Melbourne, Lord, 104
Middleton, Lady, 60
Miege, Guy, 74, 79
Miller, Sanderson, 7, 22, 45
Milnes Family, 8
Miss Lucy in Town, 139
Monmouth Street, 157
Monson, Lord, 185, 198
Montagu, Elizabeth, 52, 71, 126, 136, 182
Montagu, George, 207
Monument yard, 107
Moore, John, 45
Mordant, John, on steward, 39; on agent-in-chief, 40; on beer required by servants, 113; on wages, 152; on promotion to stewardship, 184–5, 186
More, Hannah, 168, 170
Morgan, Sir Thomas, 218
Moritz, Carl, 119
Morris, Dr. Claver, 99, 100, 127
Mortimer, Thomas, 138
Moryson, Fynes, 4
Mungo, Senegambia, 214, 215
Mure, Hutchinson, 104

Murphy, Arthur, 213
Murray, Lord, 193
Muse in Livery, 191

Negro servants, 19
Nelson, Lord, 126
Newcastle, Duke of, 5, 211
Newport, Mr., 188
Norfolk, 6, 17, 166
Norfolk, Duke of, 5, 104
Northcote, James, 135
North, Lord, 33, 34, 45, 175
Northumberland, 153, 165
Northumberland, Earl of, 4
Northumberland, Duke of, 188
Nottingham, 56
Nottingham, Earl of, 42, 43, 50, 56, 58, 163
'Numa', 113

Observations and Facts Relative to Public-houses, 189
O'Keeffe, John, 36, 55, 56
'Oliver Tiridates', 112
O'Neil, James, 187
Opera Club, 165
Opera-house, 217
Orcades, 50
Orlebar, Richard, 174
Orphan Working School, 21
Ossory, Lady, 49, 96
Oxenden, Sir Henry, 186, 190
Oxfordshire, 55, 126

Paddington, 55
Page, Sir Francis, 174
Page, the, 60
Pall Mall, 200
Palmerston, Lord, 188
Parish apprentices, 21–2
Parkinson, Mr., 186
Park-keeper, the, 58–9, 104
Paternalism, 75–7, 96–101, 102, 123–6, 186, 190–4
'Patience Giddy', 66
Peel, Sir Robert, 1
Pennington, Mrs., 26
Perquisites, 157–8

INDEX

Peters, Nanny, 98
Petre, Lord, 102
Pettingal, Dr., 79
Philanthropic Society, 21
'Philanthropist', 131
'Philanthropus', 81
Philips, Thomas, 182
'Philo-Britanniae', 12
Pilkington, Letitia, 170, 195
Piozzi, Mrs., 26, 97, 127
Pitt, William, the younger, 33, 176, 184
Pleasure resorts, 135, 201, 214
Pöllnitz, Baron de, 159, 161, 201
Pope, Alexander, 191, 192
Porter, the, 57–8, 104, 170–1
Postilion, the, 159–60
Poundage, 172–3
Powys, Mrs. Lybbe, 6, 82
Poynter, Mr., 198
Prescott's Manchester Journal, 196
Present for a Servant Maid, 87
Present for Servants, 87
Price of an Equipage, 114
'Pro Bono Publico', 11
Promotion of servants, 181–7, 188
Public houses, 131–2, 188–90
Pultney, General, 174
Purefoy, Elizabeth, 9, 26, 68, 100, 189
Purefoy, Henry, 7, 10, 82, 117

Queensberry, Duchess of, 66, 198
Queensberry, 3rd Duke of, 198
Queensberry, 4th Duke of, 56, 57, 175

Raby, Lord, 54
Raffald, Elizabeth, 196–7
Ranelagh, 167, 201, 214
Red Lion Inn, Bagshot, 189
Reed, Joseph, 31
Reeve, Clara, 18, 224
Register offices, 29–32
Reid, Mr., 98
Religious training of servants, 99
Renfrew, 166
Reynolds, Frances, 52, 135

Reynolds, Sir Joshua, 52, 62, 135
Richmond, Duke of, 194
Ringland, 6
Riots, 137, 167–8
Robotham, Mrs., 189
Rochester Bridge, 55
Rochford, Earl of, 194
Rogers, Benjamin, 126
Rosemary Lane, 157
Rowlandson, Thomas, 203
Ruggles, Thomas, 92
Running footman, 55–7
Rushbrook Hall, 108

Sadler's Wells, 135
St. Bride's, 200
St. Clement Danes, 90
St. James's Park, 201
St. James's Square, 105, 200
St. Thomas's Hospital, 98
Sancho, Ignatius, 216
Saussure, Ceasar de, 105, 161, 170, 210
Scarborough, J., 190
Scarsdale, Lord, 103
Scotland, 19
Scottish Masons, 164
Scottish move against vails, 164, 166
Scottish servants, 19, 49–50, 116
Scullery maid, the, 37, 68–9
Scullion, the, 68
Selby, Mr., 11
Select Society, 164
Serious Advice and Warning to Servants, 87
Servant's Friend, 87
Servant tax, 33, 34
Service, as refuge, 19–23, 117, 123–4; status of as occupation, 177–81; as means of accumulating capital, 190; recruitment for, 10, 26–33; length of, 81–2
Servitude, 73, 74, 191, 212
Shardeloes, 107
Shebbeare, Dr. John, 80, 160, 163, 172
Sheffield Place, 127

INDEX

Shenstone, William, 49, 114
Shuldham, Mrs., 185
Silliman, Benjamin, 54, 178
Sinecures, 175-6, 197
Sion, 196
Sitwell, Francis, 7
Skip, John, 214, 215
Slipslop, Mrs., 66
Smollett, Tobias, 3, 14, 49, 202, 212
Snuff, 222, 227
Society for the Encouragement and Encrease of Good Servants, 94
Society for the Encouragement of Good Servants, 93-4
Society of Arts, 136
Somerset, Duke of, 5, 41
Southwell, Edward, 189
Southwell, Lord, 161
Spain, Mr., 99
Spectator, 203
Spencer, John, 35
Spencer, Lord, 106
Spooner, Mrs., 128
Staffordshire, 55
Stamp Office, 176
Stapley, Anthony, 82, 151
Statute fairs, 27-9
Statute halls, 30
Statute of Apprentices, 27
Statute of Labourers, 27
Steele, Richard, 85, 132, 155, 212, 218, 219
Sterne, Laurence, 19
Stewart, Keith, 125
Stone, Mrs., 19
Stormont, Lady, 208
Stormont, 208
Stowe, 127, 195
Stow-in-the-Hole, 126
Strafford, Earl of, 188
Strafford, Lady, 117
Strawberry Hill, 6, 171
Streatham, 8
Strickland, Mr., 218
Strutt, Jedediah, 1
Stuart, Col., 208
Stuart, Sir John, of Allan Bank, 187

Suffolk, 7
Sussex, Lord, 193
Swift, Jonathan, 19, 66, 79, 87, 193, 216, 218
Swiss servants, 58

Tancred, Christopher, 88, 92
Tansley, Jonathan, 128
Tatler, 203
Tea, 222-3, 227
Tea Money, 153, 156-7
Temple, Rev. William, 62
Testimonials, 83-5, 94-5
Thames Street, 201
Thanet, Lady, 202
Thanet, Lord, 126
Thearie, Mr., 193
Theatre, 136-9, 201
Thoresby, 110, 113
Thorndon, 102
Thorne, Dr., 97
Thrale family, 190
Thrale, Henry, 8
Thrale, 'Queeny', 127
Tompion, Thomas, 108
Tony Lumpkin in Town, 36
Tooke, Mrs., 111
Townley, James, 37, 87, 129, 138, 163, 164, 215
Townshend, Charles, 207
Townshend family, 187
Townshend, Viscount, 194
Toy-shop, 191
Tradesmen, 16, 17, 26-7, 172-3
Travistock, Lord, 136
Trimmer, Sarah, 87
Troutbeck, Mrs., 128
Trueman, Thomas, 136, 139, 173
Trusler, Dr. John, on number of a squire's servants, 7; on London lower classes, 11; on register offices, 30; on newspaper advertisements, 32; on self-interestedness of servants, 80-1; on wages of postilion, 152; on board wages, 155; on perversion of perquisites, 157; on vails, 165
Tucker, Josiah, 161

INDEX

Tunbridge Wells, 202
Tyburn, 55

Under-butler, the, 57
Under-coachman, the, 57
Universal Spectator, 204

Vails, 158–68, 169
Valet, the, 42, 45–6, 61
Vauxhall, 135, 201, 214
Veblen, Thorstein, 55
Vernon, Mr., 193
Von la Roche, Sophie, 109

Wages, 141–53
Walpole, Horace, size of his household, 6; seeks steward-butler, 26; notes Scottish gardeners, 49; is held up, 53; is concerned about servant, 96–7; on bequests to servants, 101; forbids servant visitors, 127–8; on vails riots, 168; on admittance fees, 172; on Dodsley, 195; disapproves indiscretions before servants, 207–8
Walpole, Horace, the elder, 193, 195
Walter, Mr., 129
Waltham Abbey, 28
Ward, William, 128
Ware, Isaac, 8, 102, 103, 105
Warwick, Earl of, 3
Watering places, 202–3
Watts, Tom, 11
Weekly Register, 208
Weeks Preparation to the Sacrement, 99
Welch, Saunders, 17, 24, 92
Wendeborn, Frederick, 224, 226
Wentworth, Lady, 17, 18, 54

Wentworth, Lady Harriet, 100
Wesenham Hall, 82
Westminster, 21
Westminster Bridge, 55
Westminster Journal, 10
Westmorland, 3, 153, 165
Weston House, 131
Wharton, Duke of, 55
Whately family, 197
Whimsical Philosopher, 183, 192
White Conduit House, 135
Whitehead, Thomas, 109, 182, 186, 190, 198
White Swan Inn, Alnwick, 189
Wilberforce, William, 189
Wilkes, John, 208
Wilkinson, Tate, 226
Willis, Mrs., 130
Wisdom, William, 98
Withers, Mr., 100
Wood, Tom, 128
Woodforde, Nancy, 110
Woodforde, Rev. James, size of his household, 7; duties of his dairy maid, 68; turnover of his servants, 82; illness of his maid, 97; has footman educated, 99; buys cloth for maid, 116; his footman's clothes, 118; his servants' recreation, 128–9, 131; wages of his footman, 152–3; his board wages, 156; change in his servants' social status, 186–7
Woodhall Park, 104
Woodstock Cross, 55
Worksop Manor House, 104
World, 84
Wynn, Sir Watkin Williams, 105

Yearsley, Anne, 191
Yorkshire, 8, 27, 57, 165
'Yorkshire Tradesman', 178